JAVA™ DESIGN PATTERNS

JAVA™ DESIGN PATTERNS
A Tutorial

James W. Cooper

ADDISON-WESLEY

An imprint of Addison Wesley Longman, Inc.

Reading, Massachusetts • Harlow, England • Menlo Park, California
Berkeley, California • Don Mills, Ontario • Sydney
Bonn • Amsterdam • Tokyo • Mexico City

Many of the designations used by manufacturers and sellers to distinguish their products are claimed as trademarks. Where those designations appear in this book, and Addison-Wesley was aware of a trademark claim, the designations have been printed with initial capital letters or in all capitals.

The author and publisher have taken care in the preparation of this book, but make no expressed or implied warranty of any kind and assume no responsibility for errors or omissions. No liability is assumed for incidental or consequential damages in connection with or arising out of the use of the information or programs contained herein.

The publisher offers discounts on this book when ordered in quantity for special sales. For more information, please contact:

Corporate, Government, and Special Sales Group
Addison Wesley Longman, Inc.
One Jacob Way
Reading, Massachusetts 01867

Library of Congress Cataloging-in-Publication Data

Cooper, James William, 1943–
    Java design patterns : a tutorial / James W. Cooper.
        p.   cm.
    Includes bibliographical references and index.
    ISBN 0-201-48539-7
    1. Java (Computer program language) I. Title

    QA76.73.J38 C658 2000
    005.13'3—dc21

                                                                    99-056547

Acquisitions Editor: Paul Becker
Editorial Assistant: Ross Venables
Production Coordinator: Jacquelyn Doucette
Compositor: Stratford Publishing Services

ISBN 0-201-48539-7
Text printed on recycled paper

2 3 4 5 6 7 8 9 10 — MA — 04 03 02 01 00
Second printing, April 2000

CONTENTS

PREFACE

This is a practical book that tells you how to write Java programs using some of the most common *design patterns*. It is structured as a series of short chapters, each describing a design pattern and giving one or more complete, working, visual example programs that use that pattern. Each chapter also includes Unified Modeling Language (UML) diagrams illustrating how the classes interact.

This book is not a "companion" book to the well-known *Design Patterns* text [Gamma, 1995] by the "Gang of Four." Rather, it is a tutorial for people who want to learn what design patterns are about and how to use them in their work. You need not have read *Design Patterns* to gain from reading this book, but when you are done here you might want to read or reread that book to gain additional insights.

In this book, you will learn that design patterns are a common way to organize objects in your programs to make those programs easier to write and modify. You'll also see that by familiarizing yourself with these design patterns, you will gain a valuable vocabulary for discussing how your programs are constructed.

People come to appreciate design patterns in different ways—from the highly theoretical to the intensely practical—and when they finally see the great power of these patterns, they experience an "Aha!" moment. Usually this moment means that you suddenly had an internal picture of how that pattern can help you in your work.

In this book, we try to help you form that conceptual idea, or *gestalt,* by describing the pattern in as many ways as possible. The book is organized into six main sections:

- An introductory description
- A description of patterns grouped into three sections: Creational, Structural, and Behavioral

- A description of the Java Foundation Classes (JFC) showing the patterns they illustrate
- A set of case studies where patterns have been helpful

For each pattern, we start with a brief verbal description and then build simple example programs. Each example is a visual program that you can run and examine so as to make the pattern as concrete as possible. All of the example programs and their variations are on the CD-ROM that accompanies this book. In that way, you can run them, change them, and see how the variations that you create work.

All of the programs are based on Java 1.2, and most use the JFC. If you haven't taken the time to learn how to use these classes, there is a tutorial covering the basics in Section 5 where we also discuss some of the patterns that they illustrate.

Since each of the examples consists of a number of Java files for each of the classes we use in that example, we also provide a Visual SlickEdit project file for each example and place each example in a separate subdirectory to prevent any confusion.

As you leaf through the book, you'll see screen shots of the programs we developed to illustrate the design patterns; these provide yet another way to reinforce your learning of these patterns. You'll also see UML diagrams of these programs that illustrate the interactions between classes in yet another way. UML diagrams are just simple box and arrow illustrations of classes and their inheritance structure, with the arrows pointing to parent classes and dotted arrows pointing to interfaces. If you are unfamiliar with UML, we provide a simple introduction in the first chapter.

Finally, since we used JVISION to create the UML diagrams in each chapter, we provide the original JVISION diagram files for each pattern as well, so you can use the demo version of JVISION included on the CD to play with them. We also include the free Linux version of JVISION.

When you finish this book, you'll be comfortable with the basics of design patterns and will be able to start using them in your day to day Java programming work.

James W. Cooper
Wilton, CT
Nantucket, MA
November, 1999

ACKNOWLEDGMENTS

Writing a book on Java design patterns has been a fascinating challenge. Design patterns are intellectually recursive; that is, every time that you think that you've wrapped up a good explanation of one, another turn of the crank occurs to you or is suggested by someone else. So, while writing is essentially a solitary task, I had a lot of help and support.

Foremost, I thank Roy Byrd and Alan Marwick of IBM Research for encouraging me to tackle this book and providing lots of support during the manuscript's genesis and revision. I also especially thank Nicole Cooper for editing my first draft; she definitely improved its clarity and accuracy.

The design pattern community (informally called the "Pattern-nostra") were also a great help. In particular, I thank both John Vlissides and Ken Arnold for their careful and thoughtful reading of the manuscript. Among the many others, I thank Ralph Johnson, Sherman Alpert, Zunaid Kazi, Colin Harrison, and Hank Stuck. I'm also grateful to John Dorsey and Tyler Sperry at *JavaPro* magazine for their encouragement and editorial suggestions on some of the columns that I wrote that later became parts of this book. Thanks also to Herb Chong and Mary Neff for lending their names and part of their project descriptions to the case studies chapter. Finally, thanks to my wife Vicki, who provided endless support during the ups and downs of endless writing and seemingly endless revision.

SECTION 1

What Are Design Patterns?

In this first section of the book, we outline what design patterns actually are and give a few simple examples. You'll see that much of the discussion about patterns is really a discussion about various classes and how they communicate.

Then we show you how to use UML diagrams to represent the relationships between classes in your programs and how they can quickly reveal the patterns in these programs.

CHAPTER 1

Introduction

Sitting at your desk in front of your workstation, you stare into space, trying to figure out how to write a new program feature. You know intuitively what must be done and what data and which objects come into play, but you have this underlying feeling that there is a more elegant and general way to write this program.

In fact, you probably don't write any code until you can build a picture in your mind of what code does and how the pieces of the code interact. The more that you can picture this "organic whole" or *gestalt,* the more likely you are to feel comfortable that you have developed the best solution to the problem. If you don't grasp this whole right away, you might stare out of the window for a long time, even though the basic solution to the problem is quite obvious.

In one sense, you feel that the more elegant solution will be more reusable and more maintainable. However, even if you are likely to be the only programmer, you feel reassured once you have designed a solution that is relatively clean and doesn't expose too many internal inelegancies.

One of the main reasons that computer science researchers began to recognize design patterns was to satisfy this need for good, simple, and reusable solutions. The term *design pattern* sounds a bit formal to the uninitiated and can be somewhat off-putting when you first encounter it. But, in fact, a design pattern is just a convenient way of reusing object-oriented (OO) code between projects and between programmers. The idea behind design patterns is simple: to catalog common interactions between objects that programmers have often found useful.

A common pattern cited in early literature on programming frameworks is Model-View-Controller (MVC) for Smalltalk [Krasner and Pope, 1988], which divides the user interface problem into three parts (see Figure 1.1):

- **Data Model**, which contains the computational parts of the program
- **View**, which presents the user interface
- **Controller**, which interacts between the user and the view

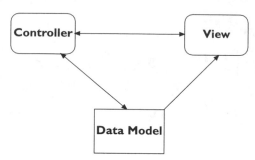

Figure 1.1   The Model-View-Controller framework.

Each aspect of the problem is a separate object, and each has its own rules for managing its data. Communication between the user, the graphical user interface (GUI), and the data should be carefully controlled; this separation of functions accomplishes that very nicely. Three objects talking to each other using this restrained set of connections is an example of a powerful design pattern.

In other words, a design pattern describes how objects communicate without becoming entangled in each other's data models and methods. Keeping this separation has always been an objective of good OO programming. If you have been trying to keep objects minding their own business, you are probably already using some of the common design patterns. It is interesting that the MVC pattern is used throughout Java 1.2 as part of the JFC, also known as Swing components.

More formal recognition of design patterns began in the early 1990s when Erich Gamma [1993] described patterns incorporated in the GUI application framework, ET++. Programmers began to meet and discuss these ideas. The culmination of these discussions and a number of technical meetings was the publication of the seminal book, *Design Patterns—Elements of Reusable Software*, by Gamma, Helm, Johnson, and Vlissides [1995]. This book, commonly called the Gang of Four, or GoF, book, became an all-time bestseller and has had a powerful impact on those seeking to understand how to use design patterns. It describes 23 common, generally useful patterns and comments on how and when you might apply them. We will refer to this groundbreaking book as *Design Patterns,* throughout this book.

Since the publication of *Design Patterns,* several other useful books have been published. One closely related book is *The Design Patterns Small-talk Companion* [Alpert, Brown, and Woolf, 1998], which covers the same

23 patterns but from the Smalltalk point of view. In this book, we refer to it as the *Smalltalk Companion.*

Defining Design Patterns

We all talk about the way that we do things in our everyday work, hobbies, and home life and recognize repeating patterns all the time.

- Sticky buns are like dinner rolls, but I add brown sugar and nut filling to them.
- Her front garden is like mine, except that in mine I use astilbe.
- This end table is constructed like that one, but in this one, the doors replace drawers.

We see the same thing in programming when we tell a colleague how we accomplish a tricky bit of programming so that the colleague doesn't have to recreate it from scratch. We simply recognize effective ways for objects to communicate while maintaining their own separate existences.

Some useful definitions of design patterns have emerged as the literature in this field has expanded.

- "Design patterns are recurring solutions to design problems you see over and over." [*Smalltalk Companion*]
- "Design patterns constitute a set of rules describing how to accomplish certain tasks in the realm of software development." [Pree, 1994]
- "Design patterns focus more on reuse of recurring architectural design themes, while frameworks focus on detailed design . . . and implementation." [Coplien and Schmidt, 1995]
- "A pattern addresses a recurring design problem that arises in specific design situations and presents a solution to it." [Buschmann and Meunier, et al., 1996]
- "Patterns identify and specify abstractions that are above the level of single classes and instances, or of components." [Gamma, Helm, Johnson, and Vlissides, 1993]

But while it is helpful to draw analogies to architecture, cabinetmaking, and logic, design patterns are not just about the design of objects; they are also about *interaction* between objects. One possible view of some of these patterns is to consider them as *communication patterns.*

Some other patterns deal not just with object communication, but also with strategies for object inheritance and containment. It is the design of simple, but elegant methods of interaction that makes many design patterns so important.

Design patterns can exist at many levels, from very low-level specific solutions to broadly generalized system issues. There are now hundreds of patterns in the literature. They have been discussed in articles and at conferences at all levels of granularity. Some are examples that apply widely. A few writers have ascribed pattern behavior to class groupings that apply to just a single problem [Kurata, 1998].

Thus you don't just write a design pattern off the top of your head. Rather, most such patterns are *discovered*. The process of looking for these patterns is called *pattern mining* and is worthy of a book of its own.

The 23 design patterns included in *Design Patterns* all had several known applications and were on a middle level of generality, where they could easily cross application areas and encompass several objects. The authors divided these patterns into three types:

- **Creational patterns**: create objects for you, rather than your having to instantiate objects directly. Your program gains more flexibility in deciding which objects need to be created for a given case.
- **Structural patterns**: help you compose groups of objects into larger structures, such as complex user interfaces and accounting data.
- **Behavioral patterns**: help you to define the communication between objects in your system and how the flow is controlled in a complex program.

We'll be looking at Java versions of these patterns in the chapters that follow. This book takes a somewhat different approach than *Design Patterns* and the *Smalltalk Companion;* we provide at least one complete, visual Java program for each of the 23 patterns. This way you can not only examine the code snippets we provide, but run, edit, and modify the complete working programs on the accompanying CD-ROM. You'll find a list of all the programs on the CD-ROM at the end of each pattern description.

The Learning Process

We have found that learning design patterns is a multiple step process:

1. Acceptance

2. Recognition

3. Internalization

First, you accept the premise that design patterns are important in your work. Then, you recognize that you need to read about design patterns in order to know when you might use them. Finally, you internalize the patterns in sufficient detail that you know which ones might help you solve a given design problem.

For some lucky people, design patterns are obvious tools, and they grasp their essential utility just by reading summaries of the patterns. For many of the rest of us, there is a slow induction period after we've read about a pattern followed by the proverbial "Aha!" when we see how we can apply them in our work. This book helps to take you to that final stage of internalization by providing complete, working programs that you can try out for yourself.

The examples in *Design Patterns* are brief and are in C++ or, in some cases, Smalltalk. If you are working in another language, it is helpful to have the pattern examples in your language of choice. This book attempts to fill that need for Java programmers.

A set of Java examples takes on a form that is a little different than in C++, because Java is more strict in its application of OO precepts—you can't have global variables, data structures or pointers. In addition, we'll see that Java interfaces and abstract classes are a major contributor to how we implement design patterns in Java.

Studying Design Patterns

There are several alternate ways to become familiar with these patterns. In each approach, you should read this book and the parent *Design Patterns* book in one order or the other. We also strongly urge you to read the *Smalltalk Companion* for completeness, since it provides an alternate description of each pattern. Finally, there are a number of Web sites on learning and discussing design patterns.

Notes on Object-Oriented Approaches

The fundamental reason for using design patterns is to keep classes separated and prevent them from having to know too much about one another. Equally important, these patterns help you to avoid reinventing the wheel and allow you to describe your programming approach succinctly in terms that other programmers can easily understand.

Recently, we obtained from a colleague some code that had been written by a very capable summer student. However, in order to use it in our project, we had to reorganize the objects to use the Java Foundation Classes (JFCs). We offered the revised code back to our colleague and were able to summarize our changes simply by noting that we had converted the toolbuttons to Command patterns and had implemented a Mediator pattern to process their actions. This is exactly the sort of concise communication that using design patterns promotes.

OO programmers use a number of strategies to achieve the separation of classes, among them *encapsulation* and *inheritance*. Nearly all languages that have OO capabilities support inheritance. A class that inherits from a parent class has access to all of the methods of that parent class. It also has access to all of its nonprivate variables. However, by starting your inheritance hierarchy with a complete, working class, you might be unduly restricting yourself, as well as carrying along specific method implementation baggage. Instead, *Design Patterns* suggest that you always

> *Program to an interface and not to an implementation.*

Putting this more succinctly, you should define the top of any class hierarchy with an *abstract* class or an *interface,* which implements no methods but simply defines the methods that the class will support. Then, in all of your derived classes you will have more freedom to implement these methods to best suit your purposes.

The other major concept that you should recognize is *object composition.* This is simply the construction of objects that contain other objects, that is, encapsulation of several objects inside another one. While many beginning OO programmers use inheritance to solve every problem, as you begin to write more elaborate programs, the merits of object composition become apparent. Your new object can have the interface that is best for what you want to accomplish without having all of the methods of the parent classes. Thus the second major precept suggested by *Design Patterns* is

> *Favor object composition over inheritance.*

At first this seems contrary to the customs of OO programming, but you will see any number of cases among the design patterns where we find that inclusion of one or more objects inside another is the preferred method.

The Java Foundation Classes

The Java Foundation Classes, which were introduced after Java 1.1 and incorporated into Java 1.2, are a critical part of writing good graphical Java programs. They were also known during their development as the Swing classes and still are informally referred to that way. They provide easy ways to write very professional-looking user interfaces and allow you to vary the look and feel of your interface to match the platform on which your program is running. Further, they, too, utilize a number of the basic design patterns and thus make extremely good examples for study.

Nearly all the example programs in this book use the JFC to produce the interfaces you see in the example code. Since not everyone may be familiar with these classes and since we are going to build some basic classes from the JFC to use throughout our examples, we include an appendix introducing the JFC and showing the patterns that it implements. While not a complete tutorial in every aspect of the JFC, it does present the most useful interface controls and shows how to use them.

Java Design Patterns

Each of the 23 patterns in *Design Patterns* is discussed in the following chapters, and each discussion includes at least one working program example that has some sort of visual interface to make it more immediate to you. Each also uses the JFC to improve the elegance of its appearance and make it a little more concrete and believable. This occurs despite the fact that the programs are necessarily simple so that the coding doesn't obscure the fundamental elegance of the pattern we are describing. However, even though Java is our target language, this isn't a book on the Java language. We make no attempt to cover all of the powerful ideas in Java; only those which we can use to exemplify patterns. For that reason, we say little or nothing about either exceptions or threads, two of Java's most important features.

CHAPTER 2

UML Diagrams

We have illustrated the patterns in this book with diagrams drawn using Unified Modeling Language (UML). This simple diagramming style was developed out of work done by Grady Booch, James Rumbaugh, and Ivar Jacobson and resulted in a merging of ideas into a single specification and eventually a standard. You can read details of how to use UML in any number of books, such as those by Booch, Rumbaugh, and Jacobson [1999], Fowler and Scott [1997], and Grand [1998]. We'll outline the basics you'll need in this introduction.

Basic UML diagrams consist of boxes that represent classes. Let's consider the following class (which has very little actual function):

```
public abstract class Person {
    protected String personName;
    private   int     age;

    public Person (String name) {
        personName = name;
    }
        static public String makeJob () {return "hired";}
        public int getAge () {return age;}
        private void splitNames () { }
        abstract String getJob ();
}
```

We can represent this class in UML as shown in Figure 2.1.

The top part of the box contains the class name and the package name (if any). The second part lists the class's variables, and the bottom lists its methods. The symbols in front of the names indicate that member's visibility, where + means public, – means private, and # means protected. In UML, methods whose names are written in italics are abstract. The class name is also abstract, since it

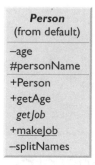

Figure 2.1   The *Person* class, showing private, protected, and public variables and static and abstract methods.

contains an abstract class, so it, too, is in italics. Static methods are shown underlined.

You can also show all of the type information in a UML diagram, where that is helpful, as illustrated in Figure 2.2(a).

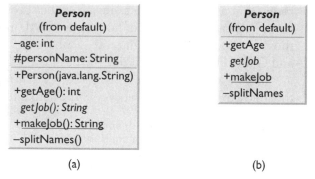

(a)   (b)

Figure 2.2(a)(b)   The *Person* class UML diagram shown both with and without the method types.

UML does not require that you show all of the attributes of a class; usually only the ones of interest to the discussion at hand are shown. For example, in Figure 2.2(b), we have omitted all the variables and the constructor declaration from the methods compartment.

Inheritance

Inheritance is represented using a solid line and a hollow triangular arrow. For the simple Employee class, which is subclass of Person, we write the following code:

```
public class Employee extends Person {

    public Employee (String name) {
        super (name);
    }

    public String getJob () {
        return "Research Staff";
        }
}
```

This is represented in UML as shown in Figure 2.3.

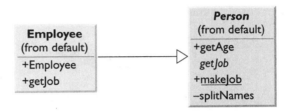

Figure 2.3   UML diagram showing Employee derived from Person.

Note that the Employee class name is not in italics. This is because the class is now a concrete class because it includes a concrete method for the formerly abstract *getJob* method. While it has been conventional to show inheritance with the arrow pointing *up* to the superclass, UML does not require this, and sometimes a different layout is clearer or uses space more efficiently.

Interfaces

An interface looks much like inheritance, except that the arrow has a dotted line tail, as shown in Figure 2.4

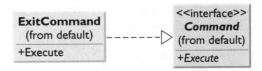

Figure 2.4   ExitCommand implements the Command interface.

Note that the name <<*interface*>> is shown enclosed within double angle brackets (or *guillemets*).

Composition

Much of the time, a useful representation of a class hierarchy must include how objects are contained in other objects. For example, a Company might include one Employee and one Person (perhaps a contractor).

```
public class Company {
  Employee emp1;
  Person    per1;
  public Company() {
    }
}
```

We represent this in UML as shown in Figure 2.5

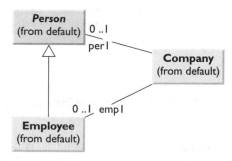

Figure 2.5   Company contains instances of Person and Employee.

The lines between classes show that there can be 0 to 1 instances of Person in Company and 0 to 1 instances of Employee in Company. If there can be many instances of a class inside another, such as the array of Employees shown here,

```
public  class  Company1 {
  Employee [ ] emp1;
  public Company1() {
    }
}
```

we represent that object composition as a single line with either an * or 0, * on it, as shown in Figure 2.6.

Figure 2.6   Company 1 contains any number of instances of Employee.

Some writers use a hollow and a solid diamond arrowhead to indicate containment of aggregates and a circle arrowhead for single object composition, but this is not required.

Annotation

You will also find it convenient to annotate your UML or insert comments to explain which class is calling a method in which other class. You can place a comment anywhere you want in a UML diagram, either enclosed in a box with a turned-down corner or just entered as text. Text comments are usually shown along an arrow line, which indicates the nature of the method that is called, as shown in Figure 2.7.

Figure 2.7   A comment is often shown in a box with a turned-down corner.

UML is a powerful way of representing object relationships in programs, and the full specification contains more diagram features. The previous discussion covers the markup methods used in this text.

JVISION UML Diagrams

All of the UML diagrams in this book were drawn using the JVISION program from Object Insight. This program reads in the actual compiled classes and then generates the UML class diagrams. Many of these class diagrams have been edited to show only the most important methods and relationships. However, the complete JVISION diagram files for each design pattern are stored in that pattern's directory on the accompanying CD-ROM. Thus you can run your copy of JVISION and read in and investigate the detailed UML diagram starting with the same drawings you see here in the book.

Visual SlickEdit Project Files

All of the programs in this book were written using Visual SlickEdit 4.0 using the project file feature. Each subdirectory on the CD-ROM contains the project file for that project so that you can load the project and compile it as we did.

SECTION 2

Creational Patterns

All of the Creational patterns deal with ways to create instances of objects. This is important because your program should not depend on how objects are created and arranged. In Java, of course, the simplest way to create an instance of an object is by using the new operator:

```
fred = new Fred();    //instance of Fred class
```

However, doing this really amounts to hard coding, depending on how you create the object within your program. In many cases, the exact nature of the object that is created could vary with the needs of the program. Abstracting the creation process into a special "creator" class can make your program more flexible and general. The six Creational patterns follow:

- **Factory Method pattern**: provides a simple decision-making class that returns one of several possible subclasses of an abstract base class, depending on the data that are provided. We'll start with the Simple Factory pattern as an introduction to factories and then introduce the Factory Method pattern as well.
- **Abstract Factory pattern**: provides an interface to create and return one of several families of related objects.
- **Builder pattern**: separates the construction of a complex object from its representation so that several different representations can be created, depending on the needs of the program.
- **Prototype pattern**: starts with an instantiated class, which it copies or clones to make new instances. These instances can then be further tailored using their public methods.
- **Singleton pattern**: is a class of which there may be no more than one instance. It provides a single global point of access to that instance.

CHAPTER 3

The Factory Pattern

One type of pattern that we see again and again in OO programs is the Simple Factory pattern. A Simple Factory pattern returns an instance of one of several possible classes depending on the data provided to it. Usually all classes that it returns have a common parent class and common methods, but each performs a task differently and is optimized for different kinds of data. This Simple Factory serves as an introduction to the somewhat more subtle *Factory Method* GoF pattern we'll discuss shortly. It is, in fact, a special subset of that pattern.

How a Factory Works

To understand the Simple Factory pattern, let's look at the diagram in Figure 3.1.

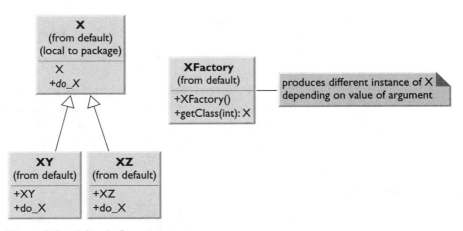

Figure 3.1   A Simple Factory pattern.

In this figure, X is base class and classes XY and XZ are derived from it. The XFactory class decides which of these subclasses to return depending on the arguments you give it. On the right, we define a `getClass` method to be one that passes in some value *abc,* and that returns some instance of the class **x**. Which one it returns doesn't matter to the programmer since they all have the same methods, but different implementations. How it decides which one to return is entirely up to the factory. It could be some very complex function, but it is often quite simple.

Sample Code

Let's consider a simple case in which we could use a Factory class. Suppose we have an entry form and we want to allow the user to enter his name either as "firstname lastname" or as "lastname, firstname." We'll make the further simplifying assumption that we will always be able to decide the name order by whether there is a comma between the last and first name.

This is a pretty simple sort of decision to make, and you could make it with a simple *if* statement in a single class, but let's use it here to illustrate how a factory works and what it can produce. We'll start by defining a simple base class that takes a String and splits it (somehow) into two names:

```
public class Namer {
    //base class extended by two child classes
    protected String last;    //split name
    protected String first;   //stored here

    public String getFirst() {
        return first;            //return first name
    }
    public String getLast() {
        return last;             //return last name
    }
}
```

In this base class, we don't compute any names as such, but we do provide implementations of the `getFirst` and `getLast` methods. We'll store the split first and last names in the Strings *first* and *last,* and, since the subclasses will need access to these variables, we'll make them *protected.*

The Two Subclasses

Now we can write two very simple subclasses that split the name into two parts in the constructor. In the FirstFirst class, we make the simplifying assumption that everything before the last space is part of the first name.

```
public class FirstFirst
extends Namer {
    //extracts first name from last name
    //when separated by a space
    public FirstFirst(String s) {
        int i = s.lastIndexOf(" ");  //find sep space
        if (i > 0) {
            first = s.substring(0, i).trim();
            last = s.substring(i + 1).trim();
        } else {
            first = "";               // if no space
            last = s;                 // put all in last name
        }
    }
}
```

And in the LastFirst class, we assume that a comma delimits the last name. In both classes, we also provide error recovery in case the space or comma does not exist.

```
public class LastFirst extends Namer {
// extracts last name from first name
// when separated by a comma
    public LastFirst(String s) {
        int i = s.indexOf(",");       //find comma
        if (i > 0) {
            last = s.substring(0, i).trim();
            first = s.substring(i + 1).trim();
        } else {
            last = s;                 //if no comma,
            first = "";               //put all in last name
        }
    }
}
```

Building the Simple Factory

Now our simple Factory class is extremely simple. We just test for the existence of a comma and then return an instance of one class or the other.

```
public class NamerFactory {
    //Factory decides which class to return based on
    //presence of a comma
    public Namer getNamer(String entry) {
        //comma determines name order
        int i = entry.indexOf(",");
        if (i > 0)
            return new LastFirst(entry);
        else
```

```
                    return new FirstFirst(entry);
        }
}
```

Using the Factory

Let's see how we put this together. The complete class diagram is shown in Figure 3.2.

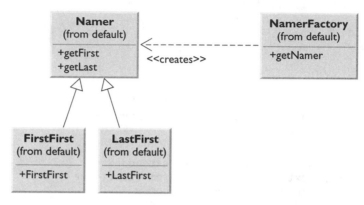

Figure 3.2   The Namer factory program.

We have constructed a simple Java user interface that allows us to enter the names in either order and see the two names separately displayed. This program is shown in Figure 3.3.

Figure 3.3   The Namer program executing.

We type in a name and then click on the Compute button, and the divided name appears in the lower two text fields. The crux of this program is the compute method that fetches the text, obtains an instance of a Namer class, and displays the results.

That's the fundamental principle of the Simple Factory pattern. You create an abstraction that decides which of several possible classes to return and returns one. Then you call the methods of that class instance without ever knowing which subclass you are actually using. This approach keeps the issues of data dependence separated from the classes' useful methods.

Factory Patterns in Math Computation

Most people who use Factory patterns tend to think of them as tools for simplifying tangled programming classes. You also can use them in programs that perform mathematical computations. For example, in the Fast Fourier Transform (FFT), you evaluate the following four equations repeatedly for a large number of point pairs over many passes through the array that you are transforming. Because of how the graphs of these computations are drawn, these equations (Equations 1–4) constitute one instance of the FFT "butterfly."

$$R_1 = R_1 + R_2 \cos(y) - I_2 \sin(y) \qquad (1)$$
$$R_2 = R_1 - R_2 \cos(y) + I_2 \sin(y) \qquad (2)$$
$$I_1 = I_1 + R_2 \sin(y) + I_2 \cos(y) \qquad (3)$$
$$I_2 = I_1 - R_2 \sin(y) - I_2 \cos(y) \qquad (4)$$

However, there are a number of times during each pass through the data where the angle y is zero. In this case, your complex math evaluation reduces to Equations 5–8.

$$R_1 = R_1 + R_2 \qquad (5)$$
$$R_2 = R_1 - R_2 \qquad (6)$$
$$I_1 = I_1 + I_2 \qquad (7)$$
$$I_2 = I_1 - I_2 \qquad (8)$$

Then, we can make a Simple Factory class that decides which class instance to return. Since we are making Butterflies, we'll call this Factory a Cocoon.

```
class Cocoon {
    public Butterfly getButterfly(float y)          {
        if (y != 0)
            return new trigButterfly(y);    //get multiply class
```

```
        else
            return new addButterfly(y);      //get add/sub class
    }
}
```

 THOUGHT QUESTIONS

1. Consider a personal checkbook management program such as Quicken. It manages several bank accounts and investments and can handle your bill paying. Where could you use a Factory pattern in designing a program like that?

2. Suppose that you are writing a program to assist homeowners in designing additions to their houses. What objects might a Factory pattern be used to produce?

Programs on the CD-ROM

Program	Description
\Base Factory\	Illustrates the Namer factory.
\FactoryIllustration\	A simple prototype showing a Simple Factory pattern.
\FFT\	Illustrates the use of the Simple Factory in FFT.

CHAPTER 4

The Factory Method

We have just seen a couple of examples of the simplest of factories. The factory concept recurs throughout OO programming, and we find examples embedded in Java itself (such as the SocketFactory class) and in other design patterns (such as the Builder pattern, discussed in Chapter 7). In these cases, a single class acts as a traffic cop and decides which subclass of a single hierarchy will be instantiated.

The Factory Method pattern is a clever but subtle extension of this idea, where no single class makes the decision as to which subclass to instantiate. Instead, the superclass defers the decision to each subclass. This pattern does not actually have a decision point where one subclass is directly selected over another subclass. Instead, a program written using this pattern defines an abstract class that creates objects but lets each subclass decide which object to create.

We can draw a pretty simple example from the way that swimmers are seeded into lanes in a swim meet. When swimmers compete in multiple heats in a given event, they are sorted to compete from slowest in the early heats to fastest in the last heat and arranged within a heat with the fastest swimmers in the center lanes. This is called *straight seeding*.

Now, when swimmers swim in championships, they frequently swim the event twice. During preliminaries, everyone competes and the top 12 or 16 swimmers return to compete against each other at finals. In order to make the preliminaries more equitable, the top heats are *circle seeded*, so that the fastest three swimmers are in the center lane in the fastest three heats, the second fastest three swimmers are in the lanes next to center lane in the top three heats, and so on.

So how do we build some objects to implement this seeding scheme and illustrate the Factory Method pattern? First, we design an abstract Event class.

```
public abstract class Event    {
    protected int     numLanes;          //used in each subclass
    protected Vector swimmers;

    public abstract Seeding getSeeding();
    public abstract boolean isPrelim();
    public abstract boolean isFinal();
    public abstract boolean isTimedFinal();
}
```

This defines the methods without our having to fill in the methods. Then we can derive concrete classes from the Event class, called PrelimEvent and Timed-FinalEvent. The only difference between these classes is that one returns one kind of seeding and the other returns a different kind of seeding.

We also define an abstract Seeding class having the following methods:

```
public abstract class Seeding {
    public abstract Enumeration getSwimmers();
    public abstract int getCount();
    public abstract int getHeats();
}
```

Next, we create two concrete seeding subclasses: StraightSeeding and Circle-Seeding. The PrelimEvent class will return an instance of CircleSeeding, and the TimedFinalEvent class will return an instance of StraightSeeding. Thus we see that we have two hierarchies: one of Events and one of Seedings. We see these two hierarchies illustrated in Figure 4.1.

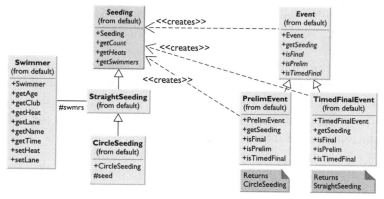

Figure 4.1   The class relationships between Event and Seeding classes.

In the Event hierarchy, you will see that both derived Event classes contain a *getSeeding* method. One of them returns an instance of StraightSeeding, and the other returns an instance of CircleSeeding. So you see, there is no real factory decision point as we had in our simple Namer example. Instead, the decision as to which Event class to instantiate determines which Seeding class will be instantiated.

While it looks like there is a one-to-one correspondence between the Seeding and Event class hierarchies, there needn't be. There could be many kinds of Events and only a few kinds of Seeding that they use.

The Swimmer Class

We haven't said much about the Swimmer class, except that it contains a name, club, age, seed time, and place to put the heat and lane after seeding. The Event class reads in the Swimmers to a Vector from some database (a file, in this example) and then passes that Vector to the Seeding class when we call the *getSeeding* method for that event.

The Event Classes

We have seen the abstract base Event class earlier. We actually use it to read in the swimmer data (here from a file) and pass it on to instances of the Swimmer class to parse.

```
public abstract class Event {
    protected int    numLanes;
                                    //number of lanes
    protected Vector swimmers;      //list of swimmers

    public Event(String filename, int lanes) {
        numLanes = lanes;
        swimmers = new Vector();
        //read in swimmers from file
        InputFile f = new InputFile(filename);
        String s = f.readLine();
        while(s != null) {
            Swimmer sw = new Swimmer(s);
            swimmers.addElement(sw);
            s = f.readLine();
        }
        f.close();
    }
    public abstract Seeding getSeeding();
    public abstract boolean isPrelim();
    public abstract boolean isFinal();
    public abstract boolean isTimedFinal();
}
```

Our PrelimEvent class just returns an instance of CircleSeeding,

```
public class PrelimEvent extends Event {

//class describes an event that will be swum twice
    public PrelimEvent(String filename, int lanes) {
        super(filename, lanes);
    }
    //return circle seeding
    public Seeding getSeeding() {
        return new CircleSeeding(swimmers, numLanes);
    }
    public boolean isPrelim() {
        return true;
    }
    public boolean isFinal() {
        return false;
    }
    public boolean isTimedFinal() }
        return false;
    }
}
```

Straight Seeding

In actually writing this program, we'll discover that most of the work is done in straight seeding; the changes for circle seeding are pretty minimal. So we instantiate our StraightSeeding class and copy in the Vector of swimmers and the number of lanes.

```
public class StraightSeeding extends Seeding {
        protected Vector    swimmers;
        protected Swimmer[] swmrs;
        protected int       numLanes;
        protected int[]     lanes;
        protected int       count;
        protected int       numHeats;

public StraightSeeding(Vector sw, int lanes) {
        Swimmers = sw;
        numLanes = lanes;
        count = sw.size();
        calcLaneOrder();
        seed();
    }
```

Then, as part of the constructor, we do the basic seeding:

```
protected void seed() {
        //loads the swmrs array and sorts it
        sortUpwards();

        int lastHeat = count % numLanes;
        if(lastHeat < 3)
           lastHeat = 3;       //last heat must have 3 or more
```

```
        int lastLanes = count - lastHeat;
        numHeats = count / numLanes;
        if(lastLanes > 0)
            numHeats++;
        int heats = numHeats;

        //place heat and lane in each swimmer's object
        int j = 0;

        for(int i = 0; i < lastLanes; i++) {
            Swimmer sw = swmrs[i];

            sw.setLane(lanes[j++]);
            sw.setHeat(heats);
            if(j >= numLanes) {
                heats--;
                j=0;
            }
        }
        //Add in last partial heat
        if(j < numLanes)
            heats--;
        j = 0;
        for(int i = lastLanes-1; i<count; i++) {

            Swimmer sw = swmrs[i];
            sw.setLane(lanes[j++]);
        }
        //copy from array back into Vector

        Swimmers = new Vector();
        for(int i = 0; i < count; i++)
            Swimmers.addElement(swmrs[i]);
    }
```

This makes the entire array of seeded Swimmers available when we call the *getSwimmers* method.

Circle Seeding

The CircleSeeding class is derived from StraightSeeding, so it copies in the same data.

```
public class CircleSeeding extends StraightSeeding {

    public CircleSeeding(Vector sw, int lanes) {
        super(sw, lanes);  //straight seed first
        seed();
    }
//---------------
    protected void seed() {
        int circle;

        super.seed();       //do straight seed as default
```

```
if(numHeats >= 2 ) {
    if(numHeats >= 3)
        circle = 3;
    else
        circle = 2;
    int i= 0;
    for(int j = 0; j < numLanes; j++) {
        for(int k = 0; k < circle; k++) {
            swmrs[i].setLane(lanes[j]);
            swmrs[i++].setHeat(numHeats - k);
        }
    }
}
}
```

Since the constructor calls the parent class constructor, it copies the swimmer Vector and lane values. Then a call to *super.seed()* does the straight seeding. This simplifies things because we will always need to seed the remaining heats by straight seeding. Then we seed the last 2 or 3 heats as shown previously, and we are done with that type of seeding as well.

The Seeding Program

In this example, we took from the Web a list of swimmers who had competed in the 500-yard freestyle and the 100-yard freestyle and used them to build our TimedFinalEvent and PrelimEvent classes. You can see the results of these two seedings in Figure 4.2.

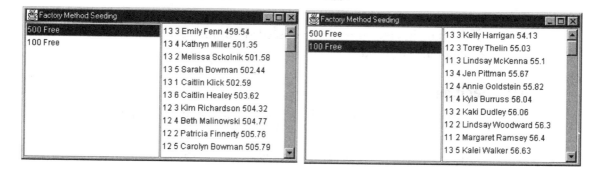

Figure 4.2   Straight seeding of the 500-yard and circle seeding of the 100-yard freestyles.

Other Factories

Now one issue that we have skipped over is how the program that reads in the swimmer data decides which kind of event to generate. We finesse this here by calling the two constructors directly:

```
events.addElement(new TimedFinalEvent("500free.txt", 6));
events.addElement(new PrelimEvent("100free.txt", 6));
```

Clearly, this is an instance where an EventFactory may be needed to decide which kind of event to generate. This revisits the simple factory we began the discussion with.

When to Use a Factory Method

You should consider using a Factory method under the following circumstances:

- A class can't anticipate which kind of class of objects that it must create.
- A class uses its subclasses to specify which objects it creates.
- You want to localize the knowledge of which class gets created.

There are several variations on the Factory pattern.

1. The base class is abstract, and the pattern must return a complete working class.

2. The base class contains default methods and is subclassed only when the default methods are insufficient.

3. Parameters are passed to the factory telling it which of several class types to return. In this case, the classes may share the same method names, but each may do something quite different.

 THOUGHT QUESTION

1. Seeding in track is carried out from inside to outside lanes. What classes would you need to develop to carry out track-like seeding?

Programs on the CD-ROM

Program	Description
\Factory\Factory Method \ShowSeeding.java	Illustrates the Factory Method pattern.

CHAPTER 5

The Abstract Factory Pattern

The Abstract Factory pattern is one level of abstraction higher than the Factory Method pattern. You can use this pattern to return one of several related classes of objects, each of which can return several different objects on request. In other words, the Abstract Factory is a factory object that returns one of several groups of classes. You might even decide which class to return from that group by using a Simple Factory.

One classic application of the Abstract Factory pattern is when your system needs to support multiple look-and-feel user interfaces, such as Windows *9x*, Motif, and Macintosh. You tell the factory that you want your program to look like Windows, and it returns a GUI factory that returns Windows-like objects. Then when you request specific objects, such as buttons, check boxes, and windows, the GUI factory returns Windows instances of these visual interface components.

In Java 1.2, the pluggable look-and-feel classes accomplish this at the system level so that instances of the visual interface components are returned correctly once the program selects the type of look and feel. In the following code, we find the name of the current windowing system and then tell the pluggable look-and-feel (PLAF) Abstract Factory to generate the correct objects.

```
String laf = UIManager.getSystemLookAndFeelClassName();
try {
      UIManager.setLookAndFeel(laf);
   }
   catch(UnsupportedLookAndFeelException exc){
      System.err.println("Unsupported L&F: " + laf);
}catch(Exception exc)
      System.err.println("Error loading " + laf);
   }
```

33

A GardenMaker Factory

Let's consider a simple example where you might want to use the Abstract factory in your application.

Suppose you are writing a program to plan the layout of gardens. These could be annual gardens, vegetable gardens, or perennial gardens. No matter the type of garden, we want to ask the same questions:

1. What are good center plants?

2. What are good border plants?

3. What plants do well in partial shade?

. . . and probably many other plant questions that we'll omit in this simple example.

We want a base Garden class that can answer these questions.

```
public abstract class Garden {
   public abstract Plant getCenter();
   public abstract Plant getBorder();
   public abstract Plant getShade();
}
```

In this case, the Plant object just contains and returns the plant name.

```
public class Plant {
String name;
   public Plant(String pname) {
     name = pname;              //save name
   }
   public String getName() {
      return name;
   }
}
```

In *Design Patterns* terms, the abstract Garden class is the Abstract Factory. It defines the methods of a concrete class that can return one of several classes, in this case one each for center, border, and shade-loving plants. The Abstract Factory could also return more-specific garden information, such as soil pH and recommended moisture content.

In a real system, for each type of garden we would probably consult an elaborate database of plant information. In this example, we'll return one kind of plant from each category. So, for example, for the vegetable garden we write the following:

```
public class VeggieGarden extends Garden {
   public Plant getShade() {
      return new Plant("Broccoli");
   }
```

```
public Plant getCenter() {
    return new Plant("Corn");
}
public Plant getBorder() {
    return new Plant("Peas");
}
}
```

Similarly, we can create Garden classes for PerennialGarden and Annual-Garden. Each of these concrete classes is a *Concrete Factory*, since it implements the methods outlined in the parent abstract class. Now we have a series of Garden objects, each of which returns one of several Plant objects. This is illustrated in the class diagram in Figure 5.1.

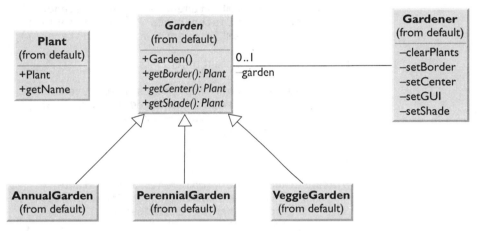

Figure 5.1   The major objects in the Gardener program.

We can easily construct Gardener, our abstract factory driver program, to return one of these Garden objects based on the radio button that a user selects, as shown in the user interface in Figure 5.2.

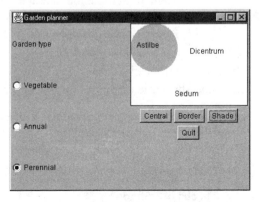

Figure 5.2   The user interface of the Gardener program.

How the User Interface Works

This simple interface consists of two parts: the left side, which selects the garden type, and the right side, which selects the plant category. When you click on one of the garden types, this causes the program to return a type of garden that depends on which button you select. At first, you might think that we would need to perform some sort of test to decide which button was selected and then instantiate the right Concrete Factory class. However, a more elegant solution is to create a different ItemListener for each radio button *as an inner class* and have each one create a different garden type.

First, we create the instances of each Listener class.

```
Veggie.addItemListener(new VeggieListener());
Peren.addItemListener(new PerenListener());
Annual.addItemListener(new AnnualListener());
```

Then we define the actual inner classes.

```
class VeggieListener implements ItemListener {
    public void itemStateChanged(ItemEvent e) {
        garden = new VeggieGarden();
        clearPlants();
    }
}
//--------------
class PerenListener implements ItemListener {
    public void itemStateChanged(ItemEvent e) {
        garden = new PerennialGarden();
        clearPlants();
    }
}
//--------------
class AnnualListener implements ItemListener {
    public void itemStateChanged(ItemEvent e) {
        garden = new AnnualGarden();
        clearPlants();
    }
}
```

Thus when a user clicks on one of the plant type buttons, the plant type is returned, and the name of that plant is displayed.

```
public void actionPerformed(ActionEvent e) {
    Object obj = e.getSource();
    if(obj == Center)
        setCenter();
    if(obj == Border)
        setBorder();
    if(obj == Shade)
        setShade();
```

```
            if(obj == Quit)
                System.exit(0);
    }
```

You can avoid the if tests in the previous *actionPerformed* method by making three different ActionListener classes, but for a program this simple, this does not seem justified. You can examine the details of drawing the garden in the code on the CD-ROM.

Adding More Classes

One of the great strengths of the Abstract Factory pattern is that you can add new subclasses very easily. For example, if you need a GrassGarden or a Wildflower Garden, you can subclass Garden and produce these classes. The only real change that you'd need to make in any existing code is to add some way to choose these new kinds of gardens.

Consequences of the Abstract Factory Pattern

One of the main purposes of the Abstract Factory is that it isolates the concrete classes that are generated. The actual names of these classes are hidden in the factory and need not be known at the client level.

Because of the isolation of classes, you can change or interchange these product class families freely. Further, since you generate only one kind of concrete class, this system keeps you from inadvertently using classes from different families of products. However, adding new class families takes some effort because you must define new, unambiguous conditions that cause such a new family of classes to be returned.

While all of the classes that the Abstract Factory pattern generates have the same base class, nothing prevents some subclasses from having additional methods that differ from the methods of other classes. For example, a BonsaiGarden class might have a *Height* or *WateringFrequency* method that is not present in other classes. This creates the same problem as occurs in any subclasses. That is, you don't know whether you can call a class method unless you know whether the subclass is one that allows those methods. This problem has the same two solutions as does any similar case. Either you can define all of the methods in the base class, even if they don't always have an actual function. Or, if you can't change the base class, you can derive a new base class that contains all of the methods that you need and then subclass that for all of your garden types.

THOUGHT QUESTION

1. Suppose that you are writing a program to track investments, such as stocks, bonds, metal futures, and derivatives. How could you use an Abstract Factory pattern?

Programs on the CD-ROM

Program	Description
\Abstract Factory\Gardener.java	Launches the user interface given in this chapter and exercises the Abstract Factory pattern and the various Garden classes.

CHAPTER 6

The Singleton Pattern

In this chapter, we'll take up the Singleton pattern. This pattern is grouped with the other Creational patterns, although it is to some extent a pattern that limits, rather than promotes, the creation of classes. Specifically, it ensures that there is one and only one instance of a class and provides a global point of access to that instance. Any number of cases in programming in which you need to ensure that there can be one and only one instance of a class are possible. For example, your system might have only one window manager or print spooler or one point of access to a database engine. Or, your computer might have several serial ports, but there can only be one instance of COM1.

Creating a Singleton Using a Static Method

The easiest way to create a class that can have only one instance is to embed a static variable inside of the class that is set on the first instance and then check for it each time that you enter the constructor. A *static variable* is a variable for which there is only one instance, no matter how many instances of the class exist. To prevent instantiating the class more than once, make the constructor private so that an instance can be created only from within the static method of the class. Then we create a method called *Instance*, which will return an instance of *Spooler*, or *null*, if the class has already been instantiated. This is illustrated in the following code:

```
public class PrintSpooler {
    private static PrintSpooler spooler;

    private PrintSpooler() {
    }
```

```
                //return only one spooler instance
                public static synchronized PrintSpooler getSpooler() {
                    if (spooler == null)              //if none created
                        spooler = new PrintSpooler(); //create one
                    return spooler;                   //return it
                }
                public void print(String s) {
                    System.out.println(s);
                }
            }
```

This approach has the major advantage that you don't have to worry about exception handling if the Singleton already exists—you always get the same instance of the spooler.

And, should you try to create instances of the PrintSpooler class directly, creating instances will fail at compile time because the constructor has been declared as private.

```
            //fails at compile time because constructor is privatized
            PrintSpooler pr3 = new PrintSpooler();
```

Finally, should you need to change the program to allow two or three instances, this class is easily modified to allow this.

If instead you want to know whether a spooler has been created and that you cannot create another, you can return a null if the spooler already exists, or you can throw an exception.

Exceptions and Instances

If you want to know whether you have created a new instance, you must check the *getSpooler* method return to make sure it is not null. Assuming that programmers will always remember to check for errors is the beginning of a slippery slope that many prefer to avoid.

Instead, you can create a class that throws an exception if you attempt to instantiate it more than once. This requires the programmer to take action and is thus a safer approach.

Let's create our own exception class for this case.

```
public class SingletonException extends RuntimeException {
    //new exception type for singleton classes
    public SingletonException() {
        super();
    }
    public SingletonException(String s) {
        super(s);
    }
}
```

Note that other than calling its parent classes through the *super* method, this new exception type doesn't do anything in particular. However, it is convenient to have our own named exception type so that the compiler will warn us of the type of exception we must catch when we attempt to create an instance of PrintSpooler.

Throwing an Exception

Let's write the skeleton of our Spooler class—we'll omit all of the printing methods and just concentrate on correctly implementing the Singleton pattern:

```
public class Spooler {
    //this is a prototype for a printer-spooler class
    //such that only one instance can ever exist
    static boolean instance_flag = false;    //true if one instance

    public Spooler() throws SingletonException
    {
        if(instance_flag)
            throw new SingletonException("Only one printer
            allowed");
        else
            instance_flag = true;          //set flag for one instance
          System.out.println("printer opened");
    }
}
```

Creating an Instance of the Class

Now that we've created our simple Singleton pattern in the PrintSpooler class, let's see how we use it. Remember that we must enclose every method that may throw an exception in a try-catch block.

```
public class singleSpooler
{
    static public void main(String argv[])
    {
        Spooler pr1, pr2;
        //open one printer--should always work
        System.out.println("Opening one spooler");
        try {
        pr1 = new Spooler();
        }
        catch (SingletonException e)
        (System.out.println(e.getMessage());}
        //try to open another printer--should fail
        System.out.println("Opening two spoolers");
        try {
```

```
                pr2 = new Spooler();
                }
                catch (SingletonException e)
                {System.out.println(e.getMessage());}
        }
}
```

If we execute this program, we get the following results:

```
Opening one spooler
printer opened
Opening two spoolers
Only one spooler allowed
```

The last line indicates that an exception was thrown as expected. The complete source of this program is on the example CD-ROM as singleSpooler.java.

Providing a Global Point of Access to a Singleton Pattern

Since a Singleton pattern is used to provide a single point of global access to a class, your program design must provide for a way to reference the Singleton throughout the program, even though Java has no global variables.

One solution is to create such Singletons at the beginning of the program and pass them as arguments to the major classes that might need to use them.

```
pr1 = new Spooler();
Customers cust = new Customers (pri);
```

The disadvantage is that you might not need all of the Singletons that you create for a given program execution. This could have performance implications. A more elaborate solution is to create a registry of all of the program's Singleton classes and make the registry generally available. Each time a Singleton is instantiated, it notes that in the registry. Then any part of the program can ask for the instance of any Singleton using an identifying string and get back that instance variable.

The disadvantage of the registry approach is that type checking might be reduced, since the table of Singletons in the registry probably keeps all of the Singletons as objects, for example in a Hashtable object. And, of course, the registry itself is probably a Singleton and must be passed to all parts of the program using the constructor of various set functions.

Probably the most common way to provide a global point of access is by using static methods of a class. The class name is always available, and the static methods can be called only from the class and not from its instances, so there is never more than one such instance no matter how many places in your program call that method. This is the approach used in the Java serial port package, javax.comm, discussed next.

The javax.comm Package as a Singleton

The javax.comm package is provided separately from the Java Software Development Kit (SDK) and is downloadable from the Sun Web site. This package is designed to provide control over the serial and parallel ports of a computer. Each supported platform has a different implementation of this package, since it must include native code to handle the actual system hardware.

Serial ports are a good example of a resource that should be represented by a Singleton, since only one program at a time can access a serial port, and even within a program only one module or group of modules should be communicating over the port.

Actually, two Singletons are possible here: one that manages the collection of ports and lets out only one instance of each port and one that manages the port objects themselves, which must each refer to a single port.

In the javax.comm package, the CommPortIdentifier class has a static method for returning an enumeration of all ports in the system:

```
public static Enumeration getPortIdentifiers()
```

This enumeration contains a CommPortIdentifier object for each element in the system. This package handles both parallel and serial ports, so you also need to filter the returned objects to allow only the serial ports.

```
//get enumeration of ports--static method
portEnum = CommPortIdentifier.getPortIdentifiers();

while (portEnum.hasMoreElements()) {
   portId = (CommPortIdentifier) portEnum.nextElement();
   if (portId.getPortType() == CommPortIdentifier.PORT_SERIAL)
      ports.addElement (portId.getName()); //add to list
}
```

The *getPortIdentifiers* method is static, so it provides the single global point of access required by the Singleton definition. Further, since it is a static method, multiple instances are not allowed. You can call this method only from the class and not from its instances. Each CommPortIdentifier instance returned from this enumeration has a distinct port name, which you can access using the *getName* method.

This enumeration consists of all possible ports for the system, whether opened or not, implemented or not. For example, on a PC the enumeration returns COM1, COM2, COM3, and COM4, regardless of whether cards for all of these ports are installed.

The only way you can make sure that a port is available is only by attempting to open it. If the port doesn't exist at all, the *open* method throws the NoSuchPortException; if the port is in use by another program, it throws the PortInUseException. The code for handling this looks like the following:

```
//try to get port ownership
portId = CommPortIdentifier.getPortIdentifier(portName);

//if successful, open the port
    Commport cp = portId.open("SimpleComm",100);
//report success
    status.add("Port opened: "+portName);
}
catch(NoSuchPortException e){
    status.add("No such port:"+portName);
}
catch(PortInUseException e) {
    status.add (portName+" in use by: " +
                portId.getCurrent Owner());
}
```

Note that we are sending the error messages to some sort of status display. The important thing is that the CommPort *cp* is non-null only if no exceptions are thrown. We illustrate the use of these ports in the SimpleComm program shown in Figure 6.1.

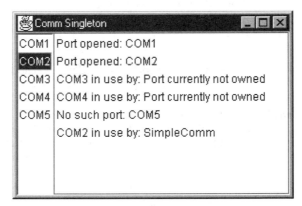

Figure 6.1   The SimpleComm program executing, showing how it represents ports that do not exist and those that are not owned.

An enumeration of the four legal ports that the PC BIOS recognizes is shown on the left. In addition, we added the bogus COM5 port to show the error message it generates. Clicking on each port in turn opens that port and assigns it to the SimpleComm program. When we click on COM3 and COM4, the system throws the PortInUseException, as if ports 3 and 4 were assigned to the system and in use by it. However, the *getCurrentOwner* method returns the message "Port currently not owned," which means it really didn't exist in the first place. When we click on COM5, we get the NoSuchPortException. When we again click on COM2, we find that it is now in use as well, and by this program.

You might ask whether each port is a Singleton. There can be many instances of a port, but you can have only one open at a time. This certainly is providing a single global point of access and making sure that only one can be used at a time. Thus we can probably view the opened ports as Singletons as well.

Building a CommPortManager

Let's consider constructing an enclosing class for these Singleton methods and calling it a PortManager. We expect the class to allow us to enumerate the available ports and open any of them. Some of the methods in such a class might be as follows:

```
public abstract class PortManager {
public static Enumeration  getAllPorts();
public static Enumeration  getAvailablePorts();
public static CommPort     openPort(String portName);
public static CommPort     openPort();
}
```

Because of the Java syntax rules, we can't have abstract static classes, so we actually declare each of them in the parent abstract class to return null.

The *getAllPorts* method is just like the one shown previously, when we enumerated the ports. However, the *getAvailablePorts* method is interesting because we don't need to do anything at all when we catch the port exceptions. We get the port and try to open it. If neither operation fails, we add the port name to the list of available ports.

```
public static Enumeration getAvailablePorts() {
    Vector portOpenList = new Vector();
    CommPortIdentifier portId;

    Enumeration enum = getAllPorts();
    while (enum.hasMoreElements ()) {
        String portName = (String) enum.nextElement () ;
        try {
            //try to get port ownership
            portId =
                CommPortIdentifier.getPortIdentifier(portName);
            //if successful, open the port
```

```
            CommPort cp = portId.open("SimpleComm",100);
            //report success
            portOpenList.addElement(portName);
            cp.close();
            }
        catch(NoSuchPortException e){}
        catch(PortInUseException e){}
        }
    return portOpenList.elements ();
}
```

The *getAvailablePorts* method is illustrated in Figure 6.2.

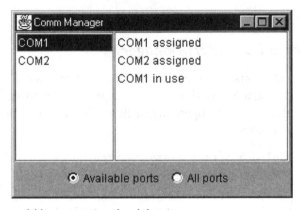

Figure 6.2   The available ports assigned and then in use.

Which are the Singletons here? We really just wrapped the *CommPortIdentifier* methods so that we could handle the exceptions internally. The static *CommPortIdentifier* method might be considered a Singleton registry, since it provides access to four or more different ports. However, as a static method it does provide the single point of access. The ports themselves remain the Singletons, since only one instance of an opened port can exist.

Other Consequences of the Singleton Pattern

The Singleton Pattern has the following additional consequences:

1. Subclassing a Singleton can be difficult, since this can work only if the base Singleton class has not yet been instantiated.

2. You can easily change a Singleton to allow a small number of instances, where this is allowed and meaningful.

THOUGHT QUESTION

1. Consider a system for processing ATM card transactions. A thief is using a stolen ATM card number to steal funds, concurrent with the legitimate user's withdrawing funds. How could you design a Singleton to reduce this risk?

Programs on the CD-ROM

Program	Description
\Singleton\singleSpooler\ SingleSpooler.java	Shows how to write a print spooler throwing an exception.
\Singleton\finalSpool\ finalspool.java	Returns a single instance of a spooler and will not create more.
\Singleton\InstanceSpooler\ InstanceSpooler.java	Creates one instance or returns null.
\Singleton\Comm SimpleComm.java	Simple illustration of Comm class uses.
\Singleton\PortManager\ ManageComm.java	Uses the CommPortManager class.

CHAPTER 7

The Builder Pattern

In this chapter we'll consider how to use the Builder pattern to construct objects from components. We have already seen that the Factory Pattern returns one of several different subclasses, depending on the data passed in arguments to the creation methods. But suppose we don't want just a computing algorithm, but rather a whole different user interface, depending on the data we need to display. A typical example might be your e-mail address book. You probably have both people and groups of people in your address book, and you expect the display for the address book to change so that the People screen has places for first and last names, company name, e-mail address, and telephone number.

On the other hand, if you were displaying a group address page, you'd like to see the name of the group, its purpose, and a list of its members and their e-mail addresses. You click on a person's name and get one display and click on a group's name and get the other display. Let's assume that all e-mail addresses are kept in an Address object and that People and Group classes are derived from this base class, as shown in Figure 7.1.

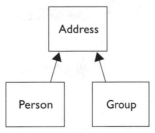

Figure 7.1   Both Person and Group are derived from Address.

Depending on which type of Address object we click on, we'd like to see a somewhat different display of that object's properties. This is little more than just a Factory pattern because the objects returned are not simple descendents of a base display object, but rather totally different user interfaces made up of different combinations of display objects. The Builder pattern assembles a number of objects, such as display widgets, in various ways depending on the data. Furthermore, since Java is one of the few languages with which you can cleanly separate the data from the display methods into simple objects, Java is the ideal language to implement the Builder pattern.

An Investment Tracker

Let's consider a somewhat simpler case in which it would be useful to have a class build our GUI for us. Suppose that we want to write a program to keep track of the performance of our investments, for example, stocks, bonds, and mutual funds. We want to display a list of our holdings in each category so that we can select one or more of the investments and plot their comparative performances.

Even though we can't predict in advance how many of each kind of investment we might own at any given time, we want a display that is easy to use for either a large number of funds (such as stocks) or a small number of funds (such as mutual funds). In each case, we want some sort of multiple choice display so that we can select one or more funds to plot. If there is a large number of funds, we'll use a multichoice list box; if there are three or fewer funds, we'll use a set of check boxes. We want our Builder class to generate an interface that depends on the number of items to be displayed and yet have the same methods for returning the results.

Our displays are shown in Figure 7.2. The first display, Figure 7.2(a), contains a large number of stocks, and the second, Figure 7.2(b), a small number of bonds.

(a)   (b)

Figure 7.2   (a) Display of stocks showing the list interface and (b) display of bonds showing the check box interface.

Now, let's consider how we can build the interface to carry out this variable display. We'll start with a multiChoice abstract class that defines the methods that we need to implement.

```
public abstract class multiChoice {
    //the abstract base class
    //from which the list box and check box choice panels
    //are derived
    private Vector choices;            //array of labels
    public multiChoice(Vector choiceList) {
        choices = choiceList;          //save list
    }
    //to be implemented in derived classes
    abstract public Panel getUI();        //return Panel of components
    abstract public String[] getSelected(); //get list
    abstract public void clearAll();         //clear all
}
```

The *getUI* method returns a Panel container that has a multiple choice display. The two displays we're using here—a check box panel and a list box panel—are derived from this abstract class.

```
class listBoxChoice extends multiChoice
```

or

```
class checkBoxChoice extends multiChoice
```

Then we create a simple Factory class that decides which of the following two classes to return:

```
public class choiceFactory {
    multiChoice ui;
    //class returns a Panel containing
    //a set of choices displayed by one of
    //several UI methods
    public multiChoice getChoiceUI(Vector choices) {
        if (choices.size() <=3)
            //return a panel of check boxes
            ui = new checkBoxChoice(choices);
        else
            //return a multiselect list box panel
            ui = new listBoxChoice(choices);
        return ui;
    }
}
```

In the language of *Design Patterns*, this simple factory class is called the Director, and each actual class derived from multiChoice is a Builder.

Calling the Builders

Since we're going to need one or more builders, we might call our main class Architect or Contractor. However, here we're dealing with lists of investments, so we'll just call it wealthBuilder. In this main class, we create the user interface, consisting of a BorderLayout with the center divided into a 1-x-2 GridLayout.

The left part of the grid contains our list of investment types and the right an empty panel that we'll fill depending on the kinds of investments selected.

```
public class wealthBuilder extends JxFrame
  implements ListSelectListener, ActionListener {
    private JawtList stockList;                 //list of funds
    private JButton Plot;                        //plot command button
    private JPanel choicePanel;                  //right panel
    private multiChoice mchoice;                 //ui for right panel
    private Vector Bonds, Stocks, Mutuals;       //3 lists
    private choiceFactory cfact;                 //the factory

    public wealthBuilder() {
      super("Wealth Builder");                   //frame title bar
      setGUI();                                  //set up display
      buildStockLists();                         //create stock lists
      cfact = new choiceFactory(                 //create builder factory
}

//--------------
  private void setGUI() {
      JPanel jp = new JPanel();
      getContentPane().add (jp);
      jp.setLayout(new BorderLayout());
      JPanel p = new JPanel();
      jp.add("Center", p);

      //center contains left and right panels
      p.setLayout(new GridLayout(1,2));
      stockList= new JawtList(10)                //left list of stocks
      stockList.addListSelectionListener(this);
      p.add(stockList);
      stockList.add("Stocks");
      stockList.add("Bonds");
      stockList.add("Mutual Funds");
      stockList.addListSelectionListener(this);

      JPanel p1 = new JPanel();
      p1.setBackground(Color.lightGray);
      jp.add("South", p1);
      Plot = new JButton("Plot");
      Plot.setEnabled(false);                    //disabled until picked
      Plot.addActionListener(this);
      p1.add(Plot);
```

```
                                       //right is empty at first
    choicePanel = new JPanel();
    choicePanel.setBackground(Color.lightGray);
    p.add(choicePanel);

    setBounds(100, 100, 300, 200);
    setVisible(true);
}
```

In this simple program, we keep our three lists of investments in three Vectors—Stocks, Bonds, and Mutuals. We load them with arbitrary values as part of program initializing.

```
Vector Mutuals = new Vector();
Mutuals.addElement("Fidelity Magellan");
Mutuals.addElement("T Rowe Price");
Mutuals.addElement("Vanguard PrimeCap");
Mutuals.addElement("Lindner Fund");
```

In a real system, we'd probably read them in from a file or database. Then, when the user clicks on one of the three investment types in the left list box, we pass the equivalent Vector to our Factory, which returns one of the Builders:

```
private void stockList_Click() {
    Vector v = null;
    int index = stockList.getSelectedIndex();
    choicePanel.removeAll(); //remove previous gui panel

    //switches between three different Vectors
    //and passes the selected one to the Builder pattern
    switch (index) {
    case 0:
        v = Stocks; break;
    case 1:
        v = Bonds; break;
    case 2:
        v = Mutuals;
    }
    mchoice = cfact.getChoiceUI(v);      //get one of the guis
    choicePanel.add(mchoice.getUI());    //insert on right
    choicePanel.validate();              //re-layout and display
    choicePanel.repaint ();
    Plot.setEnabled(true);               //allow plots
}
```

We show this *switch* code for simplicity. We could just as easily have attached a different ActionListener to each of the three buttons. We do save the multiChoice panel that the factory creates in the mchoice variable so that we can pass it to the Plot dialog.

The List Box Builder

The simpler of the two builders is the list box builder. The getUI method returns
a panel containing a list box showing the list of investments.

```
public class listBoxChoice extends multiChoice {
    JawtList list;
//--------------
    public listBoxChoice(Vector choices) {
        super(choices);
    }
//--------------
    public JPanel getUI() {
        //create a panel containing a list box
        JPanel p = new JPanel();
        list = new JawtList(choices.size());
        list.setMultipleMode(true);
        p.add(list);
        for (int i = 0; i < choices.size(); i++)
            list.add((String)choices.elementAt(i));
        return p;
    }
```

The other important method is the *getSelected* method, which returns a String
array of the investments that the user selects.

```
public String[] getSelected() {
        String[] slist = list.getSelectedItems ();
        return(slist);
}
```

The Check Box Builder

The Check box Builder is even simpler. Here we need to find out how many elements are to be displayed and then create a horizontal grid of that many divi-
sions. Then we insert a check box in each grid line.

```
public class checkBoxChoice extends multiChoice {
    //This derived class creates
    //vertical grid of check boxes
    int count;                          //number of check boxes
    JPanel p;                           //contained here
//--------------
    public checkBoxChoice (Vector choices) {
        super(choices);
        count = 0;
        p = new JPanel();
    }
//--------------
    public JPanel getUI() {
        String s;
```

```
    //create a grid layout 1 column x n rows
    p.setLayout(new GridLayout (choices.size(), 1));
    //and add labeled check boxes to it
    for (int i = 0; i< choices.size(); i++) {
        s =(String)choices.elementAt(i);
        p.add(new JCheckBox(s));
        count++;
    }
    return p;
}
```

This *getSelected* method is analogous to the method shown previously and is included in the example code on the CD-ROM. We illustrate the final UML class diagram in Figure 7.3.

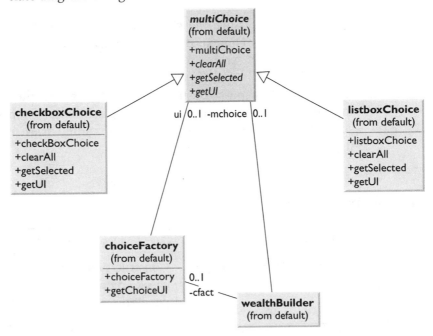

Figure 7.3   The Builder class diagram.

Consequences of the Builder Pattern

Using a Builder pattern has the following consequences:

1. A Builder pattern lets you vary the internal representation of the product that it builds. It also hides the details of how the product is assembled.

2. Each specific Builder is independent of any others and of the rest of the program. This improves modularity and makes the addition of other Builders relatively simple.

3. Because each Builder constructs the final product step by step, depending on the data, you have more control over each final product that a Builder constructs.

A Builder pattern is somewhat like an Abstract Factory pattern in that both return classes made up of a number of methods and objects. The main difference is that while the Abstract Factory returns a family of related classes, the Builder constructs a complex object step by step depending on the data presented to it.

THOUGHT QUESTIONS

1. Some word processing and graphics programs construct menus dynamically based on the context of the data being displayed. How could you use a Builder effectively here?

2. Not all Builders must construct visual objects. For the personal finance industry, what could you construct using a Builder? Suppose that you are scoring a track meet made up of five to six different events. How can you use a Builder in such a situation?

Programs on the CD-ROM

Program	Description
\Builder\wealthBuilder.java	Constructs the last box and check box multiple choice panels discussed in this chapter.

CHAPTER 8

The Prototype Pattern

With the Prototype pattern, you can specify the general class needed in a program but defer specifying the exact class until execution time. It is similar to the Builder pattern in that some class decides what components or details make up the final class. However, it differs in that the target classes are constructed by cloning one or more prototype classes and then changing or filling in the details of the cloned class to behave as desired.

Prototypes can be used whenever you need classes that differ only in the type of processing that they offer, for example, when parsing strings that represent numbers in different radixes. In this sense, the Prototype is nearly the same as the Exemplar pattern described by Coplien [1992].

Let's consider the case in which you need to make a number of queries to an extensive database to construct an answer. Once you have this answer as a table or ResultSet, you might want to manipulate it to produce other answers without your having to issue additional queries.

For example, consider a database of a large number of swimmers in a league or statewide organization. Each swimmer swims several strokes and distances throughout a season. The best times for swimmers are tabulated by age group. Within a single four-month season, many swimmers will have birthdays and therefore move into new age groups. Thus the query to determine which swimmers did the best in their age groups that season depends on the date of each meet and on each swimmer's birthday. The computational cost of assembling this table of times is therefore fairly high.

Once you have a class containing this table, sorted by sex, you might want to examine this information sorted by time or by actual age rather than by age group. Recomputing this data isn't sensible, and you don't want to destroy the original data order, so some sort of copy of the data object is desirable.

Cloning in Java

You can make a copy of any Java object using the *clone* method.

```
JObj j1 = (JObj)j0.clone();
```

The *clone* method always returns an object declared to have a return type of Object. Thus you must cast it to the actual type of the object that you are cloning. Three other significant restrictions apply to this method:

1. It is a protected method and can be called only from within the same class or a subclass.

2. You can clone only objects that are declared to implement the Cloneable interface. All arrays are considered to implement the Cloneable interface.

3. Any object whose class is Object does not implement Cloneable and throws the CloneNotSupported Exception.

Since the *clone* method is protected, this suggests packaging the public, visible *clone* method inside of the class, where it can access that protected *clone* method.

```
public abstract class SwimData implements Cloneable {

    public Object cloneMe() throws CloneNotSupportedException {
        return super.clone();
    }
}
```

You can also create special cloning procedures that change the data or processing methods in the cloned class, based on arguments that you pass to the *clone* method. In this case, method names such as *make* are probably more descriptive and suitable.

Using the Prototype

Now let's write a simple program that reads data from a database and then clones the resulting object. In our example program, SwimInfo, we just read these data from a file, but the original data were derived from a large database as we mentioned previously.

Then we create a class called Swimmer that holds one swimmer's name, age, sex, club, and time.

```
public class Swimmer {
    String name;    //name of swimmer
    int    age;     //age of swimmer
    String club;    //name of club
    float  time;       //result of time
    boolean female;    //sex
```

```
float   time;      //result of time
boolean female;    //sex
```

We also create a class called SwimData that maintains a Vector of the Swimmers we read in from the database.

```
public class TimeSwimData extends SwimData
implements Cloneable , Serializable {
    protected Vector swimmers;

    public TimeSwimData(String filename) {
        String s = "";
        swimmers     = new Vector();
        InputFile f = new InputFile(filename);
        s= f.readLine();
        while (s != null) {
            swimmers.addElement(new Swimmer(s));
            s= f.readLine();
        }
        f.close();
    }
```

We also provide a *getSwimmer* method in SwimData and *getName, getAge,* and *getTime* methods in the Swimmer class. Once we've read the data into Swim-Info, we can display it in a list box.

Then, when the user clicks on the Clone button, we'll clone this class and sort the data differently in the new class. Again, we clone the data because creating a new class instance would be much slower, and we want to keep the data in both forms.

```
private void cloneAndLoad() {
        try{
            sxdata = (SwimData)sdata.cloneMe();
            sxdata.sort();
        }
        catch(CloneNotSupportedException e){}

        cloneList.removeAll();
        //now list sorted values from clone
        for (int i = 0; i < sxdata.size(); i++) {
            sw = sxdata.getSwimmer(i);
            cloneList.add(sw.getName()+" "+sw.getTime());
        }
    }
```

In the original class, the names are sorted by sex and then by time, while in the cloned class they are sorted only by time. In Figure 8.1, we see the simple user interface that allows us to display the original data on the left and the sorted data in the cloned class on the right.

In the original class, the names are sorted by sex and then by time, while in the cloned class they are sorted only by time. In Figure 8.1, we see the simple user interface that allows us to display the original data on the left and the sorted data in the cloned class on the right.

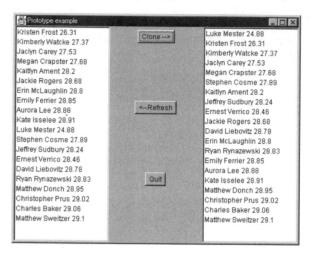

Figure 8.1   Prototype example.

The left-hand list box is loaded when the program starts, and the right-hand list box is loaded when you click on the Clone button. Now let's click on the Refresh button to reload the left-hand list box from the original data. The somewhat disconcerting result is shown in Figure 8.2.

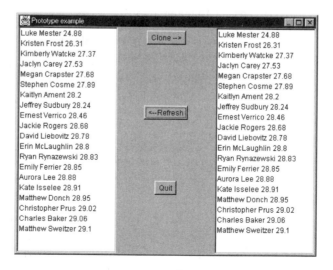

Figure 8.2   Prototype example, after clicking on Clone and then on Refresh.

Why have the names in the left-handed list box also been re-sorted? This occurs in Java because the *clone* method is a *shallow copy* of the original class. In other words, the references to the data objects are copies, but they refer to the same underlying data. Thus any operation performed on the copied data will also be done on the original data in the Prototype class.

In some cases, this shallow copy might be acceptable, but if you want to make a deep copy of the data, you must write a deep cloning routine of your own as part of the class you want to clone. In this simple class, you just create a new Vector using a constructor that creates the new instance and copies the elements of the old class's Vector into the new one.

```java
public TimeSwimData(Vector sw) {
    //this constructor copies vector as a clone
    swimmers = new Vector();
    for (int i = 0; i < sw.size (); i++) {
        swimmers.add (sw.elementAt (i));
    }
}
//--------------
public SwimData myClone() {
    return new TimeSwimData(swimmers);
}
```

Using the Prototype Pattern

You can use the Prototype pattern whenever any of a number of classes might be created or when the classes are modified after being created. As long as all of the classes have the same interface, they can actually be from entirely different class hierarchies.

Let's consider a more elaborate example of the listing of swimmers we discussed previously. Instead of just sorting the swimmers, let's create subclasses that operate on the data, modifying it and presenting the result for display in a list box. We start with the abstract class SwimData, which has all abstract methods except for the *deepClone* method we just described.

```java
//abstract class defining interface and deepClone routine
public abstract class SwimData
        implements Cloneable , Serializable {
public abstract int     size ();
public abstract Swimmer getSwimmer(int i);
public abstract String  getName(int i);
public abstract void    sort();
public abstract void    setFemale(boolean f);
```

```
public SwimData deepClone() {
    //as above
  }
}
```

Then it becomes possible to write different concrete SwimData classes depending on the application's requirements. We always start with the TimeSwimData class and then clone if for various other displays. For example, the SexSwimData class re-sorts the data by sex and displays only one sex, as shown in Figure 8.3.

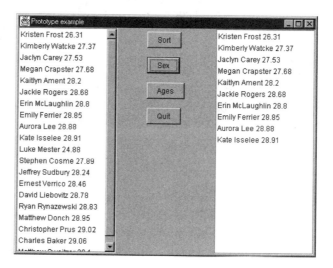

Figure 8.3   The SexSwimData class displays only one sex, shown on the right.

In the SexSwimData class, we sort the data based on whether we want to display girls or boys. This class has the following additional method:

```
public void setFemale(boolean f) {
    female = f;
  }
```

Each time that you click on the button labeled Sex, the boolean representing whether to display females is complemented. Thus when you use the prototype to clone a copy of the base TimeSwimData class to make an instance of SexSwimData, we can also tell it which sex to display.

Classes do not even have to be that similar, however. The AgeSwimData class takes the cloned input data array and creates a simple histogram by age. If you have been displaying the boys, you see their age distribution, and if you have been displaying the girls, you see their age distribution, as shown in Figure 8.4.

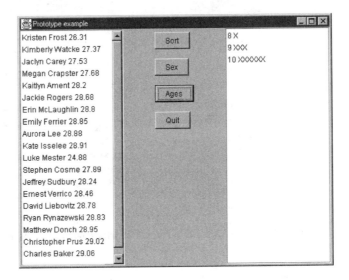

Figure 8.4   The AgeSwimData class displays an age distribution.

In this case, the concrete class resulting from the prototype is two subclasses away from the base class; the first subclass selects a single sex, and the second subclass creates a histogram. In other words, the Prototype pattern effectively hides the concrete products from the client, in this case the display list. The same *getName* and *size* methods are used as in the superclasses, but here the displayed data are quite different. As long as the concrete product classes have the same interface, the Prototype is a suitable pattern choice. We have defined a different concrete class (female or male swimmer list) by creating a class and setting parameters within that class.

The UML diagram in Figure 8.5 illustrates this system fairly clearly. The SwimInfo class is the main GUI class. It keeps two instances of SwimData but does not specify which ones. The TimeSwimData and SexSwimData classes are concrete classes derived from the abstract SwimData class. The AgeSwimData class, which creates the histograms, is derived from the SexSwimData class.

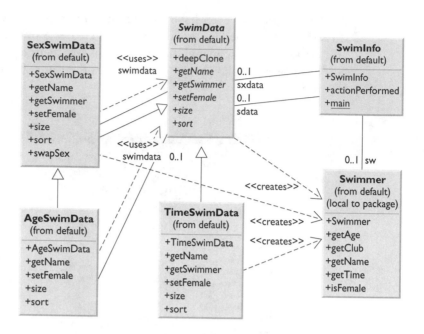

Figure 8.5   The UML diagram for the various SwimData classes.

You should also note that you are not limited to the few subclasses demonstrated here. You could easily create additional concrete classes and register them with whatever code selects the appropriate concrete class. In our previous example program, the user is the deciding point or factory, because he simply clicks on one of several buttons. In a more elaborate case, each concrete class could have an array of characteristics, and the decision point could be a class registry or *prototype manager,* which examines these characteristics and selects the most suitable class. In Java, you can load additional classes dynamically at runtime and make them available through this registry.

You could also combine the Factory Method pattern with the Prototype pattern to have each of several concrete classes use a concrete class different from those available.

Prototype Managers

A prototype manager class can be used to decide which of several concrete classes to return to the client. It can also manage several sets of prototypes at once. For example, in addition to returning one of several classes of swimmers, it could return different groups of swimmers who swam different strokes and distances. It could also manage which list boxes (of several types) are returned and to display them, including tables, multicolumn lists, and graphical displays. It is important that whichever subclass is returned does not require casting to a new class type in order to be used in the program. In other words, the methods of the parent abstract or base class should be sufficient, and the client should never need to know which actual subclass it is dealing with.

Cloning Using Serialization

Here is a clever trick, which some have called a "hack," for cloning using the serializable interface. A class is said to be *serializable* if you can write it out as a stream of bytes and then read those bytes back in to reconstruct the class. This is how Java remote method invocation (RMI) and Java Beans are implemented.

However, if we declare both the Swimmer and SwimData classes as Serializable,

```
public class SwimData
     implements Cloneable, Serializable

class Swimmer implements Serializable
```

we can write the bytes to an output stream and reread them to create a complete data copy of that instance of a class.

```
public Object deepClone() {
    try{
        ByteArrayOutputStream b = new ByteArrayOutputStream();
        ObjectOutputStream out = new ObjectOutputStream(b);
        out.writeObject(this);
        ByteArrayInputStream bIn = new
                ByteArrayInputStream(b.toByteArray());
        ObjectInputStream oi = new ObjectInputStream(bIn);
        return (oi.readObject());
    }
    catch (Exception e) {
        System.out.println("exception:"+e.getMessage());
        return null;
    }
}
```

This *deepClone* method allows you to copy an instance of a class of any complexity and have data be completely independent between the two copies, as long as all of the classes that class contains can be declared serializable.

Consequences of the Prototype Pattern

Using the Prototype pattern,

1.   You can add and remove classes at runtime by cloning them as needed.

2.   You can revise the internal data representation of a class at runtime based on program conditions.

3.   You can also specify new objects at runtime without creating a proliferation of classes and inheritance structures.

One difficulty in implementing the Prototype pattern in Java is that if the classes already exist, you might not be able to change them to add the required *clone* or *deepClone* methods. Using the deepClone method can be particularly difficult if all of the class objects contained in a class cannot be declared serializable. In addition, classes that have circular references to other classes cannot be cloned.

Similar to Singletons, discussed in Chapter 6, you can create a registry of Prototype classes that can be cloned and then ask the registry object for a list of possible prototypes. You might be able to clone an existing class rather than writing one from scratch. Note, however, that every class that you might use as a prototype must itself be instantiated (perhaps at some expense) in order for you to use a Prototype registry. This can be a performance drawback.

Finally, the idea of having Prototype classes to copy implies that you have sufficient access to the data or methods in these classes to change them after cloning. This might require adding data access methods to these prototype classes so that you can modify the data once you have cloned the class.

 THOUGHT QUESTION

1.   An entertaining banner program shows a slogan starting at different places on the screen at different times and in different fonts and sizes. Design the program using a Prototype pattern.

Programs on the CD-ROM

Program	Description
\Prototype\MyClone\ SwimInfo.java	Clones using the constructor to create a new instance by copying the Vector.
\Prototype\DeepProto\ SwimInfo.java	Clones using serialization.
\Prototype\SimpleProto\ SwimInfo.java	Example of shallow cloning and prototype.
\Prototype\AgeProto\ SwimInfo.java	Shows the prototype used to display swimmers by time and sex, and which also gives the age distinction.

Summary of Creational Patterns

Following is a summary of the Creational patterns:

- **Factory pattern**: used to choose and return an instance of a class from a number of similar classes based on data you provide to the factory.
- **Abstract Factory pattern**: returns one of several groups of classes. In some cases, it actually returns a Factory pattern for that group of classes.
- **Builder pattern**: assembles a number of objects to make a new object, based on the data with which it is presented. Often the choice of which way the objects are assembled is achieved using a Factory pattern.
- **Prototype pattern**: copies or clones an existing class rather than creating a new instance, when creating new instances is more expensive.
- **Singleton pattern**: ensures that there is one and only one instance of an object and that it is possible to obtain global access to that one instance.

SECTION 3

Structural Patterns

A *structural pattern* describes how classes and objects can be combined to form larger structures. Class and object patterns differ in that a *class pattern* describes how inheritance can be used to provide more useful program interfaces. An *object pattern* describes how objects can be composed into larger structures using object composition or by including objects within other objects.

- **Adapter pattern:** can be used to make one class interface match another for easier programming.

We'll also look at a number of other structural patterns where we combine objects to provide new functionality.

- **Composite pattern:** creates an object (a composition of objects), each of which may be a simple or a composite object.
- **Proxy pattern:** creates a simple object that takes the place of a more complex object which may be invoked later, such as when the program runs in a networked environment.
- **Flyweight pattern:** for sharing objects, where each instance does not contain its own state, but stores it externally. This approach allows efficient sharing of objects to save space when there are many instances, but only a few different types.
- **Façade pattern:** used to make a single class represent an entire subsystem.
- **Bridge pattern:** separates an object's interface from its implementation so you can vary them separately.
- **Decorator pattern:** lets you add responsibilities to objects dynamically.

You'll see that there is some overlap among these patterns and even some overlap with the Behavioral patterns in the next section. We'll summarize these similarities after we have described all of the patterns.

CHAPTER 9

The Adapter Pattern

The Adapter pattern converts the programming interface of one class into that of another. You use adapters whenever you want unrelated classes to work together in a single program. The concept of an adapter is thus pretty simple: You write a class that has the desired interface and then make it communicate with the class that has a different interface. There are two ways to do this: by inheritance and by object composition. In the first, you derive a new class from the nonconforming one and add the methods that you need to make the new derived class match the desired interface. In the second, you include the original class inside the new one and create the methods to translate calls within the new class. These two approaches, termed class adapters and object adapters, are both fairly easy to implement in Java.

Moving Data between Lists

Let's consider a simple Java program that allows you to enter names into a list and then select some of those names to be transferred to another list. The initial list in the example consists of a class roster, and the second list consists of class members who will be doing advanced work.

In this simple program, shown in Figure 9.1, you enter names into the top entry field and then click on Insert to move the names into the left-hand list box. Then, to move a name to the right-hand list box, you click on it and then click on Add. To remove a name from the right-hand list box, click on it and then on Remove. This moves the name back to the left-hand list.

This is a very simple program to write in Java 1.2. It consists of a GUI creation constructor and an *actionListener* routine for the three buttons. A Command pattern, or even a simple set of if statements, can then call the following actions on the two lists:

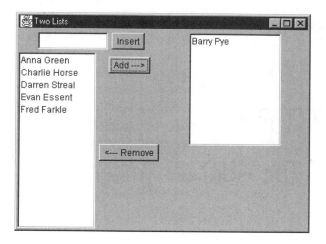

Figure 9.1   A simple program to enter and choose names.

```
//add a name to the left-hand list
  private void addName() {
        if (txt.getText().length()> 0) {
            leftList.add(txt.getText());
            txt.setText("");
        }
   }
//--------------
//move a name from the left to the right list box
  private void moveNameRight() {
        String sel[] = leftList.getSelectedItems();
        if (sel != null) {
            rightList.add(sel[0]);
            leftList.remove(sel[0]);
        }
}
//--------------
//move a name from the right to the left list box
  public void moveNameLeft() {
        String sel[] = rightList.getSelectedItems();
        if (sel != null) {
            leftList.add(sel[0]);
            rightList.remove(sel[0]);
        }
   }
```

This program, called TwoList.java, is included on the CD-ROM that accompanies this book.

Using the JFC JList Class

You will note that the previous example used the AWT List class. This is all quite straightforward, but suppose you would like to rewrite the program using the Java Foundation Classes (JFC or "Swing"). Most of the methods you use for creating and manipulating the user interface remain the same. However, the JFC JList class is markedly different from the AWT List class. In fact, because the JList class was designed to represent far more complex kinds of lists, there are virtually no methods in common between the classes.

AWT List Class	JFC JList Class
add(String);	na
remove(String)	na
String[] getSelectedItems()	Object[] getSelectedValues()

Both classes have quite a number of other methods, and almost none of them are closely correlated. However, since we have already written the program once and make use of two different list boxes, writing an adapter to make the JList class look like the List class will provide a rapid solution to our problem.

The JList class is a window container that has an array, Vector, or other ListModel class associated with it. It is this ListModel that actually contains and manipulates the data. Further, the JList class does not contain a scroll bar but instead relies on being inserted in the viewport of the JScrollPane class. Data in the JList class and its associated ListModel are not limited to strings; they may be almost any kind of objects, as long as you provide the cell drawing routine for them. This makes it possible to have list boxes with pictures illustrating each choice in the list.

In this case, we are going to create a class that only emulates the List class, which here needs only the three methods shown in the previous table.

We can define the needed methods as an interface and then make sure that the class that we create implements those methods.

```
public interface awtList {
    public void      add(String s);
    public void      remove(String s);
    public String[]  getSelectedItems();
}
```

Interfaces are important in Java because Java does not allow multiple inheritance as C++ does. So you cannot create a class that inherits from JList and List at the same time. However, you can create a class that inherits from one class hierarchy and *implements* the methods of another. In most cases, this is quite a powerful solution. Thus, by using the *implements* keyword, we can have the class take on the methods and appearance of being a class of either type.

The Object Adapter

In the object adapter approach, shown in Figure 9.2, we create a class that *contains* a JList class but which implements the methods of the previous awtList interface. Since the outer container for a JList is not the list element at all but the JScrollPane that encloses it, we are really adding methods to a subclass of JScrollPane that emulate the methods of the List class. These methods are in the interface awtList.

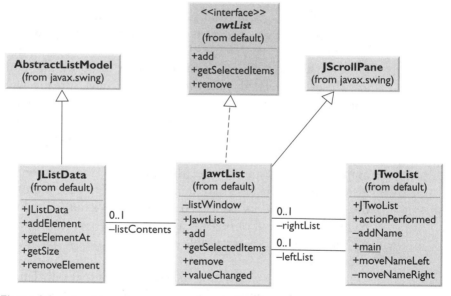

Figure 9.2   An object adapter approach to the list adapter.

So, our basic JawtList class looks as follows:

```
public class JawtList extends JScrollPane
implements ListSelectionListener, awtList {
    private JList listWindow;
    private JListData listContents;

    public JawtList (int rows) {
        listContents = new JListData();
        listWindow  = new JList(listContents);
        listWindow.setPrototypeCellValue("Abcdefg Hijkmnop");
        getViewport().add(listWindow);
    }
}
public class JawtList extends JScrollPane
```

```
implements ListSelectionListener, awtList {
    private JList listWindow;
    private JListData listContents;

    public JawtList (int rows) {
        listContents = new JlistData();
        listWindow = new JList (listContents);
        listWindow.setPrototypeCellValue("Abcdefg Hijkmnop");
        getViewport().add(listWindow);
    }
//------------------------------------------------
    public void add(String s) {
        listContents.addElement(s);
    }
//------------------------------------------------
    public void remove(String s) {
        listContents.removeElement(s);
    }
//------------------------------------------------
    public String[] getSelectedItems() {
        Object[] obj = listWindow.getSelectedValues();
        String[] s   = new String[obj.length];
        for (int i   = 0; i < obj.length; i++)
            s[i] = obj[i].toString();
        return s;
    }
//------------------------------------------------
    public void valueChanged(ListSelectionEvent e) {
    }
}
```

Note, however, that the actual data handling takes place in the JListData class. This class is derived from the AbstractListModel, which defines the methods listed in the following table:

Method	Purpose
addListDataListener(1)	Adds a listener for changes in the data.
removeListDataListener(1)	Removes a listener.
fireContentsChanged(obj,min,max)	Tells the JList window to redraw. Calls this after any change occurs between the two indexes min and max.
fireIntervalAdded(obj,min,max)	Tells the JList window to redraw. Calls this after any data have been added between min and max.

Method	Purpose
`fireIntervalRemoved(obj,min,max)`	Tells the JList window to redraw. Calls this after any data have been removed between min and max.

The three *fire* methods provide the communication path between the data stored in the ListModel and the actual displayed list data. Firing them causes the displayed list to be updated.

In this case, the *addElement*, and *removeElement* methods are all that are needed, although you could imagine a number of other useful methods. Each time that we add data to the data vector, we call the *fireIntervalAdded* method to tell the list display to refresh that area of the displayed list.

```java
public class JListData extends AbstractListModel {
    private Vector data;

    public JListData() {
        data = new Vector();
    }
//----------------
    public int getSize() {
        return data.size();
    }
//----------------
    public Object getElementAt (int index) {
        return data.elementAt(index);
    }
//----------------
    public void addElement(String s) {
        data.addElement(s);
        fireIntervalAdded(this, data.size()-1, data.size());
    }
//----------------
    public void removeElement(String s) {
        data.removeElement(s);
        fireIntervalRemoved(this, 0, data.size());
    }
}
```

The Class Adapter

In Java, the class adapter approach isn't all that different from the object adapter. If we create a class JawtClassList that is derived from JList, then we have to create a JScrollPane in our main program's constructor.

```
leftList           =  new JClassAwtList(15);
JScrollPane lsp =  new JScrollPane();
pLeft.add("Center", lsp);
lsp.getViewport().add(leftList);
```

This class-based adapter is much the same, except that some of the methods now refer to the enclosing class instead of an encapsulated class.

```
public class JclassAwtList extends JList
    implements ListSelectionListener, awtList {
    private JListData listContents;

    public JclassAwtList (int rows) {
        listContents = new JListData();
        setModel(listContents);
        setPrototypeCellValue("Abcdefg Hijklmnop");
    }
```

This is illustrated in Figure 9.3.

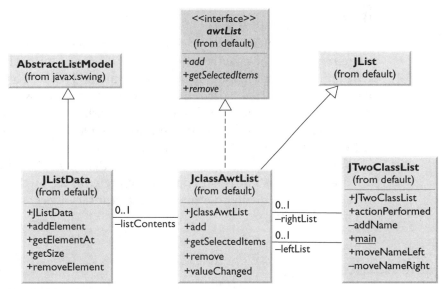

Figure 9.3 A class adapter approach to the List adapter.

Some differences between the List and the adapted JList classes are not so easy to adapt, however. The List class constructor allows you to specify the length of the list in lines. There is no way to specify this directly in the JList class. You can compute the preferred size of the enclosing JScrollPane class based on the font size of the JList, but depending on the layout manager, this might not be honored exactly.

The example class JawtClassList, called by JTwoClassList, is on the accompanying CD-ROM.

There are also some differences between the class and the object adapter approaches, although they are less significant than in C++.

- The class adapter
  - Won't work when you want to adapt a class and all of its subclasses, since you define the class that it derives from when you create it.
  - Lets the adapter change some of the adapted class's methods but still allows the others to be used unchanged.
- The object adapter
  - Could allow subclasses to be adapted by simply passing them in as part of a constructor.
  - Requires that you specifically bring to the surface any of the adapted object's methods that you wish to make available.

Two-Way Adapters

The two-way adapter is a clever concept that allows an object to be viewed by different classes as being either of type awtList or type JList. This is most easily carried out by a class adapter, since all of the methods of the base class are automatically available to the derived class. However, this can work only if you do not override any of the base class's methods with methods that behave differently. As it happens, the JawtClassList class is an ideal two-way adapter because the List and JList classes have no methods in common.

Note in the UML diagram in Figure 9.3 that JawtClassList inherits from JList and *implements* awtList. Thus you can refer to the awtList methods or to the JList methods equally conveniently and treat the object as an instance either of JList or of awtList.

ggable Adapters

A *pluggable adapter* is an adapter that adapts dynamically to one of several classes. Of course, the adapter can adapt only to classes that it can recognize, and usually the adapter decides which class it is adapting to based on differing constructors or *setParameter* methods.

Java has yet another way for adapters to recognize which of several classes it must adapt to: *reflection.* You can use reflection to discover the names of public methods and their parameters for any class. For example, for any arbitrary object you can use the *getClass* method to obtain its class and the *getMethods* method to obtain an array of the method names.

```
JList list = new JList();
    Method[] methods = list.getClass().getMethods();
    //print out methods
    for (int i = 0; i < methods.length; i++) {
        System.out.println(methods[i].getName());
        //print to parameter types
        Class cl[] = methods[i].getParameterTypes();
        for(int j = 0; j < cl.length; j++)
            System.out.println(cl[j].toString());
}
```

A "method dump" like the one produced by this code can generate a very large list of methods. It is easier to use if you know the name of the method that you are looking for and simply want to find out the arguments that it requires. From that method signature, you can then deduce the adaptations that you need to carry out.

However, because Java is a strongly typed language, you more likely would simply invoke the adapter using one of several constructors, with each constructor tailored for a specific class that needs adapting.

Adapters in Java

In a broad sense, a number of adapters are already built into the Java language. In this case, the Java adapters serve to simplify an unnecessarily complicated event interface. One of the most commonly used of these Java adapters is the WindowAdapter class.

One inconvenience of Java is that windows do not close automatically when you click on the Close button or window Exit menu item. The general solution to this problem is to have your main Frame window implement the WindowListener interface and leave all of the Window events empty except for windowClosing.

```
public void mainFrame extends Frame
        implements WindowListener {

    //frame listens for window events
    public void mainFrame() {
        addWindowListener(this);
    }

    public void windowClosing(WindowEvent wEvt) {
        System.exit(0);   //exit on System exit box click
    }
    public void windowClosed(WindowEvent wEvt) {}
    public void windowOpened(WindowEvent wEvt) {}
    public void windowIconified(WindowEvent wEvt) {}
```

```
        public void windowDeiconified(WindowEvent wEvt) {}
        public void windowActivated(WindowEvent wEvt) {}
        public void windowDeactivated(WindowEvent wEvt) {}
}
```

As you can see, this code is awkward and hard to read. The Window Adapter class is provided to simplify this procedure. This class contains empty implementations of all seven of the previous WindowEvents. You then need only to override the windowClosing event and insert the appropriate exit code.

One such simple program is shown next.

```
//illustrates using the WindowAdapter class
//make an extended window adapter which
//This class closes the frame
//when the closing event is received
class WindAp extends WindowAdapter {
    public void windowClosing(WindowEvent e) {
        System.exit(0);
    }
}
//==============
public class Closer extends Frame {
    public Closer() {
        WindAp windap = new WindAp();
        addWindowListener(windap);
        setSize(new Dimension(100,100));
        setVisible(true);
    }
    static public void main(String argv[]) {
        new Closer();
    }
}
```

You can, however, make a much more compact but less readable version of the same code by using an anonymous inner class.

```
//create window listener for window close click
    addWindowListener(new WindowAdapter()
    {
        public void windowClosing(WindowEvent e)
            {System.exit(0);}
    });
```

Adapters like these are common in Java when a simple class can be used to encapsulate a number of events. They include ComponentAdapter, ContainerAdapter, FocusAdapter, KeyAdapter, MouseAdapter, and MouseMotionAdapter.

THOUGHT QUESTION

1. How would you write a class adapter to make the JFC JTable look like a two-column list box?

Programs on the CD-ROM

Program	Description
\Adapter\TwoLists\TwoList.java	An AWT version of two lists.
\Adapter\JTwoLists\JTwoList.java	An object adapter version.
\Adapter\JTwoClassList\ JTwoClassList.java	A class adapter version.
\Adapter\showMethods.java	Illustrates reflection methods.

In addition, the Window adapter is illustrated in both the JTwoList and JTwoClassList programs on the accompanying CD-ROM.

CHAPTER 10

The Bridge Pattern

At first sight, the Bridge pattern looks much like the Adapter pattern in that a class is used to convert one kind of interface to another. However, the Adapter pattern is intended to make one or more classes' interfaces look the same as that of a particular class. By contrast, the Bridge pattern is designed to separate a class's interface from its implementation so that you can vary or replace the implementation without changing the client code.

The participants in the Bridge pattern are

- the Abstraction, which defines the class's interface,
- the Refined Abstraction, which extends and implements that interface,
- the Implementor, which defines the interface for the implementation classes, and
- the ConcreteImplementors, which are the implementation classes.

Suppose that you have a program that displays a list of products in a window. The simplest interface for that display is a JList box. But once a significant number of products have been sold, you might want to display the products in a table along with their sales figures.

Since we have just discussed the adapter pattern, you think immediately of the class-based adapter, where we adapt the fairly elaborate interface of the JList to our simpler needs in this display. In simple programs, this will work fine, but as we'll see, there are limits to that approach.

Further, let's suppose that we need to produce two kinds of displays from our product data, a customer view that is just the list of products we've mentioned and an executive view that also shows the number of units shipped. We'll display the product list in an ordinary JList box and the executive view in a JTable display. These two displays are the implementations of the display classes, as shown in Figure 10.1.

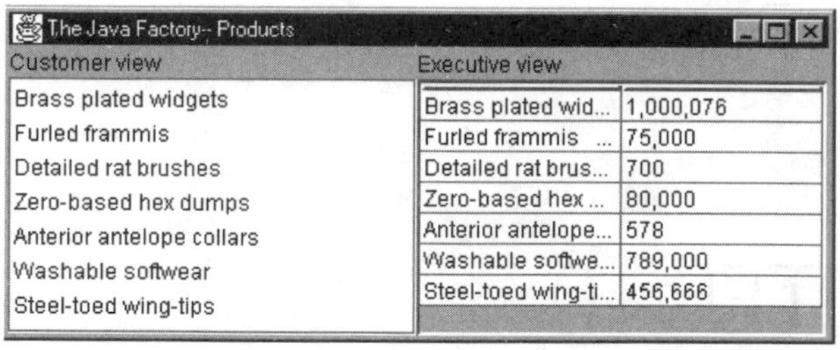

Figure 10.1   Two displays of the same information using a Bridge pattern.

Now, we want to define a single, simple interface that remains the same regardless of the type and complexity of the actual implementation classes. We'll start by defining an abstract Bridger class.

```
public abstract class Bridger extends JPanel {
    public abstract void addData(Vector v);
}
```

This class is so simple that it receives only a Vector of data and passes it on to the display classes.

On the other side of the bridge are the implementation classes, which usually have a more elaborate and somewhat lower-level interface. Here we'll have them add the data lines to the display one at a time.

```
public interface visList {
    public void addLine(String s);
    public void removeLine(int num);
}
```

Implicit in the definition of these classes is some mechanism for determining which part of each string is the name of the product and which part is the quantity shipped. In this simple example, we separate the quantity from the name with two dashes and parse these apart within the list classes.

The Bridge between the interface on the left and the implementation on the right is the listBridge class, which instantiates one or the other of the list display classes. Note that it extends the Bridger class for the use of the application program.

```
public class listBridge extends Bridger {
    protected visList list;

    public listBridge(visList jlist) {
        setLayout(new BorderLayout());
        list = jlist;
        add("Center", (JComponent)list);
    }
    public void addData(Vector v) {
        for (int i = 0; i < v.size(); i++) {
            String s = (String)v.elementAt (i);
```

```
            list.addLine (s);
        }
    }
}
```

Then, at the top programming level, we just create instances of a table and a list using the listBridge class.

```
//add in customer view as list box
        listBridge lList = new listBridge(new productList());
        lList.add Data (prod);
        pleft.add("North", new JLabel("Customer view"));
        pleft.add("Center," lList);

        //add in executive view as table
        listBridge lTable = new listBridge(new productTable());
        lTable.addData (prod);
        pright.add("North", new JLabel("Executive view"));
        pright.add("Center", lTable);
```

The Class Diagram

The UML diagram in Figure 10.2 for the Bridge pattern shows the separation of the interface and the implementation. The Bridger class on the left is the Abstraction, and the listBridge class is the implementation of that abstraction. The visList interface describes the public interface to the list classes productList and productTable. The visList interface defines the interface of the Implementor, and the Concrete Implementors are the productList and productTable classes.

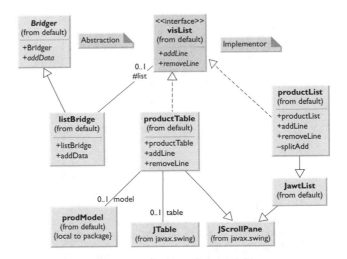

Figure 10.2   The UML diagram for the Bridge pattern used in the two displays of product information.

Note that these two concrete implementors are quite different in their specifics even though they both support the visList interface.

Extending the Bridge

Now suppose that we need to make some changes in the way these lists display the data. For example, you might want to have the products displayed in alphabetical order. You might think you'd need to either modify or subclass *both* the list and table classes. This can quickly get to be a maintenance nightmare, especially if more than two such displays eventually are needed. Instead, we simply make the changes in the extended interface class, creating a new *sortBridge* class from the parent *listBridge* class.

```java
public class sortBridge extends listBridge {

    public sortBridge(visList jlist) {
        super(jlist);
        }
//----------------
    public void addData(Vector v) {
        Vector sv = sortData(v);

        for(int i = 0; i < sv.size(); i++) {
            String s = (String)sv.elementAt (i);
            list.addLine (s);
        }
    }
//  -----------
    private Vector sortData(Vector v) {
        String s[] = new String[v.size()];
        for(int i = 0; i < v.size(); i++)
            s[i] = (String)v.elementAt (i);
        for(int i = 0; i < v.size(); i++) {
            for(int j = i; j < v.size(); j++) {
                if(s[i].compareTo (s[j]) > 0) {
                    String tmp = s[i];
                    s[i] = s[j];
                    s[j] = tmp;
                }
            }
        }
        Vector v1 = new Vector();
        for (int i = 0; i < v.size(); i++) {
            v1.addElement(s[i]);
            System.out.println(i+" "+s[i]);
        }
```

```
        return vl;
    }
}
```

This code shows that you can vary the interface without changing the implementation. The converse is also true. For example, you could create another type of list display and replace one of the current list displays without any other program changes, as long as the new list also implements the visList interface.

In the example in Figure 10.3, we have created a tree list component that inplements the visList interface. The ordinary list is replaced without any change in the public interface to the classes.

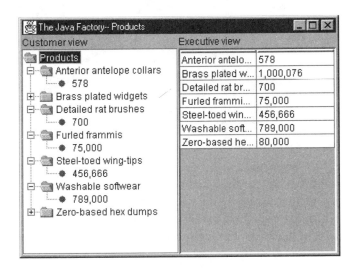

Figure 10.3   Another display using a Bridge to a tree list.

Java Beans as Bridges

The Java Beans programming model is an ideal example of a Bridge pattern implementation. A *Java Bean* is a reusable software component that can be manipulated visually in a Builder tool. All of the JFC components are written as Beans, which means that they support a query interface (using the Introspector class) that enables builder programs to enumerate their properties and display them for easy modification. Figure 10.4 shows a screen from Symantec Visual Café, showing a panel with a text field and a check box. The builder panel to the right shows how you can modify the properties of either of those components by using a simple visual interface.

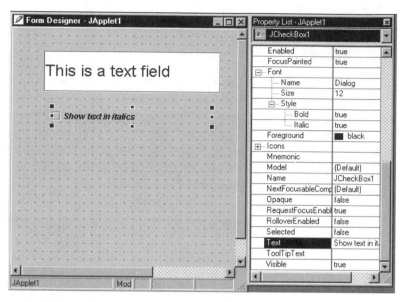

Figure 10.4   A screen from Symantec Visual Café showing a Java Bean interface. The property lists are implemented using a Bridge pattern.

In other words, all Java Beans have the same interface used by the builder program, and you can substitute any Bean for any other and still manipulate its properties using the same convenient interface. The actual program you construct uses these classes in a conventional way, each having its own rather different methods. However, from the builder's point of view, they all appear to be the same.

Consequences of the Bridge Pattern

Using the Bridge pattern has the following consequences:

1. The Bridge pattern is intended to keep the interface to your client program constant while allowing you to change the actual kind of class that you display or use. This can help you to avoid recompiling a complicated set of user interface modules and require only that you recompile the bridge itself and the actual end display class.

2. You can extend the implementation class and the Bridge class separately and usually without their having much interaction with each other.

3. You can hide implementation details from the client program much more easily.

THOUGHT QUESTION

1. In plotting a stock's performance, you usually display the price and price-earnings ratio over time, while in plotting a mutual fund, you usually show the price and the earnings per quarter. Suggest how you can use a Bridge pattern to do both.

Programs on the CD-ROM

Program	Description
Bridge\BasicBridge\ ProductDisplay.java	Displays a list box and a table of unsorted product names.
Bridge\SortBridge\ SproductDisplay.java	Displays a list box and a table of sorted product names.
Bridge\TreeBridge\ TproductDisplay.java	Displays a tree list and a table of sorted product names and amounts.

CHAPTER 11

The Composite Pattern

Programmers often develop systems in which a component may be an individual object or may represent a collection of objects. The Composite pattern is designed to accommodate both cases. You can use it to build part-whole hierarchies or to construct data representations of trees. In summary, a composite is a collection of objects, any one of which may be either a composite or a primitive object. In tree nomenclature, some objects may be nodes with additional branches, and some may be leaves.

A problem that develops is the dichotomy between having a single, simple interface to access all of the objects in a composite and the ability to distinguish between nodes and leaves. Nodes have children and can have children added to them, while leaves do not at the moment have children and in some implementations may be prevented from having children added to them.

Some authors have suggested creating a separate interface for nodes and leaves, where a leaf could have the following methods:

```
public String getName();
public String getValue();
```

A node could have the following methods:

```
public Enumeration elements();
public Node getChild(String nodeName);
public void and(Object obj);
public void remove(Object obj);
```

This then leaves us with the programming problem of deciding which elements will be which when we construct the composite. However, *Design Patterns* suggests that each element should have the *same* interface, whether it is a composite or a primitive element. This is easier to accomplish, but we are left with the question of what the *getChild* operation should accomplish when the object is actually a leaf.

Java makes this quite easy for us, since every node or leaf can return an Enumeration of the contents of the Vector where the children are stored. If there are no children, the *hasMoreElements* method returns false at once. Thus if we simply obtain the Enumeration from each element, we can quickly determine whether it has any children by checking the *hasMoreElements* method.

Just as difficult is the issue of adding or removing leaves from elements of the composite. A nonleaf node can have child leaves added to it, but a leaf node cannot. However, we would like all of the components in the composite to have the same interface. Attempts to add children to a leaf node must not be allowed, and we can design the leaf node class to throw an exception if the program attempts to add to such a node.

An Implementation of a Composite

Let's consider a small company that was started by one person who got the business going. He was, of course, the CEO, although he might have been too busy to think about it at first. Then he hired a couple of people to handle the marketing and manufacturing. Soon each of them hired some assistants to help with advertising, shopping, and so on, and they became the company's first two vice-presidents. As the company's success continued, the firm continued to grow until it had the organizational chart we see in Figure 11.1.

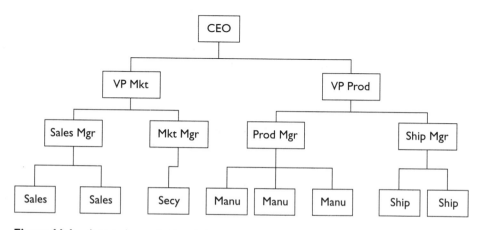

Figure 11.1   A typical organizational chart.

Computing Salaries

Now, if the company is successful, each of these company members receives a salary, and we could at any time ask for the cost of the control span of any employee to the company. We define this control span cost as the salary of that person as well as the combined salaries of all of his or her subordinates. Here is an ideal example for a composite:

- The cost of an individual employee is that employee's salary (and benefits).
- The cost of an employee who heads a department is that employee's salary plus the salaries of all employees that the employee controls.

We would like a single interface that will produce the salary totals correctly, whether or not the employee has subordinates.

```
public float getSalaries();
```

At this point, we realize that the idea of all Composites having the same standard method names in their interfaces is probably naïve. And, in fact, we'd prefer that the public methods be related to the kind of class that we are actually developing. So rather than have generic methods such as *getValue,* we'll use *get-Salaries.*

The Employee Classes

We could now imagine representing the company as a Composite made up of nodes: managers and employees. We could use a single class to represent all employees, but since each level might have different properties, defining at least two classes might be more useful: Employees and Bosses. Employees are leaf nodes and cannot have employee nodes under them; Bosses are nodes that may have Employee nodes under them.

We'll start with the AbstractEmployee class and derive our concrete employee classes from it.

```
public abstract class AbstractEmployee {
    protected String      name;
    protected long        salary;
    protected Employee    parent = null;
    protected boolean     leaf = true;

    public abstract long getSalary();
    public abstract String getName();
    public abstract boolean add(Employee e)
        throws NoSuchElementException;
```

```
    public abstract void remove(Employee e);
        throws NoSuchElementException;
    public abstract Enumeration subordinates();
    public abstract Employee getChild(String s);
    public abstract long getSalaries();
    public boolean isLeaf() {
        return leaf;
    }
}
```

Our concrete Employee class stores the name and salary of each employee and allows us to fetch them as needed.

```
public Employee(String _name, float _salary) {
    name    =    _name;
    salary =    _salary
    leaf    =    true;
}
//---------------
public Employee(Employee _parent, String _name, float _salary) {
    name    =    _name;
    salary =    _salary;
    parent =    _parent;
    leaf    =    true;
}
//---------------
public float getSalary() {
    return salary;
}
//---------------
public String getName() {
    return name;
}
```

The Employee class must have concrete implementations of the add, remove, getChild, and subordinates methods classes. Since an Employee is a leaf, all of these will return some sort of error indication. For example, *subordinates* could return null, but programming will be more consistent if it returns an empty Enumeration.

```
public Enumeration subordinates () {
    return v.elements ();
}
```

The *add* and *remove* methods must generate errors, since members of the basic Employee class cannot have subordinates.

```
public boolean add(Employee e) throws NoSuchElementException {
    throw new NoSuchElementException("No subordinates");
    }
    //
```

```
public void remove(Employee e) throws NoSuchElementException {
    throw new NoSuchElementException("No subordinates");
}
```

The Boss Class

Our Boss class is a subclass of Employee and allows us to store subordinate employees as well. We'll store them in a Vector called *subordinates*, which we return through an Enumeration. Thus if a particular Boss has temporarily run out of Employees, the Enumeration will be empty.

```
public class Boss extends Employee {
    Vector employees;

    public Boss(String _name, long _salary) {
        super(_name, _salary);
        leaf = false;
        employees = new Vector();
    }
    //--------------------
    public Boss(Employee _parent, String _name, long _salary) {
        super(_parent, _name, _salary);
        leaf = false;
        employees = new Vector();
    }
    //--------------------
    public Boss(Employee emp) {
        //promotes an employee position to a Boss
        //and thus allows it to have employees
        super(emp.getName (), emp.getSalary());
        employees = new Vector();
        leaf = false;
    }
    //--------------------
    public boolean add(Employee e) throws NoSuchElementException {
        employee.add(e);
        return true;
    }
    //--------------------
    public void remove(Employee e) throws NoSuchElementException {
        employees.removeElement(e);
    }
    //--------------------
    public Enumeration subordinates () {
        return employees.elements ();
    }
```

If you want to get a list of employees of a given supervisor, you can obtain an Enumeration of them directly from the subordinates Vector. Similarly, you can use this same Vector to return a sum of salaries for any employee and his or her subordinates.

```
public long getSalaries() {
      long sum = salary;
      for (int i = 0; i < employees.size(); i++) {
      sum +=
            ((Employee)employees.elementAt(i)).getSalaries();
   }
   return sum;
}
```

Note that this method starts with the salary of the current Employee and then calls the *getSalaries* method on each subordinate. This is, of course, recursive, and any employees who themselves have subordinates will be included. A diagram of these classes in shown in Figure 11.2.

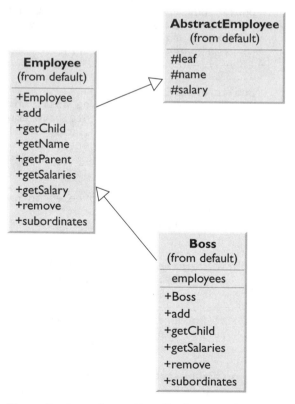

Figure 11.2   The AbstractEmployee class and how Employee and Boss are derived from it.

Building the Employee Tree

We start by creating a CEO Employee and then add that employee's subordinates and their subordinates as follows:

```
private void makeEmployees() {
    prez = new Boss("CEO", 200000);
    prez.add(marketVP = new Boss("Marketing VP", 100000));
    prez.add(prodVP = new Boss("Production VP", 100000));

    marketVP.add(salesMgr = new Boss("Sales Mgr", 50000));
    marketVP.add(advMgr = new Boss("Advt Mgr", 50000));
    //add salesmen reporting to sales manager
    for (int i = 0; i < 5; i++)
        salesMgr .add(new Employee("Sales "+ i,
                rand_sal(30000)));
    advMgr.add(new Employee("Secy", 20000));

    prodVP.add(prodMgr = new Box("Prod Mgr", 40000));
    prodVP.add(shipMgr = new Boss("Ship Mgr", 35000));
    //add manufacturing staff
    for (int i = 0; i < 4; i++)
        prodMgr.add( new Employee("Manuf "+i,
                rand_sal(25000)));
    //add shipping clerks
    for (int i = 0; i < 3; i++)
        shipMgr.add( new Employee("ShipClrk "+i,
                rand_sal(20000)));
    }
```

Once we have constructed this Composite structure, we can load a visual JTree list by starting at the top node and calling the *addNode* method recursively until all of the leaves in each node are accessed.

```
private void addNodes(DefaultMutableTreeNode pnode, Employee emp)
{
        DefaultMutableTreeNode node;

        Enumeration e = emp.subordinates();
        if (e != null) {
            while (e.hasMoreElements()) {
                Employee newEmp = (Employee)e.nextElement();
                node = new
                    DefaultMutableTreeNode(newEmp.getName());
                pnode.add(node);
                addNodes(node, newEmp);
            }
        }
    }
```

The final program display is shown in Figure 11.3.

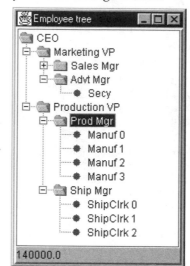

Figure 11.3   The corporate organization shown in a TreeList control.

In this implementation, the cost (sum of salaries) is shown in the bottom bar for any employee you click on. This simple computation calls the *getChild* method recursively to obtain all of the subordinates of that employee.

```
public void valueChanged(TreeSelectionEvent evt) {
      TreePath path = evt.getPath();
      String selectedTerm =
          path.getLastPathComponent().toString();
      Employee emp = prez.getChild(selectedTerm);
      if (emp != null)
          cost.setText(new Float(emp.getSalaries()).toString());
   }
```

Self-Promotion

Sometimes, an Employee will stay in a current job but acquire new subordinates. For example, a Salesman might be asked to supervise sales trainees. For such a case, we can conveniently provide a Boss constructor that creates a Boss from an Employee.

```
public Boss(Employee emp) {
    //promotes an employee position to a Boss
    //and thus allows it to have employees
    super(emp.getName (), emp.getSalary());
    employees = new Vector();
    leaf = false;
}
```

The problem of replacing the Employee instance with the Boss instance means replacing a Vector element with a new one using the *setElementAt* method.

Doubly Linked List

In the previous implementation, we keep a reference to each subordinate in the Vector in each Boss class. This means that you can move down the chain from the CEO to any employee, but that there is no way to move back up to identify an employee's supervisor. This is easily remedied by providing a constructor for each AbstractEmployee subclass that includes a reference to the parent node.

```
public Employee(Employee _parent, String _name,
        float _salary) {
    name   = _name;
    salary = _salary;
    parent = _parent; //save parent node
    leaf   = true;
}
```

Then you can quickly walk up the tree to produce a reporting chain.

```
list.add (emp.getName ()); //employee name
while(emp.getParent () != null) {
    emp = emp.getParent (); //get boss
    list.add (emp.getName ());
}
```

This is shown in Figure 11.4.

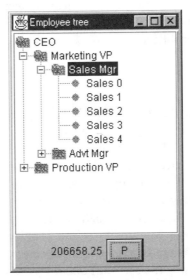

Figure 11.4   The tree list display of the composite, with a display of the parent nodes on the right.

Consequences of the Composite Pattern

The Composite pattern allows you to define a class of hierarchy of simple objects and more-complex composite objects so that they appear to be the same to the client program. Because of this simplicity, the client can be that much simpler, since nodes and leaves are handled in the same way.

The Composite pattern also makes it easy for you to add new kinds of components to your collection, as long as they support a similar programming interface. On the other hand, this has the disadvantage of making your system overly general. You might find it harder to restrict certain classes, where this would normally be desirable.

A Simple Composite

The intent of the Composite pattern is to allow you to construct a tree of various related classes, even though some have different properties than others and some are leaves that do not have children. However, for very simple cases you can sometimes use a single class that exhibits both parent and leaf behavior. In the SimpleComposite example, we create an Employee class that always contains the Vector employees. This Vector of employees will either be empty or be populated, and this determines the nature of the values that are returned from the *getChild* and *remove* methods. In this simple case, you do not throw exceptions, and you always allow leaf nodes to be promoted to have child nodes. In other words, you always allow the execution of the *add* method.

While you might not regard this automatic promotion as a disadvantage, in a system that has a very large number of leaves, keeping a Vector initialized and unused in each leaf node is wasteful. When there are relatively few leaf nodes, this is not a serious problem.

Composites in Java

In Java, you will note that the *DefaultMutableTreeNode* class we use to populate the JList pane is, in fact, just such a simple composite pattern. You will also find that the Composite describes the hierarchy of JFrame, JPanel, and JComponents in any user interface program. JFrames, Jtoolbars, and JPanels are all containers, and each may contain any number of other containers.

Any container may then contain components such as JButtons, JCheckboxes, and JTextPanels, each of which is a leaf node that cannot have further children. They may also contain JLists and JTables that may be treated as leaf nodes or that may contain further graphical components. You can walk down the Composite tree using the *getComponent* method and up the Composite tree using the *getParent* method.

Other Implementation Issues

Other composite implementation issues you might consider are

- **Ordering of Components.** In some programs, the order of the components may be important. If that order differs somehow from the order in which they were added to the parent, then the parent must do additional work to return them in the correct order. For example, you might sort the original Vector alphabetically and return the Enumerator to a new sorted Vector.
- **Caching results.** If you often ask for data that must be computed from a series of child components, as was done earlier with salaries, it might be advantageous to cache these computed results in the parent. However, unless the computation is relatively intensive and you are quite certain that the underlying data have not changed, doing this might not be worth the effort.

 THOUGHT QUESTIONS

1. A baseball team can be considered an aggregate of its individual players. How could you use a composite to represent individual and team performance?

2. The produce department of a supermarket needs to track its sales performance by food item. Suggest how a composite might be helpful in accomplishing this.

Programs on the CD-ROM

Programs	Description
\Composite\StdComposite\ empTree.java	The Composite pattern using the Boss and Employee classes.
\Composite\parentComposite\ pempTree.java	The Composite pattern using a doubly linked list to show the reporting chain.
\Composite\SimpleComposite\ empTree.java	The SimpleComposite using just the Employee class.

CHAPTER 12

The Decorator Pattern

The Decorator pattern provides us with a way to modify the behavior of individual objects without having to create a new derived class. Suppose we have a program that uses eight objects, but three of them need an additional feature. You could create a derived class for each of these objects, and in many cases this would be a perfectly acceptable solution. However, if each of these three objects requires *different* features, you would have to create three derived classes. Further, if one of the classes has features of *both* of the other classes, you begin to create complexity that is both confusing and unnecessary.

For example, suppose we wanted to draw a special border around some of the buttons in a toolbar. If we created a new derived button class, this means that all of the buttons in this new class would always have this same new border, when this might not be our intent.

Instead, we create a Decorator class that *decorates* the buttons. Then we derive any number of specific Decorators from the main Decorator class, each of which performs a specific kind of decoration. In order to decorate a button, the Decorator would have to be an object derived from the visual environment so that it can receive paint method calls and forward calls to other useful graphics methods to the object that it is decorating. This is another case in which object containment is favored over object inheritance. The Decorator is a graphical object, but it contains the object that it is decorating. It might intercept some graphical method calls and perform some additional computation, and then it might pass them on to the underlying object that it is decorating.

Decorating a CoolButton

Recent Windows applications such as Internet Explorer and Netscape Navigator have a row of flat, unbordered buttons that highlight themselves with outline borders when you move your mouse over them. Some Windows programmers call this toolbar a CoolBar and the buttons CoolButtons. There is no analogous button behavior in the JFC, but we can obtain that behavior by *decorating* a JButton. In this case, we decorate it by drawing plain gray lines over the button borders, erasing them.

Let's consider how to create this Decorator. *Design Patterns* suggests that Decorators should be derived from some general Visual Component class and then every message for the actual button should be forwarded from the Decorator. In Java, this is completely impractical because there are literally hundreds of method calls in this base JComponent class that we would have to reimplement. Instead, we derive our Decorator from the JComponent class. Then, since JComponent itself behaves as a Container, it will forward all method calls to the components that it contains. In this case, we simply add the button to the JComponent, and that button will receive all of the GUI method calls that the JComponent receives.

Design Patterns suggests that classes such as Decorator should be abstract and that you should derive all of your actual working (or concrete) Decorators from the abstract class. In this Java implementation, this is not necessary because the base Decorator class has no public methods other than the constructor, since all methods are of JComponent itself.

```
public class Decorator extends JComponent {
    public Decorator (JComponent c) {
        setLayout(new BorderLayout());
        add("Center", c);
    }
}
```

Now, let's look at how we could implement a CoolButton. All we really need to do is to draw the button as usual from the base class and then draw gray lines around the border to remove the button highlighting.

```
/** this class decorates a CoolButton so that
the borders are invisible when the mouse
is not over the button
*/
public class CoolDecorator extends Decorator {
    boolean    mouse_over;     //true when mouse over button
    JComponent thisComp;

    public CoolDecorator(JComponent c) {
    super(c);
    mouse_over = false;
    thisComp   = this;          //save this component
    //catch mouse movements in an inner class
```

```
        c.addMouseListener(new MouseAdapter() {
            //set flag when mouse over
            public void mouseEntered(MouseEvent e) {
                mouse_over = true;
                thisComp.repaint();
            }
            //clear flag when mouse is not over
            public void mouseExited(MouseEvent e) {
                mouse_over = false;
                thisComp.repaint();
            }
        });
    }
//---------------
//paint the button
public void paint(Graphics g) {
        super.paint(g);     //first draw the parent button
        //if the mouse is not over the button
        //erase the borders
        if (! mouse_over) {
            Dimension size = super.getSize();
            size.setColor(Color.lightGray);
            g.drawRect(0, 0, size.width-1, size.height-1);
            g.drawLine(size.width-2, 0, size.width-2,
                    size.height-1-);
            g.drawLine(0, size.height-2, size.width-2,
                    size.height-2);
        }
    }
}
```

Using a Decorator

Now that we've written a CoolDecorator class, how do we use it? We simply create an instance of the CoolDecorator and pass it the button that it is to decorate. We can do all of this right in the constructor. Let's consider a simple program that has two CoolButtons and one ordinary JButton. We create the layout as follows:

```
super ("Deco Button");
JPanel jp = new JPanel();
getContentPane().add(jp);

jp.add( new CoolDecorator(new JButton("Cbutton")));
jp.add( new CoolDecorator(new JButton("Dbutton")));
jp.add(Quit = new JButton("Quit"));
Quit.addActionListener(this);
```

This program is shown in Figure 12.1, with the mouse hovering over one of the buttons.

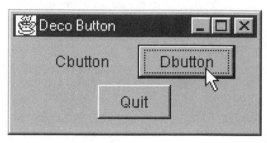

Figure 12.1   Cbutton and Dbutton are CoolButtons, which are outlined when a mouse hovers over them. Here, Dbutton is outlined.

Now that we see how a single decorator works, what about multiple decorators? Suppose that we want to decorate our CoolButtons with another decoration, say, a red diagonal line. Since the argument to any Decorator is just a JComponent, we could create a new Decorator with a Decorator as its argument. Let's consider the SlashDecorator, which draws that red diagonal line.

```
public class SlashDecorator extends Decorator {
    int x1, y1, w1, h1;

    public SlashDecorator(JComponent c) {
        super(c);
    }
    public void setBounds(int x, int y, int w, int h) {
        x1 = x; y1 = y;
        w1 = w; h1 = h;
        super.setBounds(x, y, w, h);
    }
    public void paint(Graphics g) {
        super.paint(g);
        g.setColor(Color.red);
        g.drawLine(0, 0, w1, h1);
    }
}
```

Here, we save the size and position of the button when it is created and then use those saved values to draw the diagonal line.

You can create the JButton with these two Decorators by just calling one and then the other.

```
jp.add(new SlashDecorator(
new CoolDecorator(new JButton("Dbutton"))));
```

This gives us a final program that displays the two buttons, as shown in Figure 12.2.

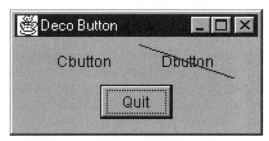

Figure 12.2   Dbutton is decorated with a SlashDecorator.

The Class Diagram

The class diagram in Figure 12.3 shows how we derived the Decorator base class from JComponent and how the concrete Decorators take another JComponent as an argument to determine the visual extent of the object that they decorate.

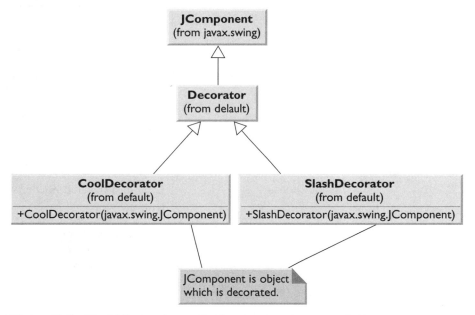

Figure 12.3   The UML class diagram for Decorators and two specific Decorator implementations.

Decorating Borders in Java

One problem with this particular implementation of Decorators is that it is not easy to expand the size of the component being decorated because you add the component to a container and allow it to fill the container completely. If you attempt to draw lines outside the area of this component, they are clipped by the graphics procedure and not drawn at all.

The JFC provides its own series of Border objects that are a kind of decorator. As with a Decorator pattern, you can add a new Border object to any JComponent. There also is a way to add several borders. However, unlike the Decorator pattern, the Borders are not JComponents, and you do not have the flexibility to intercept and change specific events. In fact, it is more an example of the Strategy pattern than a Decorator.

The JFC defines several standard Border classes, given in the following table:

Class	Description
BevelBorder(*n*)	Simple two-line bevel; can be LOWERED or RAISED.
CompoundBorder (*inner, outer*)	Allows you to add two borders.
EmptyBorder(*top, left, bottom, right*)	Provides a blank border width specified on each side.
EtchedBorder	Creates an etched border.
LineBorder(*width, color*)	Creates a simple line border.
MatteBorder	Creates a matte border of a solid color or a tiled icon.
SoftBeveledBorder	Creates a beveled border with rounded corners.
TitledBorder	Creates a border containing a title. Used to surround and label a JPanel.

These borders are simple to use in conjunction with the *setBorder* method of each JComponent. Figure 12.4 shows a normal JButton with a 2-pixel solid-line border, combined with a 4-pixel EmptyBorder and an EtchedBorder.

Figure 12.4   Dbutton has a 2-pixel solid line border, and Quit has a 4-pixel EmptyBorder and an EtchedBorder.

This was created with the following simple code:

```
JPanel jp = new JPanel();
getContentPane().add(jp);
jp.add( Cbutton = new JButton("Cbutton"));
jp.add( Dbutton = new JButton("Dbutton"));
EmptyBorder ep   = new EmptyBorder(4,4,4,4);
LineBorder lb    = new LineBorder(Color.black, 2);
Dbutton.setBorder(new CompoundBorder(lb, ep));
jp.add(Quit      = new JButton("Quit"));
EtchedBorder eb = new EtchedBorder();
Quit.addActionListener(this);
Quit.setBorder(eb);
```

One drawback of these Border objects is that they replace the default Insets values that determine the spacing around the component. Note that we had to add a 4-pixel Empty Border to the Dbutton to make it similar in size to the CButton. We did not do this for the Quit button, and it is therefore substantially smaller than the others.

You can also affect the border around a JButton, rather like a CoolButton, using the *setBorderPainted(b)* method. If *b* is false, the border is not drawn. You then can turn it back on and repaint when the button receives a mouseOver event.

Nonvisual Decorators

Decorators, of course, are not limited to objects that enhance visual classes. You can add or modify the methods of any object in a similar fashion. In fact, nonvisual objects can be easier to decorate because there may be fewer methods to intercept and forward.

While coming up with a single example is difficult, a series of Decorators do occur naturally in the java.io classes. Note the following in the Java documentation:

The class FilterInputStream itself simply overrides all methods of InputStream with versions that pass all requests to the underlying input stream. Subclasses of FilterInputStream may further override some of these methods as well as provide additional methods and fields.

The FilterInputStream class is thus a Decorator that can be wrapped around any input stream class. It is essentially an abstract class that doesn't do any processing but provides a layer on which the relevant methods have been duplicated. It normally forwards these method calls to the enclosed parent stream class.

The interesting classes derived from FilterInputStream include those in the following table:

Class	Description
BufferedInputStream	Adds buffering to the stream so that every call does not cause I/O to occur.
CheckedInputStream	Maintains a checksum of bytes as they are read.
DataInputStream	Reads primitive types (Long, Boolean, Float, and so on) from the input stream.
DigestInputStream	Computes a MessageDigest of any input stream.
InflateInputStream	Implements methods or uncompressing data.
PushbackInputStream	Provides a buffer from which data can be "unread," if during parsing you discover that you need to back up.

These Decorators can be nested, so a pushback, buffered input stream is quite possible.

As an example, consider a program to filter an e-mail stream to make it more readable. The user of an e-mail program types quickly and perhaps all in one case. The sentences can be made more readable if the first word of each sentence is capitalized. We accomplish this by interposing a FileFilter class, derived from FilterInputStream to read the data and transform it to mixed case. In Figure 12.5, we show a simple display, illustrating the original text on the left and the filtered text on the right.

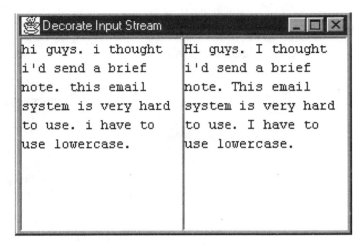

Figure 12.5 An input stream and a filtered input stream.

The left-hand stream was read with the ordinary FileInputStream class as follows:

```
private String readNormal(File fl) {
        FileInputStream fread = null;
        String s = "";
        try {
            fread = new FileInputStream(fl);
            byte b[] = new byte[1000];
            int length = fread.read (b);
            fread.close ();
            s = new String(b, 0, length);
        }
        catch(FileNotFoundException e) {}
        catch(IOException ie) {}
    return s;
    }
```

The right-hand pane was read by creating the same FileInputStream but passing it in a constructor to the FileFilter class. This class is derived from File-Filter class, where the *readLine* method simply calls the parent *read* method and then goes through the stream, inserting capitals after periods.

```
try {
        fread = new FileInputStream(f1);
        FileFilter ff = new FileFilter(fread);
        s = ff.readLine ();
        ff.close ();
    }
```

Note that we create a new *readLine* method that returns an already converted String rather than an array of bytes, as the parent classes do. We illustrate the class relationships in Figure 12.6.

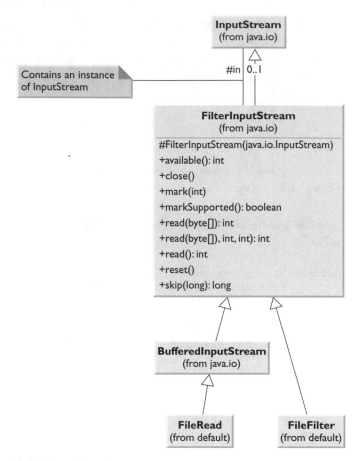

Figure 12.6   The relationships between FileFilter, FilterInputStream, and the base classes.

Note that FilterInputStream *contains* an instance of InputStream.

Decorators, Adapters, and Composites

As noted in *Design Patterns,* an essential similarity exists among these classes that you might have recognized. Adapters also seem to "decorate" an existing class. However, their function is to change the interface of one or more classes to one that is more convenient for a particular program. Decorators add methods to particular instances of classes, rather than to all of them. Also possible is that a Composite consisting of a single item is essentially a Decorator. Once again, however, the intent is different.

Consequences of the Decorator Pattern

The Decorator pattern provides a more flexible way to add responsibilities to a class than by using inheritance, since it can add these responsibilities to selected instances of the class. It also allows customizing a class without creating subclasses high in the inheritance hierarchy. *Design Patterns* points out two disadvantages of the Decorator pattern. One is that a Decorator and its enclosed component are not identical; thus tests for object type will fail. The second is that Decorators can lead to a system with lots of little objects that look alike to the programmer trying to maintain the code. This can be a maintenance headache.

The Decorator and the Façade pattern, discussed next, evoke similar images in building architecture. However, in design pattern terminology, Façade is a way of hiding a complex system inside a simpler interface, while Decorator adds function by wrapping a class.

THOUGHT QUESTIONS

1. When someone enters an incorrect value in a cell of a JTable, you might want to change the color of the row to indicate the problem. Suggest how you could use a Decorator for this purpose.

2. A mutual fund is a collection of stocks. Each one consists of an array or Vector of prices over time. Suggest how a Decorator can be used to produce a report of stock performance for each stock and for the whole fund.

Programs on the CD-ROM

Programs	Description
\Decorator\decoWindow.java	Shows the CoolButton Decorator.
\Decorator\slashWindow.java	Shows the SlashButton decorator.
\Decorator\borderWindow.java	Shows how the JFC Border classes are used.
\Decorator\FilterStream \DecoStream.java	Shows a use of the FilterInputStream class as a Decorator.

CHAPTER 13

The Façade Pattern

In this chapter, we take up the Façade pattern. This pattern is used to wrap a set of complex classes into a simpler enclosing interface.

Frequently, as your programs evolve and develop, they grow in complexity. In fact, for all the excitement about the benefits of design patterns, these patterns sometimes generate so many classes that it is difficult to understand the program's flow. Furthermore, there may be a number of complicated subsystems, each of which has its own complex interface.

The Façade pattern allows you to simplify this complexity by providing a simplified interface to those subsystems. This simplification might in some cases reduce the flexibility of the underlying classes, but usually it provides all of the function needed for all but the most sophisticated users. These latter users can, of course, still access the underlying classes and methods.

Fortunately, we don't have to write a complex system to provide an example of where a Façade can be useful. Java provides a set of classes that connect to databases using an interface called JDBC. You can connect to any database for which the manufacturer has provided a JDBC connection class—almost every database on the market. Some databases have direct connections using JDBC, and a few allow connection to an ODBC driver using the JDBC-ODBC bridge class.

These database classes, in the java.sql package, provide an excellent example of a set of quite low-level classes that interact in a convoluted manner, as shown in Figure 13.1.

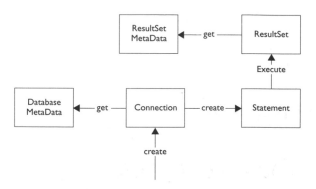

To connect to a database, you use an instance of the Connection class. Then, to find out the names of the database tables and fields, you need to get an instance of the DatabaseMetadata class from the Connection. Next, to issue a query, you compose the SQL (Structured Query Language) query string and use the Connection to create a Statement class. By executing the Statement, you obtain a ResultSet class, and to find out the names of the column rows in that ResultSet, you need to obtain an instance of the ResultSetMetadata class. Thus juggling all of these classes can be quite difficult, and since most of the calls to their methods throw exceptions, the coding can be messy at the least.

However, by designing a Façade (Figure 13.2) consisting of a Database class and a Results class, we can build a much more usable system.

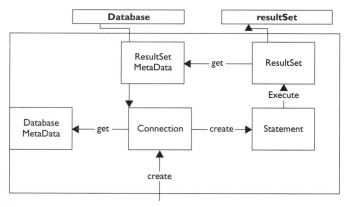

Figure 13.2   A Façade that encloses many of the java.sql.* classes.

Building the Façade Classes

Let's consider how we connect to a database. We first must load the database driver.

```
try{Class.forName(driver);} //load the Bridge driver
```

```
      catch (Exception e)
{System.out.println(e.getMessage());}
```

Then we use the Connection class to connect to a database. We also obtain the database metadata to find out more about the database.

```
try {
    con = DriverManager.getConnection(url);
    dma = con.getMetaData(); //get the meta data
}catch (Exception e) {
    System.out.println(e.getMessage());
}
```

If we want to list the names of the tables in the database, we then need to call the *getTables* method on the database metadata class, which returns a ResultSet object. Finally, to get the list of names, we must iterate through that object, making sure that we obtain only user table names, and exclude internal system tables.

```
public String[] get TableNames() {
      String[] tbnames = null;
      Vector tname = new Vector();
   //add the table names to a Vector
   //since we don't know how many there are
      try {
          results = new Results(dma.getTables(catalog,
                                    null, "%", types));
      } catch (Exception e) {
          System.out.println(e);
      }

          while (results.hasMoreElements())
          tname.addElement(results.getColumnValue
                                ("TABLE_NAME"));

      //copy the table names into a String array
      tbnames = new String[tname.size()];
      for (int i=0; i< tname.size(); i++)
          tbnames[i] = (String)tname.elementAt(i);
      return tbnames;
   }
```

This quickly becomes quite complex to manage, and we haven't even issued any queries.

We can make one simplifying assumption: The exceptions that all of these database class methods throw do not need complex handling. For the most part, the methods will work without error unless the network connection to the database fails. Thus we can wrap all of these methods in classes in which we simply print out the infrequent errors and take no further action.

This makes it possible to write two simple enclosing classes that contain all of the significant methods of the Connection, ResultSet, Statement, and Meta-Data classes. These are the Database class methods:

```
class Database {
    public Database(String driver)()   //constructor
    public void          Open(String url, String cat);
    public String[]      getTableNames();
    public String[]      getColumnNames(String table);
    public String        getColumnValue(String table,
                         String columnName);
    public String        getNextValue(String columnName);
    public resultSet     Execute(String sql);
}
```

Following is the Results class:

```
class Results
{
    public Results(ResultSet rset);     //constructor
    public String[]      getMetaData();
    public boolean       hasMoreElements();
    public String[]      nextElement();
    public String        getColumnValue(String columnName);
    public String        getColumnValue(int i);
}
```

These simple classes allow us to write a program for opening a database; displaying its table names, column names, and contents; and running a simple SQL query on the database.

Our example program using this Façade pattern is the dbFrame.java program. This program, shown in Figure 13.3, accesses a database that contains food prices at three local markets.

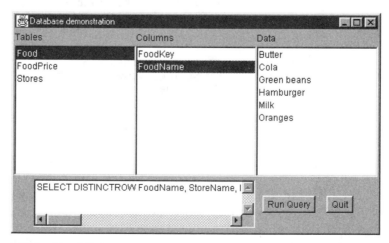

Figure 13.3   The dbFrame program showing the selection of a table, the column names, and the contents of that column in the database.

Clicking on a table name displays the column names, and clicking on a column name displays the content of that column. Clicking on Run Query displays the food prices sorted by store for oranges, as shown in Figure 13.4.

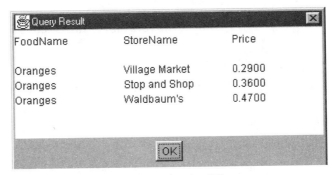

Figure 13.4 A result of the query executed in the dbFrame program.

This program starts by connecting to the database and getting a list of the table names.

```
db = new Database("sun.jdbc.odbc.JdbcOdbcDriver");
db.Open("jdbc:odbc:Grocery prices", null);
String tnames[] = db.getTableNames();
loadList(Tables, tnames);
```

Clicking on one of the lists runs a query for table column names or contents.

```
public void itemStateChanged(ItemEvent e) {
    Object obj = e.getSource();
    if (obj == Tables)
        showColumns();
    if (obj == Columns)
        showData();
}
//––––––––––––––––––
private void showColumns() {
        String cnames[] =
            db.getColumnNames(Tables.getSelectedItem());
        loadList(Columns, cnames);
}
//––––––––––––––––––
private void showData() {
        String colname = Columns.getSelectedItem();
        String colval =
            db.getColumnValue(Tables.getSelectedItem(),
                colname);
        Data.setVisible(false);
        Data.removeAll();
        Data.setVisible(true);
```

```
colval =
    db.getNextValue(Columns.getSelectedItem());

while (colval.length()>0) {
    Data.add(colval);
    colval =
        db.getNextValue(Columns.getSelectedItem());
    }
}
```

The diagram in Figure 13.5 shows a complete representation of the Façade classes.

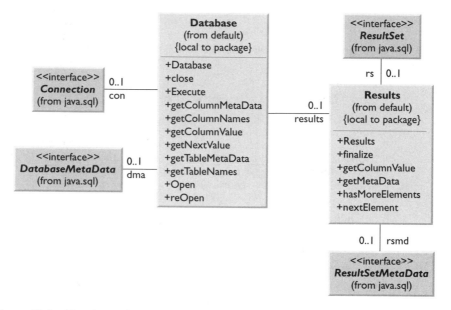

Figure 13.5   The classes that the programmer actually uses outside of the Façade.

Note that the Database class *contains* instances of Connection, DatabaseMetaData, and Results and that the Results class contains instances of ResultSet and ResultSetMetaData.

Consequences of the Façade Pattern

The Façade pattern shields clients from complex subsystem components and provides a simpler programming interface for the general user. However, it does not prevent the advanced user from going to the deeper, more complex classes when necessary.

In addition, the Façade allows you to make changes in the underlying subsystems without requiring changes in the client code and reduces compilation dependencies.

Notes on Installing and Running the dbFrame Program

In order for Java to communicate with a database, you must have ODBC and the JDBC-ODBC drivers for Java installed. This example program will work only in a Windows environment because it requires the Microsoft Access database groceries.mdb. If you have Java 2 (version 1.2 or greater) installed, the JDBC-ODBC driver is built in. However, if you have earlier versions, you need to obtain this driver from the java.sun.com Web site.

The ODBC Data Access drivers are available to download free from Microsoft. Version 1 of these drivers was called Dataacc.exe and was packed and stored as wx1350.exe. Version 2 handles many more databases and provides more sophisticated access functions. It also requires that DCOM98 be installed. When ODBC is installed, you should see an ODBC folder in your Control Panel.

Copy the programs from the Façade folder on the accompanying CD-ROM to a convenient location on your hard disk. Then launch the ODBC program from the Control Panel. To register the groceries.mdb file, click on Add and fill out the panel, as shown in Figure 13.6. To indicate where the groceries.mdb file is located, click on Select and locate the file in the folder you just copied it to, as shown in Figure 13.6.

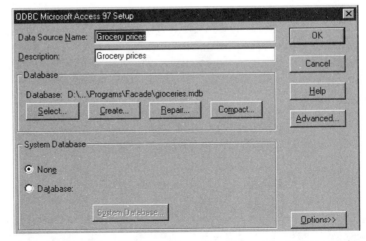

Figure 13.6   How to set up ODBC/JDBC access to the sample database used in this chapter.

If you name the Data Source something other than "Grocery Prices," you will need to change the corresponding name in line 20 of dbFrame.java.

THOUGHT QUESTION

1. Suppose that you have written a program with a File / Open menu, a text field, and some buttons controlling font (bold and italic). Now suppose that you need to have this program run from a line command with arguments. Explain how you would use a Façade pattern to accomplish this.

Programs on the CD-ROM

Programs	Description
\Façade\dbFrame.java	Reads in the groceries.mdb database and displays the grocery tables, as illustrated in the text.

CHAPTER 14

The Flyweight Pattern

In this chapter we take up the Flyweight pattern, which is used to avoid the overhead of large numbers of very similar classes.

Sometimes, you need to generate a very large number of small class instances to represent data. You can greatly reduce the number of different classes that you need to instantiate if you can determine that the instances are fundamentally the same, except for a few parameters. If you can move those variables outside of the class instance and pass them in as part of a method call, you greatly reduce the number of separate instances by sharing them.

The Flyweight pattern provides an approach for handling such classes. It refers to the instance's *intrinsic* data that make the instance unique and the *extrinsic* data that are passed in as arguments. The Flyweight is appropriate for small, fine-grained classes such as those for individual characters or icons on the screen. For example, you might be drawing a series of icons on the screen in a window, with each icon representing a person or data file as a folder, as shown in Figure 14.1.

In this case, it doesn't make sense for each folder to have an individual class instance that remembers the person's name and the icon's screen position. Typically, such an icon is one of a few similar images, and the position where it is drawn is calculated dynamically based on the window's size.

In another example in *Design Patterns*, each chapter in a Document is represented as a single instance of a character class, but the positions where the characters are drawn on the screen are kept as external data so that only one instance of each character is needed, rather than one for each appearance of that character.

Figure 14.1 A set of folders representing information about various people. Their similarity makes them candidates for the Flyweight pattern.

Discussion

A flyweight is a sharable instance of a class. At first glance, each class might appear to be a Singleton. In fact, a small number of instances might exist, such as one for every character or one for every icon type. The number of instances that are allocated must be decided as the class instances are needed; usually a FlyweightFactory class does this. This factory class usually *is* a Singleton, since it needs to keep track of whether a particular instance has been generated. It then returns either a new instance or reference to one that it has already generated.

To decide if some part of your program is a candidate for using Flyweights, consider whether it is possible to remove some data from the class and make them extrinsic. If this makes it possible to reduce greatly the number of different class instances that your program needs to maintain, then Flyweights will help.

Example Code

Suppose that we want to draw a small folder icon with a name under it for each person in an organization. If the organization is large, there could be many such icons; however, they are actually all the same graphical image. Even if we have two icons, one for "is Selected" and one for "not Selected," the number of different icons is small. In such a system, having an icon object for each person—with its own coordinates, name, and selected state—is a waste of resources. Figure 14.2 shows two such icons.

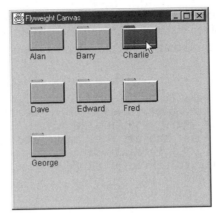

Figure 14.2 A set of folders displaying two images; one for "is Selected" and one for "not Selected."

Instead, we'll create a FolderFactory that returns either the selected or the unselected folder drawing class but does not create additional instances once one of each has been created. Since this is such a simple case, we just create them both at the outset and then return one or the other.

```
public class FolderFactory {
    Folder unSelected, Selected;
    public FolderFactory() {
        Color brown = new Color(0x5f5f1c);
        Selected = new Folder(brown);
        unSelected = new Folder(Color.yellow);
    }
//---------------
    public Folder getFolder(boolean isSelected) {
        if (isSelected)
            return Selected;
        else
            return unSelected;
    }
}
```

When more instances could exist, the factory could keep a table of the ones that it had already created and create new ones only if they aren't already in the table.

The unique thing about using Flyweights, however, is that we pass the coordinates and the name to be drawn into the folder when we draw it. These coordinates are the extrinsic data that allow us to share the folder objects and

in this case create only two instances. The complete folder class shown next creates a folder instance with one background color or the other and has a public
draw method that draws the folder at the point we specify.

```java
public class Folder extends JPanel {
    private Color color;
    final int W = 50, H = 30;
    final int tableft = 0, tabheight=4, tabwidth=20,
            tabslant=3;
    public Folder(Color c) {
        color = c;
    }
//---------------
    public void draw(Graphics g, int tx, int ty,
                        String name) {
        g.setColor(Color.black);                //outline
        g.drawRect(tx, ty, W, H);
        g.drawString(name, tx, ty + H+15);      //title
        g.setColor(Color.white);
        g.drawLine (tx, ty, tx+W, ty);

        Polygon poly = new Polygon();
        poly.addPoint (tx+tableft,ty);
        //etc...
        g.drawPolygon (poly);

        g.setColor(color);                      //fill rectangle
        g.fillRect(tx+1, ty+1, W-1, H-1);
        g.fillPolygon (poly);
        g.setColor(Color.white);
        g.drawLine (tx, ty, tx+W, ty);

        g.setColor(Color.black);                //shadow lines
        g.drawLine(tx, ty+H+1, tx+W-1, ty+H+1);
        g.drawLine(tx+W+1, ty, tx+W+1, ty+H);

        g.setColor(Color.white);                //highlight lines
        g.drawLine(tx+1, ty+1, tx+W-1, ty+1);
        g.drawLine(tx+1, ty+1, ty+H-1);
    }
}
```

To use a Flyweight class like this, our calling program must calculate the
position of each folder as part of its paint routine and then pass the coordinates
to the folder instance. This is actually rather common, since we need a different
layout depending on the window's dimensions and we do not want to have to
keep telling each instance where its new location is going to be. Instead, we
compute it dynamically during the paint routine.

Note that we could have generated an array or Vector of folders at the outset and scanned through the array to draw each folder.

```
//go through all the names and folders
    for (int i = 0; i< names.size(); i++) {
        name = (String)names.elementAt(i);
        if (name.equals(selectedName))
            f = fact.getFolder(true);
        else
            f = fact.getFolder(false);
        //have that folder draw itself at this spot
        f.draw(g, x, row, name);
```

Such an array is not as wasteful as a series of different instances because it is actually an array of references to one of only two folder instances. However, because we want to display one folder as "selected" and we want to be able to change which folder is selected dynamically, we just use the FolderFactory itself to give us the correct instance each time. The top and left variables are declared constants in the main program.

```
public void paint(Graphics g) {
    Folder f;
    String name;

    int j = 0;           //count the number in the row
    int row = Top;       //start in the upper left
    int x = Left;

    //go through all of the names and folders
    for (int i = 0; i< names.size(); i++) {
        name = (String)names.elementAt(i);
        if (name.equals(selectedName))
            f = fact.getFolder(true);
        else
            f = fact.getFolder(false);
        //have that folder draw itself at this spot
        f.draw(g, x, row, name);
        x = x + HSpace;     //change to the next position
        j++;
        if (j >= HCount) { //reset for the next row
            j = 0;
            row += VSpace;
            x = Left;
        }
    }
}
```

The Class Diagram

The diagram in Figure 14.3 shows how these claims interact.

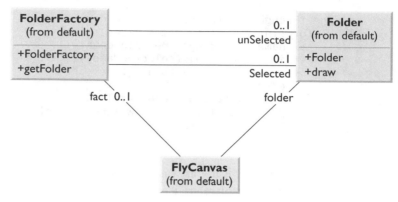

Figure 14.3   How Flyweights are generated.

The FlyCanvas class is the main GUI class, in which the folders are arranged and drawn. It contains one instance of the FolderFactory and one of the Folder class. The FolderFactory class contains two instances of Folder: *selected* and *unselected*. One or the other of these is returned to the FlyCanvas by the Folder-Factory.

Selecting a Folder

Since we have two folder instances, selected and unselected, we'd like to be able to select folders by moving the mouse over them. In the previous paint routine, we simply remember the name of the folder that was selected and ask the factory to return a "selected" folder for it. Because the folders are not individual instances, we can't listen for mouse motion within each folder instance. Even if we did, we'd need a way to tell the other instances to deselect themselves.

Instead, we check for mouse motion at the window level. If the mouse is found to be within a Rectangle, we make that corresponding name the selected name. Thus we can check each name when we redraw and create a selected folder instance where it is needed.

```
public void mouseMoved(MouseEvent e) {
        int j = 0;         //count the number in the row
        int row = Top;     //start in the upper left
        int x = Left;

        //go through all of the names and folders
        for (int i = 0; i< names.size(); i++) {
            //see if this folder contains the mouse
```

```
Rectangle r = new Rectangle(x,row,W,H);
if (r.contains(e.getX(), e.getY())) {
    selectedName=(String)names.elementAt(i);
    repaint();
}
x = x + HSpace;          //change to the next position
j++;
if (j >= HCount) {       //reset for the next row
    j = 0;
    row += VSpace;
    x = Left;
}
    }
}
```

Flyweight Uses in Java

Flyweights are not often used at the application level in Java. They are more of a system resource management technique that is used at a lower level than Java. However, it is useful to recognize that this technique exists so that you can use it if you need it.

We have already seen the Flyweight pattern in the cell renderer code used for tables and list boxes. Usually the cell renderer is just a JLabel; however, there might be two or three types of labels or renderers for different colors or fonts. But there are far fewer renderers than there are cells in the table or list. Some objects within the Java language could be implemented under the covers as Flyweights. For example, if two instances of a String constant with identical characters exist, they could refer to the same storage location. Similarly, two Integer or Float objects that contain the same value might be implemented as Flyweights, although they probably are not. To prove the absence of Flyweights here, we run the following code:

```
Integer five = new Integer(5);
Integer myfive = new Integer(5);
System.out.println(five == myfive);

String fred=new String("fred");
String fred1 = new String("fred");
System.out.println(fred == fred1);
```

Both cases print out "false." However, note that you can easily determine that you are dealing with two identical instances of a Flyweight by using the == operator. This operator compares actual object references (memory addresses) rather than the "equals" operator, which will probably be slower, if it is implemented at all.

Sharable Objects

The *Smalltalk Companion* points out that sharable objects are much like Flyweights, although their purpose differs somewhat. When you have a very large object that contains a lot of complex data, such as tables or bitmaps, you want to minimize the number of instances of that object. In such cases, you return one instance to every part of the program that asks for it and avoid creating other instances.

A problem with such sharable objects occurs when one part of a program wants to change some data in a shared object. You then must decide whether to change the object for all users, prevent any change, or create a new instance with the changed data. If you change the object for every instance, you might have to notify the users that the object has changed.

Sharable objects are also useful when you are referring to large data systems outside of Java, such as databases. The Database class we developed previously in the Façade pattern could be a candidate for a sharable object. We might not want a number of separate connections to the database from different program modules, preferring instead that only one be instantiated. However, if several modules in different threads decide to make queries simultaneously, the Database class might have to queue the queries or spawn extra connections.

Copy-on-Write Objects

The Flyweight pattern uses just a few object instances to represent many different objects in a program. All of them normally have the same base properties as intrinsic data, as well as a few properties that represent extrinsic data that vary with each manifestation of the class instance. However, these instances eventually could take on new intrinsic properties (such as shape or folder tab position) and require a new specific instance of the class to represent them. Rather than creating these in advance as special subclasses, you can copy the class instance and change its intrinsic properties when the program flow indicates that a new, separate instance is required. The class thus copies itself when the change becomes inevitable, changing those intrinsic properties in the new class. This process is called *copy-on-write*. It can be built into Flyweights as well as a number of other classes, such as the Proxy pattern discussed in the next chapter.

THOUGHT QUESTIONS

1. Consider a JTable with a cell renderer to highlight certain cells. Write a Flyweight pattern for this system.

2. Suppose that JButtons can appear on several different tabs of a JTabbedPane, but each controls the same one or two tasks. How could you use a Flyweight pattern here?

Programs on the CD-ROM

Programs	Description
\Flyweight\FlyFolders\ FlyCanvas.java	Complete code for drawing folders that are selected by a mouse-over event.
\Flyweight\FlyVectors\ FlyCanvas.java	Similar code in which the folders are generated in advance and kept in a Vector.
\Flyweight\Flytest.java	Tests Integers and Strings for Flyweight properties.

CHAPTER 15

The Proxy Pattern

The Proxy pattern is used to represent with a simpler object an object that is complex or time-consuming to create. If creating an object is expensive in time or computer resources, a Proxy allows you to postpone this creation until you need the actual object. A Proxy usually has the same methods as the full object that it represents. Once that full object is loaded, the Proxy passes on the method calls to the full object.

There are several cases where a Proxy can be useful:

1. If an object, such as a large image, takes a long time to load

2. If the object is on a remote machine and loading it over the network might be slow, especially during peak network load periods

3. If the object has limited access rights. The proxy can then validate the access permissions for that user.

Proxies can also be used to distinguish between requesting an instance of an object and the actual need to access it. For example, program initialization might set up a number of objects, all of which might not be used right away. In that case, the Proxy can load the real object only when it is needed.

Consider a program that needs to load and display a large image. When the program starts, some indication that an image is to be displayed is needed so that the screen is set out correctly; however, the actual image display can be postponed until the image is completely loaded. This is particularly important in programs such as word processors and Web browsers that lay out text around the images before the images are available.

An image proxy can note the image and begin loading it in the background, while drawing a simple rectangle or other symbol to represent the image's extent on the screen before it appears. The proxy can even delay loading the image at all until it receives a paint request and only then begin the loading process.

Sample Code

In this example program, we create a simple program to display an image on a JPanel when it is loaded. Rather than loading the image directly, we use a class we call ImageProxy to defer loading and draw a rectangle around the image area until loading is completed.

```java
public class ProxyDisplay extends JxFrame {
    public ProxyDisplay() {
        super("Display proxied image");
        JPanel p = new JPanel();
        getContentPane().add(p);
        p.setLayout(new BorderLayout());
        ImageProxy image = new ImageProxy("elliott.jpg", 321, 271);

        p.add("Center", image);
        p.add("North", new Label("        "));
        p.add("West", new Label("     "));
        setSize(370, 350);
        setVisible(true);
    }
```

Note that we create the instance of the Image Proxy just as we would have for an Image and that we add it to the enclosing JPanel as we would an actual image.

The ImageProxy class sets up the image loading and creates a MediaTracker object to follow the loading process within the constructor.

```java
public class ImageProxy extends JPanel
implements Runnable {
    private int height, width;
    private MediaTracker tracker;
    private Image img;
    private JFrame frame;
    private Thread imageCheck;        //to monitor loading
//------------------
    public ImageProxy(String filename, int w, int h) {
        height = h;
        width = w;

        tracker = new MediaTracker(this);
        img =
            Toolkit.getDefaultToolkit().
```

```
            getImage(filename);
    tracker.addImage(img, 0);          //watch for image loading

        imageCheck = new Thread(this);
        imageCheck.start();            //start 2nd thread monitor

        //this begins actual image loading
        try {
            tracker.waitForID(0,1);
        } catch (InterruptedException e) {
        }
    }
```

The *waitForID* method of the MediaTracker actually initiates loading. In this case, we put in a minimum wait time of 1 millisecond so that we can minimize apparent program delays.

The constructor also creates a separate thread *imageCheck* that checks the loading status every few milliseconds and then starts that thread running.

```
public void run() {
        /**this thread monitors image loading
        and repaints when done
        the 1000 millisecond is artificially long
        to allow the demo to display with a delay*/
        try {
            Thread.sleep(1000);
            while (! tracker.checkID(0))
                Thread.sleep(1000);
        } catch (Exception e) {
        }
        repaint ();
    }
```

For the purposes of this illustration program, we slowed the polling time down to 1 second so that we can see the program draw the rectangle and then refresh the final image.

Finally, the Proxy is derived from the JPanel component and therefore has a *paint* method. In this method, we draw a rectangle if the image is not loaded. If the image has been loaded, we erase the rectangle and draw the image.

```
public void paint(Graphics g) {
        if (tracker.checkID(0)) {
            height = img.getHeight(frame);//get height
            width = img.getWidth(frame);  //and width

            getsetColor(Color.lightGray); //erase box
            g.fillRect(0,0, width, height);
            g.drawImage(img, 0, 0, this); //draw image
```

```
        } else {
            //draw box outlining image if not loaded yet
            g.setColor(Color.black);
            g.drawRect(1, 1, width-2, height-2);
        }
    }
```

The program's two states are illustrated in Figure 15.1.

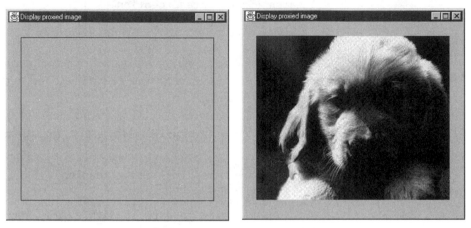

Figure 15.1   The proxy image display on the left is shown until the image on the right loads.

Copy-on-Write

You can also use Proxies to keep copies of large objects that may or may not change. If you create a second instance of an expensive object, a Proxy can decide that a copy is not needed yet, so it simply uses the original object. Then, if the program makes a change in the new copy, the Proxy can copy the original object and make the change in the new instance. This can save time and space when objects do not always change after they are instantiated.

Enterprise Java Beans

Enterprise Java Beans (EJB) are a set of classes and interfaces for writing well-encapsulated server code. They are not at all related to the Java Beans you use in client GUI programs. However, they do supply a convenient approach for accessing databases and other legacy data systems.

Each time you request a line of data from a database, you are making a new connection to an EJB. Clearly, there are a limited number of these connections available, so the remaining requests are cached within the Bean and a Proxy to the connection that eventually becomes the connection when one becomes available is returned.

Comparison with Related Patterns

Both the Adapter and the Proxy patterns constitute a thin layer around an object. However, the Adapter provides a different interface for an object, whereas the Proxy provides the same interface for the object but interposes itself where it can postpone processing or data transmission effort.

A Decorator also has the same interface as the object that it surrounds, but its purpose is to add additional (sometimes visual) function to the original object. A Proxy, by contrast, controls access to the contained class.

THOUGHT QUESTION

1. You have designed a Java server that connects to a database. If several clients connect to your server at once, how could Proxies be of help?

Programs on the CD-ROM

Program	Description
\Proxy\ProxyDisplay.java	Displays a Proxy for the image for one second and then loads the image.

Summary of Structural Patterns

Following is a summary of the Structural patterns:

- **Adapter pattern**: changes the interface of one class to that of another.
- **Bridge pattern**: separates a class's interface from its implementation so that you can vary or replace the implementation without changing the client code.
- **Composite pattern**: a collection of objects, any one of which may be a Composite or a leaf object.
- **Decorator pattern**: a class that surrounds a given class, adds new capabilities to it, and passes all of the unchanged methods to the underlying class.

- **Façade pattern**: groups a complex set of objects and provides a new, simpler interface to access those objects.
- **Flyweight pattern**: provides a way to limit the proliferation of small, similar instances by moving some of the class data outside of the class and passing them in during various execution methods.
- **Proxy pattern**: provides a simple placeholder object for a more complex object that is in some way time-consuming or expensive to instantiate.

SECTION 4

Behavioral Patterns

Behavioral patterns are those patterns that are most specifically concerned with communication between objects. This chapter covers the following patterns:

- **Chain of Responsibility pattern**: allows decoupling between objects by passing a request from one object to the next in a chain until the request is recognized.
- **Command pattern**: utilizes simple objects to represent the execution of software commands and allows you to support logging and undoable operations.
- **Interpreter pattern**: provides a definition of how to include language elements in a program.
- **Iterator pattern**: formalizes the way we move through a list of data within a class.
- **Mediator pattern**: defines how communication between objects can be simplified by using a separate object to keep all objects from having to know about each other.
- **Observer pattern**: defines how multiple objects can be notified of a change.
- **State pattern**: allows an object to modify its behavior when its internal state changes.
- **Strategy pattern**: encapsulates an algorithm inside of a class.
- **Template Method pattern**: provides an abstract definition of an algorithm.
- **Visitor pattern**: adds polymorphic functions to a class noninvasively.

CHAPTER 16

Chain of Responsibility Pattern

The Chain of Responsibility pattern allows a number of classes to attempt to handle a request, without any of them knowing about the capabilities of the other classes. It provides a loose coupling between these classes; the only common link is the request that is passed between them. The request is passed along until one of the classes can handle it.

One example of such a pattern is a Help system like the one shown in Figure 16.1. Here, every screen region of an application invites you to seek help, but in some window background areas, more generic help is the only suitable result.

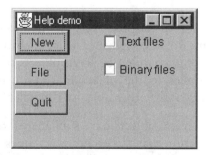

Figure 16.1 A simple application where different screen areas provide different help messages.

When you select an area for help, that visual control forwards its ID or name to the chain. Suppose that you selected the New button. If the first module can handle the New button, it displays the help message; otherwise, it forwards the request to the next module. Eventually, the message is forwarded to an All buttons class that can display a general message about how buttons work. If no general button help is available, the message is forwarded to the general help module that tells you how the system works. If that doesn't exist, the message is lost, and no information is displayed. This is illustrated in Figure 16.2.

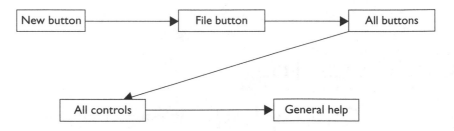

Figure 16.2   A simple Chain of Responsibility pattern.

There are two significant points we can observe from this example:

1.   The chain is organized from most specific to most general.

2.   There is no guarantee that the request will produce a response in all cases.

      We will see later that the Observer pattern defines how multiple classes can be notified of a change.

Applicability

The Chain of Responsibility is a good example of a pattern that helps to keep separate the knowledge of what each object in a program can do. That is, it reduces the coupling between objects so that they can act independently. This also applies to the object that constitutes the main program and contains instances of the other objects. You will find this pattern helpful when

- Several objects have similar methods that could be appropriate for the action that the program is requesting. However, it is more appropriate for the objects to decide which one is to carry out the action than it is for you to build this decision into the calling code.
- One of the objects might be most suitable, but you don't want to build in a series of if-else or switch statements to select a particular object.
- There might be new objects that you want to add to the list of processing options while the program is executing.
- Sometimes more than one object will have to act on a request, and you don't want to build knowledge of these interactions into the calling program.

Sample Code

The help system described previously is a little involved for a first example. So let's start with a simple visual command-interpreter program, shown in Figure 16.3, that illustrates how the chain works. This program displays the results of typed commands. While this first case is constrained to keep the example code tractable, we'll see that this Chain or Responsibility pattern is commonly used for parsers and even compilers.

In this example, the commands may be any of the following:

- Image filenames
- General filenames
- Color names
- Any other commands

In the first three cases, we can display a concrete result of the request, and in the last case, we can display only the request text itself.

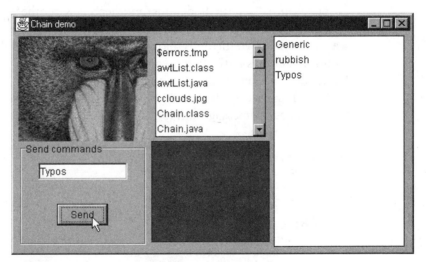

Figure 16.3 A simple visual command-interpreter program that acts on one of four panels, depending on the command you type in.

This system responds to commands as follows:

1. We type in "Mandrill," and see a display of the image Mandrill.jpg.

2. We type in "FileList," and that filename is highlighted in the center list box.

3. We type in "blue," and that color is displayed in the lower center panel.

If we type in anything that is neither a filename nor a color, that text is displayed in the right-hand list box.

This sequence of steps is shown in Figure 16.4.

Figure 16.4   The command chain for the program in Figure 16.3.

To write this simple chain of responsibility program, we start with an abstract Chain class.

```
public interface Chain {
public abstract void addChain(Chain c);
public abstract void sendToChain(String mesg);
public abstract Chain getChain();
)
```

The *addChain* method adds another class to the chain of classes. The *getChain* method returns the current class to which messages are being forwarded. These two methods allow us to modify the chain dynamically and add additional classes in the middle of an existing chain. The *sendToChain* method forwards a message to the next object in the chain.

The Imager class is derived from JPanel and implements the Chain interface. It takes the message and looks for .jpg files with that root name. If it finds one, it displays it.

```
public class Imager extends JPanel implements Chain {
    private Chain    nextChain;
    private Image    img;
    private boolean loaded;

    public Imager(){
        super();
        loaded = false;
        setBorder(new BevelBorder(BevelBorder.RAISED));
    }
//---------------
    public void addChain(Chain c) {
        nextChain = c;    //next in chain of resp
    }
//---------------
    public void sendToChain(String mesg) {
        //if there is a JPEG file with this root name
        //load it and display it.
        if (findImage(mesg))
            loadImage(mesg+".jpg");
```

```
        else
            //Otherwise, pass request along chain
            nextChain.sentToChain(mesg);
    }
//---------------
    public Chain getChain() {
        return nextChain;
    }
//---------------
    public void paint(Graphics g) {
        if (loaded) {
            g.drawImage(img, 0, 0, this);
        }
    }
```

Similarly, the ColorImage class simply interprets the message as a color name and displays it if it can. This example interprets only three colors, but you could implement any number.

```
public void sendToChain(String mesg) {
        Color c = getColor(mesg);
        if (c != null) {
            setBackground(c);
            repaint();
        } else {
            if (nextChain != null)
                nextChain.sentToChain(mesg);
        }
    }
//---------------
    private Color getColor(String mesg) {
        String lmesg = mesg.toLowerCase();
        Color c = null;

        if (lmesg.equals("red"))
            c = Color.red;
        if (lmesg.equals("blue"))
            c = Color.blue;
        if (lmesg.equals("green"))
            c = Color.green;
        return c;
    }
```

The List Boxes

Both the file list and the list of unrecognized commands are JList boxes. Since we developed an adapter JawtList in the previous chapter to give JList a simpler interface, we'll use that adapter here. The RestList class is the end of the chain, and any command that reaches it is simply displayed in the list. However, to allow for convenient extension, we are able to forward the message to other classes as well.

```java
public class RestList extends JawtList
implements Chain {
    private Chain nextChain = null;
    public RestList() {
        super(10);              //arg to JawtList
        setBorder(new LineBorder(Color.black));
    }
    public void addChain(Chain c) {
        nextChain = c;
    }
    public void sendToChain(String mesg){
        add(mesg);              //the end of the chain
        repaint();
        if (nextChain != null)
            nextChain.sendToChain(mesg);
    }
    public Chain getChain() {
        return nextChain;
    }
}
```

The FileList class is quite similar and can be derived from the RestList class to avoid replicating the *addChain* and *getChain* methods. It differs only in that it loads a list of the files in the current directory into the list when initialized and looks for one of those files when it receives a request.

```java
public class FileList extends RestList {
    String files[];
    private Chain nextChain;

    public FileList() {
        super();
        setBorder(new CompoundBorder (new EmptyBorder(5,5,5,5),
            new LineBorder(Color.black)));
        String tmp = "";
        File dir = new File(System.getProperty("user.dir"));
        files = dir.list();
        for (int i = 0; i < files.length; i++) {
            for (int j = i; j < files.length; j++) {
                if (files[i].toLowerCase().compareTo(
                        files[j].toLowerCase()) > 0) {
                    tmp = files[i];
                    files[i] = files[j];
                    files[j] = tmp;
                }
            }
        }
        for (int i = 0; i<files.length; i++)
            add(files[i]);
    }
//--------------
```

```
public void sendToChain(String mesg) {

    boolean found = false;
    int i = 0;
    while ((! found) && (i < files.length)) {
        XFile xfile = new XFile(files[i]);
        found = xfile.matchRoot(mesg);
        if (! found) i++;
    }
    if (found) {
        setSelectedIndex(i);
    } else {
        if (nextChain != null)
            nextChain.sendToChain(mesg);
    }
}
```

The Xfile class we introduce above is a simple child of the File class that contains a *matchRoot* method to compare a string to the root name of a file. Finally, we link these classes together in the constructor to form the Chain.

```
//set up the chain of responsibility
    sender.addChain(imager);
    imager.addChain(colorImage);
    colorImage.addChain(fileList);
    fileList.addChain(restList);
```

You can see the relationship between these classes in the UML diagram in Figure 16.5.

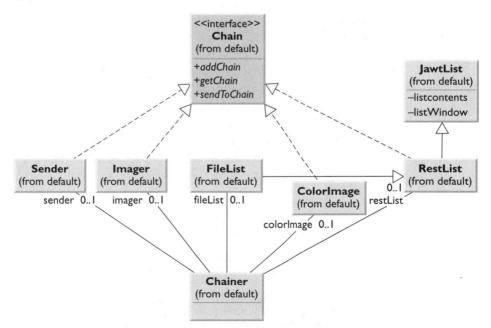

Figure 16.5 The class structure of the Chain of Responsibility program.

The Sender class is the initial class that implements the Chain interface. It receives the button clicks, obtains the text from the text field, and passes the command on to the Imager class, the FileList class, the ColorImage class, and finally to the RestList class. Note that FileList is a subclass of RestList and implements the Chain interface because the parent RestList class does.

Programming a Help System

As we noted earlier in this discussion, help systems provide good examples of how the Chain or Responsibility pattern can be used. Now that we've outlined a way to write such chains, let's consider a help system for a window that has several controls. The program, shown in Figure 16.6, pops up a help dialog message when the user presses the F1 (help) key. Which message is displayed depends on which control is selected when the F1 key is pressed.

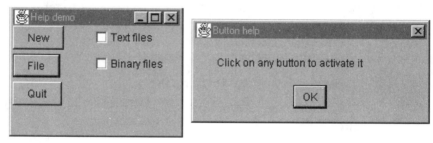

Figure 16.6   A simple help demonstration that pops up a different message, depending on which control is selected when the F1 key is pressed.

In this example, the user has selected the Quit key, which does not have a specific help message associated with it. So the chain forwards the help request to a general button help object, which displays the message shown on the right.

To write this help chain system, we begin with a general concrete Help-Window class that has empty implementations of three of the Chain interface methods. The class does, however, check for whether the next item in the chain is non-null before forwarding the message to that item.

```
public class HelpWindow implements Chain {
    protected Chain nextChain;
    protected String mesg;

    public HelpWindow() {
        mesg ="";
    }
//---------------
    public void addChain(Chain c) {
        nextChain = c;
    }
```

```
    public Chain getChain() {
        return this;
    }
    public void sendToChain(Component c) {
        sendChain(c);
    }
//--------------
    protected void sendChain (Component c) {
        if (nextChain != null) {
            nextChain.sendToChain(c);
        }
    }
}
```

Then we derive specific subclasses for each of the help message categories that we want to produce. In this case, we want help messages for

- The New button
- The File button
- A general button
- A general visual control (covering the check boxes)
- The window itself

So we write classes for these and combine them into a chain as follows:

```
chain = new FileNewHelp(this);
FileHelp fhelp = new FileHelp(this);
chain.addChain (fhelp);
ButtonHelp bhelp = new ButtonHelp(this);
fhelp.addChain(bhelp);
ControlHelp chelp = new ControlHelp(this);
bhelp.addChain (chelp);
WindowHelp whelp = new WindowHelp(this);
chelp.addChain (this);
```

Receiving the Help Command

Next, we need to assign keyboard listeners to look for the F1 keypress. You might think that we need six such listeners: one each for the three buttons, the two check boxes, and the background window. However, we really need only one listener—for the Frame window itself. This is because the Java Swing event dispatcher forwards these events to all surrounding (parent) components. In other words, the keyPress event is received successively by

1. the selected component,

2. the Panel containing the component, and

3. the Frame.

This is in fact an interval Java implementation of the Chain of Responsibility, in which the request is the keyPressed event. So in constructing the event listener in this program's user interface, we need only to define a subclass of KeyAdapter that traps the F1 key

```
//    inner class for key strokes
    class k_adapter extends KeyAdapter {
        public void keyPressed(KeyEvent e) {
            if(e.getKeyCode () == KeyEvent.VK_F1) {
                sendToChain((JComponent)getFocusOwner());
            }
        }
    }
```

and add a key event listener to the Frame

```
    helpKey = new key_adapter();
    addKeyListener(helpKey);
```

Note that we obtain the component that has the current focus by using *getFocusOwner* and then send that component along the chain to obtain the most specific help message that the system provides. Each help object has a test to check whether the object is the one described by that help message. Either the message is displayed or the object is forwarded to the next chain element. For the File button, the class looks like the following:

```
public class FileHelp extends HelpWindow {
    String message, title;
    int icon;
    JFrame frame;

    public FileHelp(JFrame f) {
        mesg = "Select to open a file";
        title ="File button help";
        icon = JOptionPane.DEFAULT_OPTION;
        frame = f;
    }
    public void sendToChain(JComponent c) {
        if (c instanceof JButton) {
            JButton b = (JButton)c;
            if( b.getText().equals("File"))
                JOptionPane.showMessageDialog(frame, mesg,
                                              title, icon);
            else
                sendChain(c);
        }
    }
}
```

Figure 16.7 shows the complete class diagram for this help system.

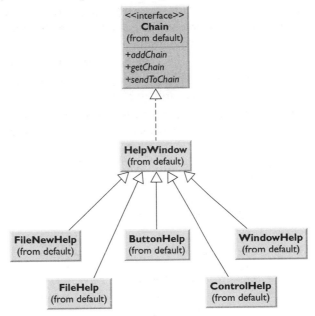

Figure 16.7   The class diagram for the help system.

A Chain or a Tree?

A Chain of Responsibility does not have to be linear. The *Smalltalk Companion* suggests that it is more generally a tree structure with a number of specific entry points, all pointing upward to the most general node, as shown in Figure 16.8.

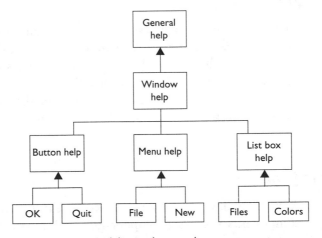

Figure 16.8   The Chain of Responsibility implemented as a tree structure.

However, this sort of structure seems to imply that each button, or its handler, knows where to enter the chain. This can complicate the design in some cases and may preclude the need for the chain at all.

Another way of handling a tree-like structure is to have a single-entry point that branches to the specific button, menu, or other widget type and then "unbranches" as described previously to more general help cases. There is little reason for that complexity. We could instead align the classes into a single chain, starting at the bottom, and proceed left to right and up a row at a time until the entire system has been traversed, as shown in Figure 16.9.

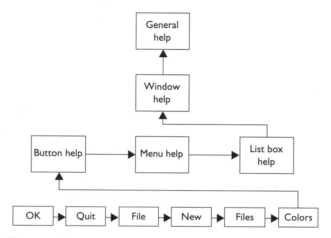

Figure 16.9   The same Chain of Responsibility implemented as a linear chain.

Kinds of Requests

The request or message passed along the Chain of Responsibility may well be a great deal more complicated than just the string that we conveniently used in this example. It could include various data types or a complete object with a number of methods. Since various classes along the chain may use different properties of such a request object, you might end up designing an abstract Request type and any number of derived classes with additional methods.

Examples in Java

As just noted, while we were discussing help systems, any sequence of contained components such as JComponent/Panel/Frame causes a cascade of events to be sent upward to the surrounding components. This is a clear implementation of the Chain of Responsibility pattern. It could also be argued that, in general, the class inheritance structure itself exemplifies this pattern. If a method is to be executed in a deeply derived class, that method is passed up the inheritance chain until the first parent class containing that method is found. The fact that further parents contain other implementations of that method does not matter.

Consequences of the Chain of Responsibility

Use of the Chain of Responsibility pattern has the following consequences:

1. This pattern's primary purpose, like that of several other patterns, is to reduce coupling between objects. An object needs to know only how to forward the request to other objects.

2. Each Java object in the chain is self-contained. It knows nothing of the others and needs only to decide whether it can satisfy the request. This makes writing each one, as well as constructing the chain, very easy.

3. You can decide whether the final object in the chain handles all requests that it receives in some default fashion or just discards them. However, for this to be effective you must know which object will be last in the chain.

4. Finally, since Java cannot provide multiple inheritance, the basic Chain class needs to be an interface rather than an abstract class so that the individual objects can inherit from another useful hierarchy (as we did here by deriving them all from JPanel). The disadvantage of this approach is that you often must implement the linking, sending, and forwarding of code in each module separately (or as we did here, by subclassing a concrete class that implements the Chain interface).

 ## THOUGHT QUESTIONS

1. How could you use the Chain of Responsibility pattern to implement an e-mail filter?

2. Write a Java servlet for processing a Common Gateway Interface (CGI) form using the Chain of Responsibility pattern.

Programs on the CD-ROM

Program	Description
\ChainOfResponsibility\ ImageChain\Chainer.java	Allows the entry of commands that cause visual objects in the screen interface to change.
\ChainOfResponsibility\ HelpChain\HelpChain.java	Shows how a simple help system can pass messages to increasingly more general components.

CHAPTER 17

The Command Pattern

The Chain of Responsibility pattern forwards requests along a chain of classes, but the Command pattern forwards a request only to a specific object. It encloses the request for a specific action inside an object and gives it a known public interface. It lets you give the client the ability to make requests without knowing anything about the actual action that will be performed and allows you to change that action without affecting the client program in any way.

Motivation

When you build a Java user interface, you provide controls—menu items, buttons, check boxes, and so on—to allow the user to tell the program what to do. When a user selects one of these controls, the program receives an ActionEvent, which it must trap by implementing the ActionListener interfaces' actionPerformed event.

Suppose that we build a very simple program that allows us to select the menu items File | Open and File | Exit and click on a button labeled Red that turns the background of the window red. This program is shown in Figure 17.1.

Figure 17.1   A simple program that receives actionPerformed events from the button and menu items.

155

The program consists of the File Menu object with the mnuOpen and mnuExit MenuItems added to it. It also contains one button called btnRed. Clicking any of these causes an ActionEvent, which generates a call to the *actionPerformed* method such as the following:

```
public void actionPerformed(ActionEvent e)     {
        Object obj = e.getSource();
        if(obj == mnuOpen)
            fileOpen();            //open file
        if (obj == mnuExit)
            exitClicked();         //exit from program
        if (obj == btnRed)
            redClicked();          //turn red
    }
```

Here are the three private methods that we call from the *actionPerformed* method:

```
    private void exitClicked()     {
        System.exit(0);
    }
//————————————
    private void fileOpen()     {
        FileDialog fDlg = new FileDialog(this, "Open a file",
                                  FileDialog.LOAD);
            fDlg.show();
    }
//————————————
    private void redClicked()     {
        p.setBackground(Color.red);
    }
```

Now, as long as there are only a few menu items and buttons, this approach works fine, but when there are dozens of menu items and several buttons, the *actionPerformed* code can get pretty unwieldy. This also seems a little inelegant, since, when using an OO language such as Java, we want to avoid a long series of if statements to identify the selected object. Instead, we want to find a way to have each object receive its commands directly.

Command Objects

One way to ensure that every object receives its own commands directly is to use the Command pattern and create individual Command objects. A Command object always has an *Execute* method that is called when an action occurs on that object. Most simply, a Command object implements at least the following interface:

```
public interface Command {
    public void Execute();
}
```

We use this interface to reduce the *actionPerformed* method to the following:

```
public void actionPerformed(ActionEvent e) {
        Command cmd = (Command)e.getSource();
        cmd.Execute();
    }
```

Then we can provide the *Execute* method for each object that carries out the desired action, thus keeping the knowledge of what to do inside of the object where it belongs, instead of having another part of the program make these decisions.

One important purpose of the Command pattern is to keep the program and user interface objects completely separate from the actions that they initiate. In other words, these program objects should be completely separate from each other and should not have to know how other objects work. The user interface receives a command and tells a Command object to carry out whatever duties it has been instructed to do. The GUI does not and should not need to know what tasks will be executed. This decouples the UI class from the execution of specific commands, thereby making it possible to modify or completely change the action code without changing the classes that contain the user interface.

You can also use the Command object to tell the program to execute the command when the resources are available rather than immediately. In such cases, you are *queuing* commands to be executed later. Finally, you can use Command objects to remember operations so that you can support Undo requests.

Building Command Objects

There are several ways to go about building Command objects for a program like this, and each has some advantages. We start with the simplest: deriving new classes from the MenuItem and Button classes and implementing the Command interface in each. Following are examples of extensions to the Button and Menu classes for our simple program.

```
class btnRedCommand extends Button
                implements Command    {
        public btnRedCommand(String caption)    {
            super(caption);    //initialize the button
```

```
        }
        public void Execute()    {
            p.setBackground(Color.red);
        }
    }
    //--------------
class flieExitCommand extends MenuItem
                  implements Command     {
        public fileExitCommand(String caption)    {
            super(caption);    //initialize the menu
        }
        public void Execute()    {
            System.exit(0);
        }
    }
```

This certainly lets us simplify the calls made in the *actionPerformed* method, but it requires that we create and instantiate a new class for each action that we want to execute.

```
mnuOpen.addActionListener(new fileOpen());
mnuExit.addActionListener(new fileExit());
btnRed.addActionListener(new btnRed());
```

We can circumvent most of the problem of passing needed parameters to those classes by making them *inner classes*. This makes the Panel and Frame objects available directly.

However, inner classes are not such a good idea as commands proliferate because any that access any other GUI components must remain inside the main class. This clutters up the code for this main class with a lot of confusing little inner classes.

Of course, if we are willing to pass the needed parameters to these classes, they can be independent. Here, we pass in the Frame object and a Panel object.

```
mnuOpen = new fileOpenCommand("Open...", this);
mnuFile.add(mnuOpen);
mnuExit = new fileExitCommand("Exit");
mnuFile.add(mnuExit);

p = new Panel();
add(p);
btnRed = new btnRedCommand("Read", p);
p.add(btnRed);
```

In this second case, the Menu and Button command classes can then be external to the main class and even stored in separate files if we prefer.

The Command Pattern

Now, while it is advantageous to encapsulate the action in a Command object, binding that object into the element that causes the action (such as the menu item or button) is not exactly what the Command pattern is about. Instead, the Command object should be separate from the invoking client so that we can vary the invoking program and the details of the command action separately. Rather than having the command be part of the menu or button, we make the Menu and Button classes *containers* for a Command object that exists separately. We thus make UI elements that implement a CommandHolder interface.

```
public interface CommandHolder (
    public void setCommand(Command comd);
    public Command getCommand();
}
```

This interface indicates that there is a method to put a Command object into the invoking object and a method to fetch that Command object and call its *Execute* method.

Then we create the cmdMenu class, which implements this interface.

```
public class cmdMenu extends JMenuItem
            implements CommandHolder {
protected Command menuCommand;        //internal copies
protected JFrame frame;

public cmdMenu(String name, JFrame frm) {
    super(name);               //menu string
    frame = frm;               //containing frame
}
public void setCommand(Command comd) {
    menuCommand = comd;     //save the command
}
public Command getCommand() {
    return menuCommand;     //return the command
}
}
```

This actually simplifies our program—we don't have to create a separate menu class for each action that we want to carry out. We just create instances of the menu and pass them different Command objects.

```
mnuOpen = new cmdMenu("Open...", this);
mnuFile.add(mnuOpen);
mnuOpen.setCommand (new fileCommand(this));
```

```
mnuExit = new cmdMenu("Exit", this);
mnuExit.setCommand (new ExitCommand());
mnuFile.add(mnuExit);
```

Creating the cmdButton class is analogous.

```
btnRed = new cmdButton("Red", this);
btnRed.setCommand (new RedCommand (this, jp));
jp.add(btnRed);
```

We still must create separate Command objects, but they are no longer part of the user interface classes. For example, the FileCommand class is the following:

```
public class fileCommand implements Command {
    JFrame frame;

public fileCommand(JFrame fr) {
    frame = fr;
}
public void Execute() {
    FileDialog fDlg = new FileDialog(frame, "Open file");
    fDlg.show();      //show file dialog
}
}
```

   Then our *actionPerformed* method needs to obtain the actual Command object from the UI object that caused the action and then execute that command.

```
public void actionPerformed(ActionEvent e)    {
    CommandHolder obj = (CommandHolder)e.getSource();
    obj.getCommand().Execute();
}
```

This is only slightly more complicated than our original routine and again keeps the *actionPerformed* method from having to perform a series of if tests.

   We can see the relationships between these classes and interfaces clearly in the UML diagram in Figure 17.2.

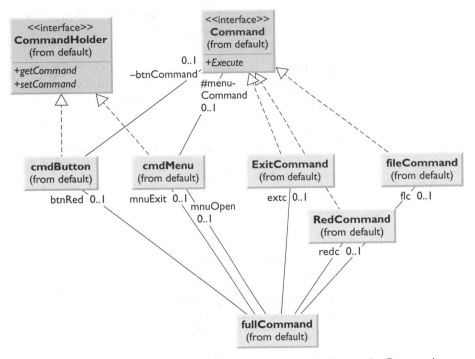

Figure 17.2　A class structure for three different objects that implement the Command interface and two that implement the CommandHolder interface.

Here you see that cmdButton and cmdMenu implement the Command-Holder interface and that there are two instances of cmdMenu in the UI class fullCommand. The diagram also shows the classes ExitCommand, RedCommand, and fileCommand, which implement the Command interface and are instantiated in the fullCommand UI class. This is, finally, the complete implementation of the Command pattern that we have been inching toward.

The Command Pattern in the Java Language

But there are still a couple of more ways to approach this. If you give every control its own ActionListener class, you are in effect creating individual command objects for each of them. And, in fact, this is really what the designers of the Java 1.1 event model had in mind. We have become accustomed to using these multiple if test routines because they occur in most simple example texts, even if they are not the best way to catch these events.

To implement this approach, we create several little classes, each of which implements the ActionListener interface.

```
class btnRed implements ActionListener    {
    public void actionPerformed(ActionEvent e)    {
        p.setBackground(Color.red);
    }
}
//--------------
class fileExit implements ActionListener    {
    public void actionPerformed(ActionEvent e {
        System.exit(0);
    }
}
}
```

Then we register them as listeners in the usual way.

```
mnuOpen.addActionListener(new fileOpen());
mnuExit.addActionListener(new fileExit());
buttonRed.addActionListener(new btnRed());
```

Here, we made these to be inner classes. However, they also could be external with arguments passed in, as we did previously.

Consequences of the Command Pattern

The Command pattern's main disadvantage is the proliferation of little classes that either clutter up the main class if they are inner classes or clutter up the program namespace if they are outer classes.

Even when we put all of the actionPerformed events in a single basket, we usually call little private methods to carry out the actual functions. It turns out that these private methods are just about as long as out little inner classes, so often there is little difference in complexity between the inner class and outer class approaches.

Anonymous Inner Classes

We can reduce the clutter of the namespace by creating unnamed inner classes. We do this by declaring an instance of a class where we need it. For example, we could create the Red button and the class for manipulating the background all at once.

```
btnRed.addActionListener(new ActionListener()    {
    public void actionPerformed(ActionListener e) {
        p.setBackground(Color.red);
    }
}   );
```

This is not very readable, however, and does not really reduce the number of runtime classes, since the compiler generates a class file even for these unnamed classes.

Providing Undo

Another main reason for using the Command pattern is that it provides a convenient way to store and execute an Undo function. Each Command object can remember what it just did and restore that state when requested to do so, provided that the computational and memory requirements are not too overwhelming. At the top level, we simply redefine the Command interface to have two methods.

```
public interface Command    {
    public void Execute();
    public void unDo();
}
```

Then we must design each Command object to keep a record of what it last did so that it can undo it. This can be a little more complicated than it first appears, since having a number of interleaved commands being executed and then undone can lead to some hysteresis. In addition, each command will need to store enough information about each execution of the command so that it can know what specifically must be undone.

The problem of undoing commands has actually two parts. First, we must keep a list of the commands that have been executed, and second, each command must keep a list of its executions. To see how we use the Command pattern to carry out undo operations, let's consider the program, shown in Figure 17.3, that draws successive red or blue lines on the screen using one of two buttons to draw a new instance of each line. We can undo the last line that we drew by clicking on the Undo button.

Figure 17.3   A program that draws red and blue lines each time you click on the Red and Blue buttons.

Clicking on Undo several times should cause the last several lines to disappear, no matter in what order the buttons are clicked. This is shown in Figure 17.4.

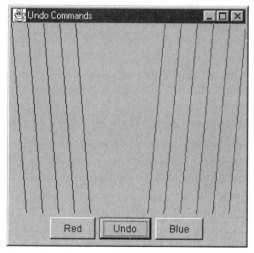

Figure 17.4   The same program as in Figure 17.3 after the Undo button has been clicked four times.

Thus any undoable program needs a single sequential list of all commands that have been executed. Each time we click on any button, we add its corresponding command to the list.

```
public void actionPerformed(ActionEvent e) {
      CommandHolder cmdh = (CommandHolder)e.getSource ();
      Command        cmd  = cmdg.getCommand ();
      u_cmd.add (cmd);       //add to list
      cmd.Execute ();        //and execute
   }
```

Further, the list that we add the Command objects to is maintained inside the Undo Command object so that it can access that list conveniently.

```
public class undoCommand implements Command {
   Vector undoList;

   public undoCommand () {
      undoList = new Vector();          //list of commands to undo
   }
   //---------------
   public void add(Command cmd) {
      if(! (cmd instanceof undoCommand))
         undoList.add(cmd);             //add commands to list
   }
   //---------------
   public void Execute() {
      int index = undoList.size () -1;

      if (index > = 0) {
         //get last command executed
         Command cmd =  (Command)undoList.elementAt (index);
         cmd.unDo  ();                  //undo it
         undoList.remove (index);       //and remove from list
      }
   }
   //---------------
   public void unDo() {                 //does nothing
   }
}
```

The undoCommand object keeps a list of Commands and not a list of actual data. Each Command object has its *unDo* method called to execute the actual undo operation. Note that since the undoCommand object implements the Command interface, it too must have an *unDo* method. However, the idea of undoing successive unDo operations is a little complex for this simple example program. Consequently, you should note that the *add* method adds all Commands to the list *except* the undoCommand itself, since we have just decided that undoing an unDo command is meaningless.

The Command objects that draw the red and blue lines are derived from the parent drawCommand class. The derived redCommand and blueCommand classes use different colors and start at opposite sides of the window. Each class keeps a list of lines to be drawn in a Vector as a series of drawData objects that contain the coordinates of each line. Undoing a line from either the red or the blue line list means removing the last drawData object from the drawList Vector. Then either command forces the screen to be repainted.

```java
//parent class for redCommand and blueCommand
public class drawCommand and implements Command {
    protected Vector drawlist;
    protected int       x, y, dx, dy;
    protected Color     color;
    protected JPanel p;

    public drawCommand(JPanel pn) {
        drawList = new Vector();
        p = pn;         //save the panel that we draw on
    }
    //---------------
    public void Execute() {
        drawList.add(new drawData(x, y, dx, dy));
        x += dx;        //increment to the next position
        y += dy;
        p.repaint();
    }
    //---------------
    public void unDo() {
        int index = drawList.size() -1;
        //remove last-drawn line from list
        if(index <= 0) {
            drawData d = (drawData)drawList.elementAt (index);
            drawList.remove (index);
            x = d.getX ();      //reset x and y
            y = d.getY ();      //to the last-used position
        }
        p.repaint();            //force redrawing
    }
    //---------------
    public void draw(Graphics g) {
        //draw all remaining lines in the list
        //called by panel's paint method
        Dimension sz = p.getSize();
        g.setColor (color);
        for (int i=0; i < drawList.size (); i++) {
            drawData d = (drawData)drawList.elementAt (i);
            g.drawLine (d.getX (), d.getY (),
                        d.getX()+dx, d.getY()+sz.height );
        }
    }
}
```

The *draw* method in the drawCommand class redraws the entire list of lines that the Command object has stored. These two *draw* methods are called from the *paint* method of the enclosing panel in the undoCmd main class.

```
public class paintPanel extends JPanel (
//inner class which draws both sets of lines
//by calling the two object's draw methods
        public void paint(Graphics g) {
        Dimension sz = getSize();
        //erase background
        g.setColor(Color.lightGray );
        g.fillRect (0, 0, sz.width , sz.height );
        //draw lines
        red_command.draw(g);
        blue_command.draw(g);
    }
}
```

The set of classes we use in this Undo program is shown in Figure 17.5.

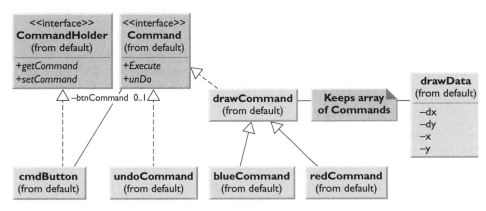

Figure 17.5 The classes used to implement Undo in a Command pattern implementation.

THOUGHT QUESTIONS

1. Mouse clicks on list box items and on radio buttons also constitute commands. Clicks on multiselect list boxes could also be represented as commands. Design a program that includes these features.

2. A lottery system used a random number generator constrained to integers between 1 and 50. The selections are made in intervals selected by a random

timer. Each selection must be unique. Design Command patterns to choose the winning numbers each week.

Programs on the CD-ROM

Program	Description
\Command\commandObject\ testCommand.java	Extends menu and button classes as simple Command objects.
\Command\actionCommand\ actionCommand.java	Uses a separate actionListener for each button or menuItem.
\Command\fullCommand\ fullCommand.java	Creates separate CommandHolder classes from buttons and menus and separate Command objects to execute the commands.
\Command\Undo\undoCmd.java	Draws a series of diagonal colored lines using two buttons and undoes them using an Undo button.

CHAPTER 18

The Interpreter Pattern

Some programs benefit from having a language to describe operations that they can perform. The Interpreter pattern generally deals with defining a grammar for that language and using that grammar to interpret statements in that language.

Motivation

When a program presents a number of different but somewhat similar cases that it can deal with, it can be advantageous to use a simple language to describe these cases and then have the program interpret that language. Such cases can be as simple as the Macro language recording facilities that various office suite programs provide or as complex as Visual Basic for Applications (VBA). VBA not only is included in Microsoft Office products but also can be easily embedded in any number of third-party products.

One problem is how to recognize when a language can be helpful. The Macro language recorder records menu and keystroke operations for later playback and just barely qualifies as a language; it might not actually have a written form or grammar. Languages such as VBA, by contrast, are quite complex but are far beyond the capabilities of the individual application developer. Further, embedding commercial languages such as VBA, Java, or SmallTalk usually requires substantial licensing fees—this makes them less attractive to all but the largest developers.

Applicability

As the *Smalltalk Companion* notes, recognizing cases in which an Interpreter can be helpful is much of the problem, and programmers without formal language/compiler training often overlook this approach. There aren't many such cases, but there are three in which languages apply:

1. When you need a command interpreter to parse user commands: The user can type queries of various kinds and obtain a variety of answers.

2. When the program must parse an algebraic string: This case is fairly obvious. The program is asked to carry out its operations based on a computation in which the user enters an equation of some sort. This often occurs in mathematical-graphics programs, where the program renders a curve or surface based on any equation that it can evaluate. Programs such as *Mathematica* and graph drawing packages such as *Origin* work in this way.

3. When the program must produce varying kinds of output: This case is a little less obvious but far more useful. Consider a program that can display columns of data in any order and sort them in various ways. These programs are often called Report Generators. The underlying data might be stored in a relational database, but the user interface to the report program is usually much simpler then the SQL that the database uses. In fact, in some cases the simple report language might be interpreted by the report program and translated into SQL.

Simple Report Example

Let's consider a report generator that can operate on five columns of data in a table and return various reports on these data. Suppose that we have the following results from a swimming competition:

```
Amanda McCarthy           12    WCA          29.28
Jamie Falco               12    HNHS         29.80
Meaghan O'Donnell         12    EDST         30.00
Greer Gibbs               12    CDEV         30.04
Rhiannon Jeffrey          11    WYW          30.04
Sophie Connolly           12    WAC          30.05
Dana Helyer               12    ARAC         30.18
```

The five column names are frname, lname, age, club, and time. If we consider the complete race results of 51 swimmers, we might want to sort these results by club, by last name, or by age. We could produce several useful reports from these data in which the order of the columns changes as well as the sorting, so a language is one useful way to handle these reports.

We'll define a very simple nonrecursive grammar of the sort

```
Print lname frname club time Sortby club Thenby time
```

For the purposes of this example, we define the three verbs given in the grammar as

```
Print
Sortby
Thenby
```

and the five column names as

```
frname
lname
age
club
time
```

For convenience, we assume that the language is case-insensitive and that its grammar is punctuation-free, amounting in brief to

> *Print var[var] [sortby var [thenby var]]*

Finally, the grammar contains only one main verb, and while each statement is a declaration, it has no assignment statement or computational ability.

Interpreting the Language

Interpreting the language takes place in three steps:

1. Parse the language symbols into tokens.

2. Reduce the tokens into actions.

3. Execute the actions.

We parse the language into tokens by scanning each statement with a StringTokenizer and then substituting a number for each word. Usually parsers push each parsed token onto a *stack*—we will use that technique here. We implement that Stack class using a Vector, which contains *push, pop, top,* and *nextTop* methods to examine and manipulate the stack contents.

After the language is parsed, the stack could look as shown in the following table:

Type	Token
Var	Time
Verb	Thenby
Var	Club
Verb	Sortby
Var	Time
Var	Club
Var	Frname
Var	Lname
Verb	Print

◄— Top of stack

However, we quickly realize that the verb *Thenby* has no real meaning other than clarification. We'd more likely parse the tokens and skip *Thenby* altogether. The initial stack then looks like this:

```
Time
Club
Sortby
Time
Club
Frname
Lname
Print
```

Objects Used in Parsing

Actually, we do not push just a numeric token onto the stack, but rather a *ParseObject* that has both a type and a value property.

```
public class ParseObject {
    public static final int VERB=1000, VAR = 1010,
              MULTVAR = 1020;
```

```
        protected int value;
        protected int type;

        public int getValue() {return value;}
        public int getType() {return type;}
}
```

These objects can take on the type VERB or VAR. Then we extend this object into ParseVerb and ParseVar objects, whose value fields can take on PRINT or SORT, for ParseVerb and FRNAME, LNAME, and so on, for Parse-Var. For later use in reducing the parse list, we then derive Print and Sort objects from ParseVerb. This gives the hierarchy shown in Figure 18.1.

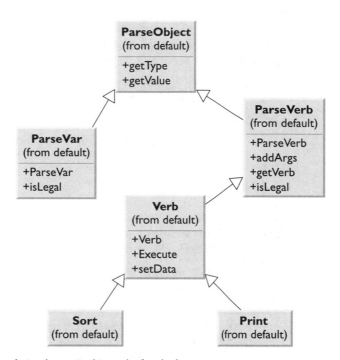

Figure 18.1   A simple parsing hierarchy for the Interpreter program.

The parsing process is just the following code, which uses the StringTokenizer and the ParseObjects:

```
public class Parser implements Command {
    private Stack stk;
    private Vector actionList;
    private KidData kdata;
```

```
        private Data data;
        private JawtList ptable;
        private Chain chain;

        public Parser(String line) {
            stk = new Stack();
            actionList = new Vector();       //actions accumulate here

            buildStack(line);
            buildChain();      //construct the interpreter chain
        }
        //---------------
        public void setData(KidData k, JawtList pt) {
            data = new Data(k.getData());
            ptable = pt;
        }
        //---------------
        //executes parse and the interpretation of command line
        public void Execute() {

            while (stk.hasMoreElements()) {
                chain.sendToChain (stk);
            }
            //now execute the verbs
            for (int i = 0; i < actionList.size() ; i++) {
                Verb v = (Verb)actionList.elementAt(i);
                v.setData(data,ptable);
                v.Execute();
            }
        }
        //---------------
        protected ParseObject tokenize (String s) {
            ParseObject obj = getVerb(s);
            if (obj == null)
                obj = getVar(s);
            return obj;
        }
        //---------------
        protected ParseVerb getVerb(String s) {
            ParseVerb v;
            v = new ParseVerb(s);
            if (v.isLegal())
                return v.getVerb(s);
            else
                return null;
        }
    //---------------
        protected ParseVar getVar(String s) {
            ParseVar v;
            v = new ParseVar(s);
            if (v.isLegal())
```

```
                return v;
           else
                return null;
      }
}
```

The ParseVerb and ParseVar classes return objects with isLegal set to true if they recognize the word.

```
public class ParseVerb extends ParseObject {
    static public final int PRINT=100, SORTBY=110, THENBY=120;
    protected Vector args;

    public ParseVerb(String s) {
        args = new Vector();
        s = s.toLowerCase();
        value = -1;
        type = VERB
        if (s.equal("print")) value = PRINT;
        if (s.equals("sortby")) value = SORTBY;
    }
//---------------
    public ParseVerb getVerb(String s) {
        switch (value) {
        case PRINT:
            return new Print(s)
        case SORTBY:
            return new Sort(s);
        }
        return null;
    }
```

Reducing the Parsed Stack

The tokens on the stack have the following forms:

```
Var
Var
Verb
Var
Var
Var
Var
Verb
```

We reduce the stack a token at a time, folding successive Vars into a MultVar class until the arguments are folded into the verb objects, as shown in Figure 18.2.

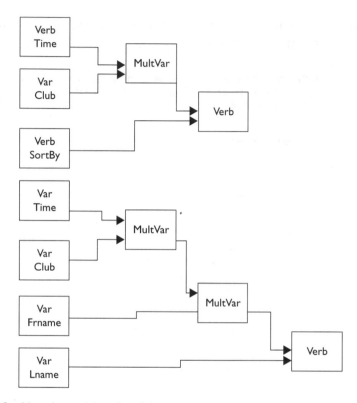

Figure 18.2   How the stack is reduced during parsing.

When the stack reduces to a verb, this verb and its arguments are placed in an action list. When the stack is empty, the actions are executed.

Creating a Parser class that is a Command object and executing it when the Go button on the user interface is clicked carry out this entire process.

```
public void actionPerformed(ActionEvent e) {
    Parser p = new Parser (tx.getText());
    p.setData(kdata, ptable);
    p.Execute();
}
```

The parser itself just reduces the tokens, as shown earlier. It checks for various pairs of tokens on the stack and reduces each pair to a single one for each of five different cases.

Implementing the Interpreter Pattern

Writing a parser for this simple grammar as a series of if statements is certainly possible. For each of the six possible stack configurations, we reduce the stack until only a verb remains. Then, since we made the Print and Sort verb classes Command objects, we can just execute them one by one as the action list is enumerated.

The real advantage of the Interpreter pattern, however, is its flexibility. By making each parsing case an individual object, we can represent the parse tree as a series of connected objects that reduce the stack successively. Using this arrangement, we can easily change the parsing rules, with few changes to the program. We just create new objects and insert them into the parse tree.

The participating objects in the Interpreter pattern are:

- **AbstractExpression**: declares the abstract Interpreter operation.
- **TerminalExpression**: interprets expressions containing any of the terminal tokens in the grammar.
- **NonTerminalExpression**: interprets all of the nonterminal expressions in the grammar.
- **Context**: contains the global information that is part of the parser, in this case, the token stack.
- **Client**: builds the syntax tree from the previous expression types and invokes the Interpret operation.

The Syntax Tree

We can construct a simple syntax tree to carry out the parsing of the previous stack. We need only to look for each defined stack configuration and reduce it to an executable form. In fact, the best way to implement this tree is to use a Chain of Responsibility pattern, which passes the stack configuration along between classes until one of them recognizes that configuration and acts on it. You can decide whether a successful stack reduction should end that pass; it is perfectly possible to have several successive chain members work on the stack in a single pass. The processing ends when the stack is empty. Figure 18.3 shows a diagram of the individual parse chain elements.

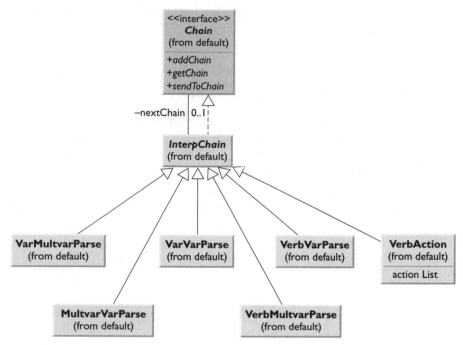

Figure 18.3   How the classes that perform the parsing interact.

This class structure begins with the AbstractExpression interpreter class Interp-
Chain.

```
public abstract class InterpChain implements Chain {

    private Chain nextChain;
    private Stack stk;
//---------------
    public void addChain(Chain c) {
        nextChain = c:     next in the chain of resp
    }
//---------------
    public abstract boolean interpret();
//---------------
    public Chain getChain() {
        return nextChain;
    }
//---------------
    public void sendToChain(Stack stack) {
        stk = stack;
        if (! interpret())     //interpret the stack
            //otherwise, pass the request along the chain
                nextChain.sendToChain(stk);
    }
```

```
//----------------
    protected void addArgsToVerb() {
        ParseObject v = stk.pop();
        ParseVerb verb = (ParseVerb)stk.pop();
        verb.addArgs(v);
        stk.push(verb);
    }
//----------------
    protected boolean toStack(int c1, int c2) {
        return(stk.top().getType() == c1) &&
        (stk.nextTop().getType()== c2);
    }
}
```

This class also contains the methods for manipulating objects on the stack. Each subclass implements the Interpret operation differently and reduces the stack accordingly. For example, the complete VarVarParse class is as follows:

```
public class VarVarParse extends InterpChain (

    public boolean interpret() {
        if (topStack(ParseObject.VAR, ParseObject.VAR)) {
            //reduce (Var Var) to Multvar
            ParseVar v = (ParseVar)stk.pop();
            ParseVar v1 = (ParseVar)stk.pop();
            MultVar mv = new MultVar(v1, v);
            stk.push(mv);
            return true;
        } else
            return false;
    }
}
```

Thus in this implementation of the pattern the stack constitutes the Context participant. Each of the first five subclasses of InterpChain are NonTerminalExpression participants. The ActionVerb class, which moves the completed verb and action objects to the actionList, is the TerminalExpression participant.

The client object is the Parser class that builds the stack object list from the typed command text and constructs the Chain or Responsibility pattern from the various interpreter classes.

```
public class Parser implements Command {
    Stack stk;
        Vector actionList;
        KidData kdata;
        Data data;
        JawtList ptable;
        Chain chain;
```

```
    public Parser(String line) {
        stk = new Stack();
        actionList = new Vector();      //actions accumulate here

        buildStack(line);       //construct a stack of tokens
        buildChain();           //construct an interpreter chain
    }
//---------------
    private void buildStack(String line) {
        //parse the input tokens and build a stack
        StringTokenizer tok = new StringTokenizer(line);
        while(tok.hasMoreElements()) {
            ParseObject token = tokenizer(tok.nextToken());
            if(token != null)
                stk.push(token);
        }
    }
//---------------
    private void buildChain() {
        chain = new VarVarParse(); //start of the chain
        VarMultvarParse vmvp = new VarMultvarParse();
        chain.addChain (vmvp);
        MultvarVarParse mvvp = new MultvarVarParse();
        vmvp.addChain(mvvp);
        VerbMultvarParse vrvp = new VerbMultvarParse();
        mvvp.addChain(vrvp);
        VerbVarParse vvp = new VerbVarParse();
        vrvp.addChain(vvp);
        VerbAction va = new VerbAction(actionList);
        vvp.addChain(va);
    }
```

The class also sends the stack through the chain until it is empty and then executes the verbs that have accumulated in the action list.

```
//executes parse and interpretation of command line
    public void Execute() {

        while (stk.hasMoreElements()) {
            chain.sendToChain (stk);
        }
        //now execute the verbs
        for (int i =0; i< actionList.size(); i++) {
            Verb v = (Verb)actionList.elementAt(i);
            v.setData(data, ptable);
            v.Execute();
        }
    }
```

Figure 18.4 shows the final visual program.

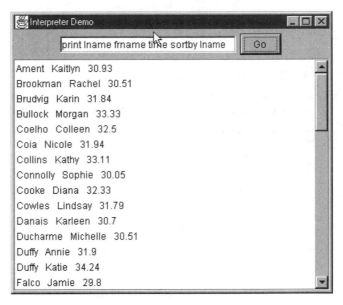

Figure 18.4   The Interpreter pattern operating on the simple command in the text field.

Consequences of the Interpreter Pattern

Use of the Interpreter pattern has the following consequences:

1. Whenever you introduce an interpreter into a program, you need to provide a simple way for the program user to enter commands in that language. This can be done via the Macro record button noted previously, or it can be done via an editable text field like the one in the previous program.

2. Introducing a language and its accompanying grammar requires fairly extensive error checking for misspelled terms or misplaced grammatical elements. This can easily consume a great deal of programming effort unless some template code is available for implementing this checking. Further, effective methods for notifying the users of these errors are not easy to design and implement.

    In the Interpreter example in this chapter, the only error handling is that keywords that are not recognized are not converted to ParseObjects and are pushed onto the stack. Thus nothing will happen because the resulting stack sequence probably cannot be parsed successfully. Even if it can, the item represented by the misspelled keyword will not be included.

3. You can also consider generating a language automatically from a user interface or radio and command buttons and list boxes. While it might seem that having such an interface obviates the necessity for a language, the same

requirements of sequence and computation still apply. When you must have a way to specify the order of sequential operations, a language is a good way to do so, even it that language is generated from the user interface.

4. The Interpreter pattern has the advantage that you can extend or revise the grammar fairly easily once you have built the general parsing and reduction tools. You can also easily add new verbs or variables once the foundation is constructed.

5. In the simple parsing scheme, shown in the previous Parser class, there are only six cases to consider and they are shown as a series of simple if statements. If you have many more than that, *Design Patterns* suggests that you create a class for each. This makes language extension easier, but it has the disadvantage of proliferating lots of similar little classes.

6. Finally, as the grammar's syntax becomes more complex, you run the risk of creating a hard to maintain program.

While interpreters are not commonly used for solving general programming problems, the Iterator pattern discussed in the next chapter is one of the most common ones you'll be using.

THOUGHT QUESTION

1. Design a system to compute the results of simple quadratic expressions such as $4x^2 + 3x -4$ in which the user can enter x or a range of x's and can type in the equation.

Programs on the CD-ROM

Program	Description
\Interpreter\ObjInterp\ Interpdemo.java	Demonstrates an object-based interpreter of report commands.
\Interpreter\BaseInterp\ InterpDemo.java	Uses all objects for the parser but shows a nonchain of responsibility version of parsing.

CHAPTER 19

The Iterator Pattern

The Iterator pattern is one of the simplest and most frequently used of the design patterns. It allows you to move through a list or collection of data using a standard interface without having to know the details of that data's internal representations. You can also define special iterators that perform some special processing and return only specified elements of the data collection.

Motivation

The Iterator pattern is useful because it provides a defined way to move through a set of data elements without exposing what is taking place inside the class. It is an *interface*; thus you can implement it in any way that is convenient for the data that you are returning. *Design Patterns* suggests that a suitable interface for an iterator might be the following:

```
public interface Iterator {
    public Object      First() ;
    public Object      Next();
    public boolean     isDone();
    public Object      CurrentItem();
}
```

Using this interface, you can move to the top of the list, move through the list, find out if there are more elements, and find the current list item. It is easy to implement and has certain advantages. However, the Iterator of choice in Java is the following:

```
public interface Enumeration {
    public boolean     hasMoreElements();
    public Object      nextElement();
}
```

Not having a method to move to the top of a list might seem restrictive at first. However, it is not a serious problem in Java because you customarily obtain a new instance of the Enumeration each time that you want to move through a list. Disadvantages of the Java Enumeration over similar constructs in C++ and Smalltalk are the strong typing of the Java language, as well as its lack of templates. This prevents the *hasMoreElements* method from returning an object of the actual type of the data in the collection without an annoying requirement to cast the returned Object type to the actual type. Thus, while the Iterator or Enumeration interface is intended to be polymorphic, this is not directly possible in Java.

Enumerations in Java

The Enumeration type is built into the Vector and Hashtable classes. Rather than these classes implementing the two methods of the Enumeration directly, both contain an *elements* method that returns an Enumeration of that class's data.

```
public Enumeration elements();
```

This *elements* method is really a kind of Factory method that produces instances of an Enumeration class.

Then you move through the list using the following simple code:

```
Enumeration e = vector.elements();
while (e.hasMoreElements()) {
    String name = (String)e.nextElement();
    System.out.println(name);
    }
```

In addition, the Hashtable also has the *keys* method, which returns an Enumeration of the keys to each element in the table:

```
public Enumeration keys();
```

This is the preferred style for implementing Enumerations in Java and has the advantage that you can have any number of simultaneous active enumerations of the same data.

Sample Code

Let's reuse the list of swimmers, clubs, and times we described for the Interpreter in Chapter 18 and add some enumeration capabilities to the KidData class. This class is essentially a collection of Kid objects, each with a name, club, and time stored in a Vector.

```
public class kidData {
    private Vector kids;
    private Hashtable clubs;
//---------------
    public kidData(String filename) {
        kids = new Vector();
        clubs = new Hashtable();
        InputFile f = new InputFile(filename);
        String s = f.readLine();
        while (s != null) {
            if (s.trim().length() > 0) {
                Kid k = new Kid(s);
                kids.addElement(k);
                clubs.put (k.getClub (), k.getClub ());
            }
            s = f.readLine();
        }
    }
```

To obtain an Enumeration of all of the Kids in the collection, we just return the Enumeration of the Vector itself.

```
public Enumeration elements() {
        return kids.elements();
    }
```

Filtered Iterators

Having a clearly defined method of moving through a collection is helpful. However, you can also define filtered Enumerations that perform some computation on the data before returning it. For example, you could return the data ordered in some particular way or return only those objects that match a particular criterion. Then, rather than have a lot of very similar interfaces for these filtered Enumerations, you provide a method that returns each type of Enumeration, with each one having the same methods.

The Filtered Enumeration

Suppose that we want to enumerate only those kids who belong to a certain club. We need a special Enumeration class that has access to the data in the Kid-Data class. This is very simple to achieve because the *elements* method just defined gives us that access. So we need to write only an Enumeration that returns kids belonging to a specified club.

```
public class kidClub
implements Enumeration {
    private String clubMask;       //name of club
    private Kid kid;               //next kid to return
```

```
        private Enumeration ke;          //gets all kids
        private kidData kdata;           //class containing kids
//---------------
    public kidClub(KidData kd, String club) {
        clubMask = club;                 //save the club
        kdata = kd;                      //copy the class
        kid = null;                      //default
        ke = kdata.elements();           //get the Enumerator
    }
//---------------
    public boolean hasMoreElements() {
        //return true if there are any more kids
        //belonging to the specified club
        boolean found = false;
        while (ke.hasMoreElements() && ! found) {
            kid = (Kid)ke.nextElement();
            found = kid.getClub().equals(clubMask);
        }
        if (! found)
            kid = null;      //set to null if none are left
        return found;
    }
//---------------
    public Object nextElement() {
        if (kid != null)
            return kid;
        else
            //throw an exception if access is past the end
                throw new NoSuchElementException();
    }
}
```

All of the work is done in the *hasMoreElements()* method. This method scans through the collection for another kid belonging to the club specified in the constructor and either saves that kid in the *kid* variable or sets it to *null* and then returns either true or false. The *nextElement()* method either returns that next kid variable or throws an exception if there are no more kids. Note that under normal circumstances, this exception is never thrown, since the *has More Elements* boolean should have already told you not to ask for another element.

Finally, we need to add a method, kidsInClub, to KidData to return this new filtered Enumeration.

```
public Enumeration kidsInClub(String club) {
        return new kidClub(this, club);
    }
```

This method passes the instance of KidClub to the Enumeration class KidClub along with the club's initials. Figure 19.1 shows a simple program. The program displays all of the kids on the left side, fills a combo box with a list of the clubs, and then allows the user to select a club. Finally, it fills the right-hand list box with the names of those kids who belong to a single club.

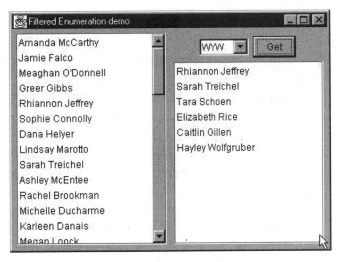

Figure 19.1   A simple program illustrating filtered Enumeration.

The class diagram is shown in Figure 19.2.

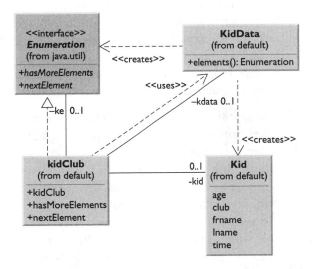

Figure 19.2   The classes used in the filtered Enumeration.

Note that the *elements* method in KidData supplies an Enumeration and the kidClub class is, in fact, itself an Enumeration class.

Consequences of the Iterator Pattern

Use of the Iterator pattern has the following consequences:

1. **Data modification:** The most significant question resulting from the use of iterators concerns iterating through data while it is being changed. If your code is wide ranging and only occasionally moves to the next element, an element might be added or deleted from the underlying collection while you are moving through it. It is also possible that another thread could change the collection. There are no simple solutions to this problem. You can make an Enumeration thread safe by declaring the loop to be *synchronized*, but if you want to move through a loop using an Enumeration and delete certain items, you must be careful of the consequences. Deleting or adding an element might mean that a particular element is skipped or accessed twice, depending on the storage mechanism that you are using.

2. **Privileged access:** Enumeration classes might need to have some sort of privileged access to the underlying data structures of the original container class so that they can move through the data. If the data are stored in a Vector or Hashtable, accomplishing this is fairly easy. But if it is some other collection structure contained in a class, you will probably have to make that structure available through a *get* operation. Alternatively, you could make the Iterator a derived class of the containment class and access the data directly. The friend class solution available in C++ does not apply in Java. However, classes defined in the same module as the containing class do have access to the containing class's variables.

3. **External versus internal Iterators:** *Design Patterns* describes two types of Iterators: external and internal. Thus far, we have described only external iterators. Internal Iterators are methods that move through the entire collection, performing some operation on each element directly, without any specific requests from the user. Internal Iterators are less common in Java, but methods that normalize a collection of data values to lie between 0 and 1 or that convert all of the strings to a particular case are possible. In general, external Iterators give you more control because the calling program accesses each element directly and can decide whether to perform an operation on it.

Composites and Iterators

Iterators, or in the current case Enumerations, are also an excellent way to move through Composite structures. In the Composite of an employee hierarchy developed in Chapter 18, each Employee contains a Vector whose *elements* method allows you to continue to enumerate down that chain. If that Employee has no subordinates, the *hasMoreElements* method correctly returns false.

Iterators in Java 1.2

Java 1.2 introduces the following Iterator interface that is quite similar to the Enumeration interface:

```
public interface Iterator {
    public boolean hasNext();
    public Object next();
    public void remove();

}
```

The Iterator and the Enumeration differ only in the Iterator's simpler names and *remove* method. The *remove* method removes the last object returned from the *next* method and can be called only once per *next* method.

In Java 1.2, the Vector class now has an *iterator* method that returns an instance of the Iterator class. The Hashtable class, however, has not been updated—rather, it has been supplanted by a series of Collection and Map classes. The HashMap class is a hash table implementation based on a Map interface that has an *elements* method. This *elements* method returns an instance of the Collection class, which in turn returns an Iterator. Thus, to iterate through a HashMap, you obtain an iterator as follows:

```
private HashMap clubs;
//.. fill hash map
Iterator enum = clubs.values().iterator();
```

THOUGHT QUESTION

1. The ListIterator interface in Java 1.2 applies to objects of type List. It allows you to move through a list in either direction and modify elements of the list. Rewrite the J2Iterator to allow and use these additional features.

Programs on the CD-ROM

Program	Description
\Iterator\IterDemo.java	Demonstrates the filtered iterator. Allows the selection of a single club from a combo box and then displays those members of that club in the right-hand list box.
\Iterator\J2Iterator\ J2IterDemo.java	Same program using the Iterator interface and the HashMap to store the list of clubs.

CHAPTER 20

The Mediator Pattern

When a program consists of a number of isolated classes, the logic and computation is divided among these classes. However, as more of these isolated classes are developed in the program, communication between them becomes more complex. The more that each class needs to know about the methods of another class, the more tangled the class structure can become, thereby making the program harder to read and harder to maintain. Further, it can become difficult to change the program, since any change might affect code in several other classes. The Mediator pattern addresses this problem by promoting looser coupling between these classes. It accomplishes this by being the only class that has detailed knowledge of the methods of other classes. Classes inform the Mediator when changes occur, and the Mediator then passes them on to any other classes that need to be informed.

An Example System

Consider a program with several buttons, two list boxes, and a text entry field for selecting a few names from a list, as shown in Figure 20.1.

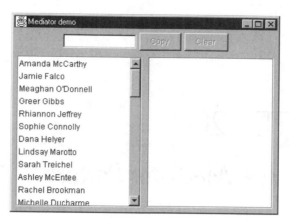

Figure 20.1   A program with two lists, two buttons, and a text field, all of which will interact.

When the program starts, the Copy and Clear buttons are disabled.

1. When you select one of the names in the left-hand box, it is copied into the text field for editing, and the Copy button is enabled.

2. When you click on the Copy button, that selected name is added to the right-hand list box, and the Clear button is enabled, as shown in Figure 20.2.

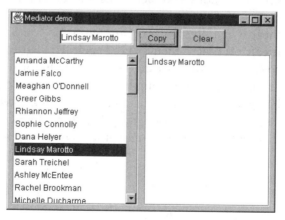

Figure 20.2   Selecting a name enables the buttons, and clicking on the Copy button copies the name to the right-hand list box.

3. When you click on the Clear button, the right-hand list box and the text field are cleared, the list box is deselected, and the two buttons are again disabled.

User interfaces such as this one are commonly used to select lists of people or products from lists. They often are more complicated, including insert, delete, and undo operations as well.

Interactions between Controls

The interactions between the visual controls are pretty complex, even in this simple example. Each visual object needs to know about two or more others. This can lead to quite a tangled relationship diagram, as shown in Figure 20.3.

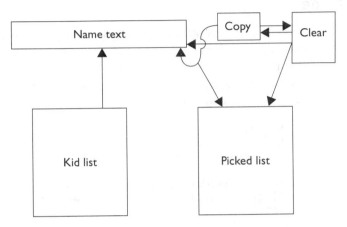

Figure 20.3 A tangled web of interactions between classes in the simple visual interface we presented in Figures 20.1 and 20.2.

The Mediator pattern simplifies this system by being the only class that is aware of the other classes in the system. Each control that the Mediator communicates with is called a *Colleague*. Each Colleague informs the Mediator when it has received a user event, and the Mediator decides which other classes should be informed of this event. This simpler interaction scheme is illustrated in Figure 20.4.

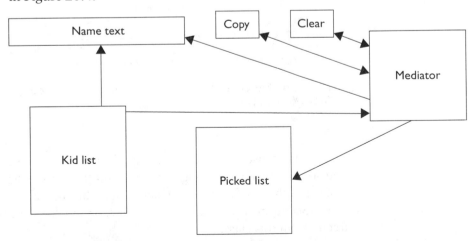

Figure 20.4 A Mediator class simplifies the interactions between classes.

The advantage of the Mediator is clear: It is the only class that knows of the other classes and thus the only one that needs to be changed when one of the other classes changes or when other interface control classes are added.

Sample Code

Let's consider this program in detail and decide how each control is constructed. The main difference in writing a program using a Mediator class is that each class needs to be aware of the existence of the Mediator. You start by creating an instance of the Mediator and then pass the instance of the Mediator to each class in its constructor.

```
Mediator med = new Mediator();
kidList = new Kidlist( med);
tx = new KTestField(med);

Move = new MoveButton(this, med);
Clear = new ClearButton(this, med);
med.init();
```

We created new classes for each control, each derived from base classes, so we can handle the mediator operations within each class. The two buttons use the Command pattern and register themselves with the Mediator during their initializations. Following is the Copy button; the Clear button is analogous:

```
public class CopyButton extends JButton
implements Command {
    private Mediator med:              //copy of the Mediator
    public CopyButton(ActionListener fr,
                     Mediator md) {
        super("Copy");                 //create the button
        addActionListener(fr);         //add its listener
        med = md;                      //copy in the Mediator instance
        med.registerMove(this);        //register with the Mediator
    }
    public void Execute() {            //execute the copy
        med.Move();
    }
}
```

The Kid name list is based on that used in the last two examples but is expanded so that the data loading of the list and the registering of the list with the Mediator both occur in the constructor. In addition, we make the enclosing class the ListSelectionListener and pass the click on any list item on to the Mediator directly from this class.

```
public class KidList extends JawtList
implements ListSelectionListener {
```

```
    private KidData kdata;
    private Mediator med;
    public KidList(Mediator md) {
        super(20);
        kdata = new KidData ("50free.txt"0;
        fillKidList();
        med = md;
        med.registerKidList(this);
        addListSelectionListener(this);
    }
    //---------------
    public void valueChanged(ListSelectionEvent ls) {
        JList obj = (JList)ls.getSource();
        if (obj.getSelectedIndex() >= 0)
            med.select();
    }
    //---------------
    private void fillKidList() {
        Enumeration ekid = kdata.elements();
        while (ekid.hasMoreElements()) {
            Kid k =(Kid)ekid.nextElement();
            add(k.getFrname()+" "+k.getLname());
        }
    }
}
```

The text field is even simpler, since all it does is register itself with the Mediator.

```
public class KTextField extends JTextField {
    private Mediator med;
    public KTextField(Mediator md) {
        super(10);
        med = md;
        med.registerText(this);
    }
}
```

The general point of all of these classes is that each knows about the Mediator and tells the Mediator of its existence so that the Mediator can send commands to it when appropriate.

The Mediator itself is very simple. It supports the *move, clear,* and *select* methods and has register methods for each control.

```
private class Mediator {
    private ClearButton        clearButton;
    private MoveButton         moveButton;
    private KTextField         ktext;
    private KidList            klist;
    private PickedKidsList     picked;
    public void move() {
        picked.add(ktext.getText());
```

```
        clearButton.setEnabled(true);
    }
    //--------------
    public void init() {
        Clear();
    }
    //--------------
    public void clear() {
        ktext.setText("");
        moveButton.setEnabled(false);
        clearButton.setEnabled(false);
        picked.clear();
        klist.clearSelection();
    }
    //--------------
    public void select() {
        String s = (String)klist.getSelectedValue();
        ktext.setText(s);
        moveButton.setEnabled(true);
    }
    //--------------
    public void registerClear(ClearButton cb) {
        clearButton = cb;
    }
    //--------------
    public void registerMove(MoveButton mv) {
        moveButton = mv;
    }
    //--------------
    public void registerText(KTextField tx) {
        ktext = tx;
    }
    //--------------
    public void registerPicked(PickedKidsList pl) {
        picked = pl;
    }
    //--------------
    public void registerKidList(KidList kl) {
        klist = kl;
    }
}
```

Initialization of the System

One further operation that is best delegated to the Mediator is the initialization
of all of the controls to the desired state. When we launch the program, each
control must be in a known, default state. Because these states might change as
the program evolves, we create in the Mediator an *init* method that sets them all
to the desired state. In this case, that state is the same as that achieved by clicking on the Clear button.

```
public void init() {
    clear();
}
```

Mediators and Command Objects

The two buttons in the program are Command objects. We register the main user interface frame as the ActionListener when we initialize them. As noted in Chapter 17, this makes processing the button click events simple.

```
public void actionPerformed(ActionEvent e) {
        Command comd = (Command)e.getSource();
        comd.Execute();
    }
```

Alternatively, we could register each derived class as its own listener and pass the results directly to the Mediator.

In either case, however, this represents the solution to one of the problems we noted in the discussion of the Command pattern in Chapter 17. That is, each button needs knowledge of many of the other user interface classes in order to execute its command. Here, we delegate that knowledge to the Mediator so that the Command buttons do not need any knowledge of the methods of the other visual objects. Figure 20.5 shows the class diagram for this program, illustrating both the Mediator pattern and the Command pattern.

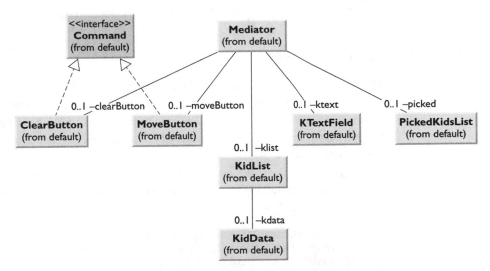

Figure 20.5 The interactions between Command objects and the Mediator object.

Consequences of the Mediator Pattern

Using the Mediator pattern has the following consequences:

1. The Mediator pattern keeps classes from becoming entangled when actions in one class need to be reflected in the state of another.

2. Using a Mediator makes it easy to change a program's behavior. For many kinds of changes, you can merely change or subclass the Mediator and leave the rest of the program unchanged.

3. New controls or other classes can be added without changing anything except the Mediator.

4. The Mediator solves the problem of each Command object's needing to know too much about the objects and methods in the rest of a user interface.

5. Sometimes, however, the Mediator can become a "god class," having too much knowledge of the rest of the program. This can make the Mediator hard to change and maintain. You can improve this situation by putting more of the function into the individual classes and less into the Mediator. Each object should carry out its own tasks, and the Mediator should manage only the interaction between objects.

6. Each Mediator is a custom-written class that has methods for each Colleague to call and knows the methods that each Colleague has available. This makes it difficult to reuse Mediator code in different projects. However, most Mediators are quite simple, and writing this code is far easier than managing the complex object interaction in any other way.

Single Interface Mediators

The Mediator pattern described here acts as a kind of Observer pattern, observing changes in each of the Colleague elements, with each element having a custom interface to the Mediator. Another approach is to have a single interface to the Mediator and pass to it various objects that tell the Mediator which operations to perform.

In this approach, we avoid registering the active components and create a single action method with different polymorphic arguments for each of the action elements.

```
public void action(MoveButton mv){}
public void action(ClearButton clrButton){}
public void action(KidList klst){}
```

Thus we need not register the action objects, such as the buttons and source list boxes, since we can pass them as part of generic *action* methods.

In the same fashion, we can have a single Colleague interface that each Colleague implements, and each Colleague then decides what operation it is to carry out.

Implementation Issues

Mediators are not limited to use in visual interface programs, although that is their most common application. You can use them whenever you are faced with the problem of resolving complex intercommunication between multiple objects.

Programs on the CD-ROM

Program	Description
\Mediator\MedDemo.java	Demonstrates the Mediator mediating between two buttons, a text field, and two list boxes.
\Mediator\SIMediator\ SIMedDemo.java	Demonstates the same program but with a single action interface to the Mediator.

CHAPTER 21

The Memento Pattern

In this chapter, we discuss how to use the Memento pattern to save data about an object so that you can restore it later. For example, you might like to save the color, size, pattern or shape of objects in a draughting or painting program. Ideally, you can save and restore this state without making each object take care of this task and without violating encapsulation. This is the purpose of the Memento pattern.

Motivation

Objects normally shouldn't expose much of their internal state using public methods, but you still want to be able to save the entire state of an object because you might need to restore it later. In some cases, you could obtain enough information from the public interfaces (such as the drawing positions of graphical objects) to save and restore that data. In other cases, the color, shading, angle, and connection relationships to other graphical objects need to be saved, and yet this information is not readily available. This saving and restoration of data is common in systems that need to support Undo commands.

If all of the data that describe an object is available in public variables, saving in some external store is not difficult. However, making this data public makes the entire system vulnerable to change by external program code, when you usually expect data inside an object to be private and encapsulated from the outside world.

The Memento pattern attempts to solve this problem by having privileged access to the state of the object that you want to save. Other objects have only a more restricted access to the object, thus preserving their encapsulation. This pattern defines the following three roles for objects:

1. **Originator:** the object whose state you want to save.

2. **Memento:** another object that saves the state of the Originator.

3. **Caretaker:** manages the timing of the saving of the state, saves the Memento, and, if needed, uses the Memento to restore the state of the Originator.

Implementation

Saving the state of an object without making all of its variables publicly available is tricky and can be done with varying degrees of success in various languages. *Design Patterns* suggests using the C++ friend construction to achieve this access. *Smalltalk Companion* notes that it is not directly possible in Smalltalk. In Java, this privileged access is possible using a little-known and seldom-used protection mode. Variables within a Java class can be declared as

- private,
- protected,
- public, or
- [package protected] (which is the default if none is declared).

Java does not allow you to declare variables as package protected, but a variable with no protection declaration is treated as having that level of visibility. Other classes can access public variables, and derived classes can access protected variables. However, another class in the same package can access protected or private-protected variables. It is this last feature of Java that you can use to build Memento objects.

For example, suppose that we have classes A and B declared in the same method.

```
public class A {
int x, y:
public Square() {}
x = 5;                              //initialize x
}
//---------------
class B {
public B() {
    A a = new A();                  //create an instance of A
    System.out.println (a.x);       //has access to variables in A
  }
}
```

Class A contains a private-protected variable *x*. In class B in the same module, we create an instance of A, which automatically initializes *x* to 5. Class B has direct access to the variable *x* in class A and can print it out without compilation or an execution error. It is exactly this feature that we will use to create a Memento.

Sample Code

Let's consider a simple prototype of a graphics drawing program that creates rectangles and allows you to select them and move them around by dragging them with the mouse. This program has a toolbar containing three buttons—Rectangle (R), Undo (U), and Clear (C)—as shown in Figure 21.1.

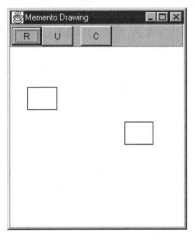

Figure 21.1   A simple graphics drawing program that allows you to draw rectangles, undo their drawing, and clear the screen.

The Rectangle button is a JToggleButton that stays selected until you click the mouse to draw a new rectangle. Once you have drawn the rectangle, you can click in any rectangle to select it, as shown in Figure 21.2.

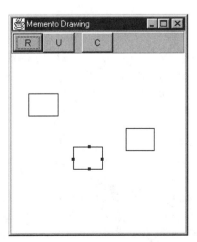

Figure 21.2   Selecting a rectangle causes handles that indicate that it is selected and can be moved to appear.

Once it is selected, you can drag that rectangle to a new position using the mouse, as shown in Figure 21.3.

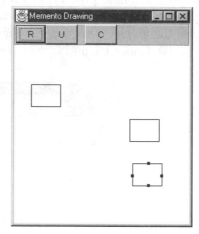

Figure 21.3   The same selected rectangle after dragging.

The Undo button can undo a succession of operations. In the current case, it can undo moving a rectangle and undo the creation of each rectangle.

We need to respond to five actions in this program:

1.   Rectangle button click

2.   Undo button click

3.   Clear button click

4.   Mouse click

5.   Mouse drag

The three buttons can be constructed as Command objects, and the mouse click and drag can be treated similarly. Because we have a number of visual objects that control the display of screen objects, this suggests an opportunity to use the Mediator pattern, and that is the way that this program is constructed.

We'll create a Caretaker class to manage the Undo action list; it can keep a list or the last *n* operations so that they can be undone. The Mediator maintains the list of drawing objects and communicates with the Caretaker object. In fact, because a program could contain any number of actions to save and undo, a Mediator is virtually required so that there is a single place to send these commands to the Undo list in the Caretaker.

In this program, we save and undo only two actions: creating new rectangles and changing the positions of rectangles. Let's start with the visRectangle class, which actually draws each instance of the rectangles.

```
public class visRectangle {
    int        x, y, w, h;          //package-protected
    private Rectangle rect;
    private boolean    selected;
    public visRectangle(int xpt, int ypt)    {
        x = xpt;    y = ypt;     //save the location
        w = 40;     h = 30;      //use the default size
        saveAsRect();
    }
    //---------------
    public void setSelected(boolean b)    {
        selected = b;
    }
    //---------------
    private void saveAsRect()    {
    //convert to rectangle so that we can use the contains method
        rect = new Rectangle(x-w/2, y-2/2, w, h);
    }
    //---------------
    public void draw(Graphics g)    {
        g.drawRect(x, y, w, h);
        if (selected)    {       //draw handles
            g.fillRect(x+w/2, y-2, 4, 4);
            g.fillRect(x-2, y+h/2, 4, 4);
            g.fillRect(x+y/2, y+h-2; 4, 4);
            g.fillRect(x+w-2, y+h/2, 4, 4);
        }
    }
    //---------------
    public boolean contains(int x, int y)    {
        return rect.contains(x, y);
    }
    //---------------
    public void move(int xpt, int ypt)    {
        x = xpt; y = ypt;
        saveAsRect();
    }
}
```

Drawing the rectangle is straightforward. Now, let's look at the Memento class, which must be contained in the same package as visRectangle.java and thus will have access to the position and size variables.

```
public class Memento {
    visRectangle rect;
    //saved fields- remember internal fields
    //of the specified visual rectangle

    private int x, y, w, h;

    public Memento(visRectangle r) {
        rect = r;
```

```
        x = rect.x;   y = rect.y;
        w = rect.w;   h = rect.h;
    }
    //---------------
    public void restore () {
        //restore the internal state of
        //the specified rectangle
        rect.x = x;   rect.y = y;
        rect.h = h;   rect.w = w;
    }
}
```

When we create an instance of the Memento class, we pass it the visRectangle instance that we want to save. It copies the size and position parameters and saves a copy of the instance of the visRectangle itself. Later, when we want to restore these parameters, the Memento knows which instance must be restored and can do it directly, as shown in the *restore* method.

The rest of the activity takes place in the Mediator class, where we save the previous state of the list of drawings as the Integer on the undo list.

```
public void createRect(int x, int y) {
    unpick();     //make sure no rectangle is selected
    if (startRect)    {    //if the Rect button is depressed
        Integer count = new Integer(drawings.size());
        caretaker.addElement(count);   //save the previous size
        visRectangle v = new visRectangle(x, y);
        drawings.addElement(v);         //add a new element
        startRect = false;              //done with a rectangle
        rect.setSelected(false);        //unclick the button
        canvas.repaint();
    }else
        pickRect(x, y);     //if not pressed look for the Rect
}
```

We also save the previous position of a rectangle before moving it into a Memento.

```
public void rememberPosition() {
    if (rectSelected) {
        Memento m = new Memento (selectedRectangle);
        caretaker.addElement(m);
        repaint();
    }
}
```

The *undo* method simply decides whether to reduce the drawing list by one or to invoke the *restore* method of a Memento.

```
public void undo() {
        if (undoList.size() > 0) {
```

```
                        //get the last element in the undo list
                        Object obj = undoList.lastElement();
                        undoList.removeElement(obj);     //and remove it
                        if (obj instanceof Integer)
                           remove ((Integer)obj); //remove the integer or
                                                   //Memento
                        else
                            remove((Memento)obj);
                    }
                }
```

The complete class structure is diagrammed in Figure 21.4.

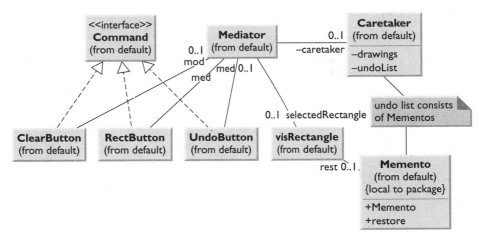

Figure 21.4   The class structure for the drawing program using the Memento pattern.

Consequences of the Memento Pattern

1. The Memento pattern provides a way to preserve the state of an object while preserving encapsulation, in languages where this is possible. Thus data that only the Originator class should have access to effectively remain private. The pattern also preserves the simplicity of the Originator class by delegating the saving and restoring of information to the Memento class.

2. However, the amount of data that a Memento must save might be quite large, thus taking up a fair amount of storage. This also affects the Caretaker class (here, the Mediator), which might have to design strategies to limit the number of objects for which it saves state. In the example in this chapter, we imposed no such limits. When objects change in a predictable manner, each Memento might be able to get by with saving only incremental changes of an object's state.

THOUGHT QUESTION

1. The Memento pattern can be used to restore an object's state when a process fails. If a database update fails because of a dropped network connection, you should be able to restore the data in your cached data to their previous state. Rewrite the Database class in the Façade pattern (Chapter 13) to allow for such failures.

Programs on the CD-ROM

Program	Description
\Memento\MemDraw.java	Allows you to draw and move rectangles and undo these operations.

CHAPTER 22

The Observer Pattern

In this chapter we discuss how you can use the Observer pattern to present data in several forms at once.

In the more sophisticated windowing world, we often want to display data in more than one form at the same time and have all of the displays reflect any changes in the data. For example, we might represent stock price changes as both a graph and a table or list box. Each time the price changes, we'd expect both representations to change at once without any action on our part.

We expect this sort of behavior because many Windows applications, such as Excel, demonstrate such behavior. However, nothing inherent in Windows allows this activity, and, as you might know, programming directly in Windows in C or C++ is quite complicated. In Java, however, you can easily use the Observer pattern to cause your program to behave in this way.

The Observer pattern assumes that the object containing the data is separate from the objects that display the data and that these data objects *observe* changes in those data. This idea is illustrated in Figure 22.1.

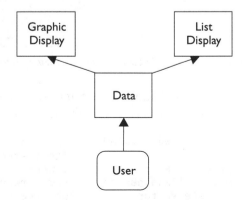

Figure 22.1   Data are displayed as a list and in some graphical mode.

When we implement the Observer pattern, we usually refer to the data as the Subject and each of the displays as Observers. Each Observer registers its interest in the data by calling a public method in the Subject, and each has a known interface that the Subject calls when the data change. We could define these interfaces as follows:

```
public interface Observer {
    //notify Observers that a change has taken place
    public void sendNotify(String s);
}
public interface Subject {
//tell the Subject that you are interested in changes
    public void registerInterest(Observer obs);
}
```

The advantages of defining these abstract interfaces are that you can write any sort of class objects you want as long as they implement these interfaces, and that you can declare these objects to be of type Subject and Observer no matter what else they do.

Watching Colors Change

Let's write a program to illustrate how to use this powerful concept. It shows a display frame containing three radio buttons named Red, Blue, and Green, as shown in Figure 22.2.

Figure 22.2   A simple control panel to create red, green, or blue "data."

This main window is the Subject, or data repository object. We create this window using the JFC in the following code:

```
public class Watch2Windows    extends JxFrame
implements ActionListener,   ItemListener, Subject {
    private JButton           Close;
    private JRadioButton      red, green, blue;
    private Vector            observers;
    private ColorFrame        cframe;
    private ListFrame         lframe;
```

```
//-----------
    public Watch2Windows() {
        super("Change 2 other frames");
        observers = new Vector();      //list of observing frames

        JPanel p = new JPanel(true);  //add a panel to the content
                                                     pane
        p.setLayout(new BorderLayout());
        getContentPane().add("Center", p);

        Box box = new Box(BoxLayout.Y_AXIS);   //vertical box layout
        p.add("Center", box);
        box.add(red = new JRadioButton("Red"));   //and three radio
                                                       buttons
        box.add(green = new JRadioButton("Green"));
        box.add(blue = new JRadioButton("Blue"));

        blue.addItemListener(this);    //listen for clicks
        red.addItemListener(this);     //on the radio buttons
        green.addItemListener(this);

        //make all part of same button group
        ButtonGroup bgr = new ButtonGroup();
        bgr.add(red);
        bgr.add(green);
        bgr.add(blue);

        //put a Close button at the bottom of the frame
        JPanel p1 = new JPanel();
        p.add("South", p1);
        p1.add( Close =new JButton("Close"));
        Close.addActionListener(this):          //listen for clicks
        setBounds(200, 200, 200, 200);
        pack();

    }
```

Note that the main frame class implements the Subject interface. Thus it must provide a public method for registering interest in the data in this class. This method is *registerInterest*, which just adds Observer objects to a Vector.

```
public void registerInterest(Observer obs) {
        //adds an Observer to the list
        observers.addElement(obs);
    }
```

Next we create two Observers, one that displays the color (and its name) and another that adds the current color to a list box.

```
//------create Observers-----
    ColorFrame cframe = new ColorFrame(this);
    ListFrame lframe = new ListFrame(this);
    setVisible(true);
```

When we create the ColorFrame window, we register out interest in the data in the main program.

```java
public class ColorFrame extends JFrame
implements Observer {
    private Color color;
    private String color_name="black";
    private Font font;

    private JPanel p = new JPanel(true);
    public ColorFrame(Subject s) {
        super("Colors");
        getContentPane().add("Center", p);
        s.registerInterest(this);
        setBounds(100, 100, 100, 100);
        font = new Font("Sans Serif", Font.BOLD, 14);
        setVisible(true);
    }
    public void sendNotify(String s) {
            color_name = s;
            if (s.equalsIgnoreCase ("RED"))
               color = Color.red;
            if (s.equalsIgnoreCase ("BLUE"))
               color = Color.blue;
            if (s.equalsIgnoreCase ("GREEN"))
               color = Color.green;
            //p.repaint();
            setBackground(color);
        }
        public void paint(Graphics g) {

            g.setFont(font);
            g.drawString(color_name, 20, 50);
    }
}
```

Meanwhile, in the main program, every time someone clicks on one of the radio buttons, it calls the *sendNotify* method of each Observer that registered interest in such a change by simply running through the objects in the Observer's Vector.

```java
public void itemStateChanged(ItemEvent e) {
    //responds to radio button clicks
    //if the button is selected
    if (e.getStateChange() == ItemEvent.SELECTED)
            notifyObservers((JRadioButton)e.getSource());
}
//——————————
private void notifyObservers(JRadioButton rad) {
    //sends text of selected button to all observers
    String color = rad.getText();
    for (int i = 0; i< observers.size(); i++) {
        ((Observer)(observers.elementAt(i))).sendNotify(color);
    }
}
```

In the case of the ColorFrame Observer, the *sendNotify* method changes the background color and the text string in the Frame panel. In the case of the ListFrame Observer, it just adds the name of the new color to the list box. Figure 22.3 shows the final program running.

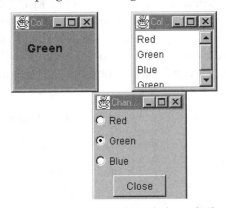

Figure 22.3   The data control pane generates data, which are displayed simultaneously as a colored panel and as a list box. This is a candidate for an Observer pattern.

The Message to the Media

Now, what kind of notification should a Subject send to its Observers? In this carefully circumscribed example, the notification message is the string representing the color itself. When we click on one of the radio buttons, we can get the caption for that button and send it to the Observers. This, of course, assumes that all of the Observers can handle that string representation. In more realistic situations, this might not always be the case, especially if the Observers could also be used to observe other data objects. Here, we undertake two simple data conversions:

1. We get the label from the radio button and send it to the Observers.

2. We convert the label to an actual color in the ColorFrame Observer.

A more complicated system might have Observers that demand specific, but different, kinds of data. Rather than have each Observer convert the message to the right data type, we could use an intermediate Adapter class to perform this conversion.

Another problem that observers might have to deal with is the case where the data of the central Subject class can change in several ways. We could delete points from a list of data, edit their values, or change the scale of the data that we are viewing. In these cases, we must either send different change messages to the Observers or send a single message and then have the Observer ask which sort of change has occurred.

The JList as an Observer

Now, what about that list box in our color changing example? We saved it for last because, as we noted in the Adapter class discussion (Chapter 9), the JList is rather different in concept than the List object in the AWT. You can display a fixed list of data in the JList by simply putting the data into a Vector or a String array. However, to display a list of data that might grow or otherwise change, you must put that data into a special data object derived from the AbstractList-Model class and then use that class in the constructor to the JList class. The List-Frame class looks like this:

```
public class ListFrame extends JFrame
implements Observer {
    private JList         list;
    private  JPanel       p;
    private JScrollPane   lsp;
    private JListData     listData;

    public ListFrame(Subject s) {
        super("Color List");
        //put the panel into the frame
        p = new JPanel(true);
        getContentPane().add("Center", p);
        p.setLayout(new BorderLayout());
        //tell the Subject that we are interested
        s.registerInterest(this);

        //Create the list
        listData = new JListData();     //the list model
        list = new JList(listData);     //the visual list
        lsp = new JScrollPane();        //the scroller
        lsp.getViewport().add(list);
        p.add("Center", lsp);
        lsp.setPreferredSize(new Dimension(100,100));
        setBounds(250, 100, 100, 100);
        setVisible(true);
    }
    //--------------
    public void sendNotify(String s) {
        listData.addElement(s);
    }
}
```

We name the ListModel class JListData. It holds the Vector that contains the growing list of color names.

```
public class JListData extends AbstractListModel {
    private Vector data;
    public JListData() {
        data = new Vector();
```

```
    }
    public int getSize() {
        return data.size();
    }
    public Object getElementAt(int index) {
        return data.elementAt(index);
    }
    public void addElement(String s) {
        data.addElement(s);
        fireIntervalAdded(this, data.size()-1, data.size());
    }
}
```

Whenever the ColorList class is notified that the color has changed, it calls the *addElement* method of the JListData class. This method adds the string to the Vector and then calls the *fireIntervalAdded* method. This base method of the AbstractListModel class connects to the JList class, telling that class that the data has changed. The JList class then redisplays the data as needed. There are also equivalent methods for two other kinds of changes: *fireInterval-Removed* and *fireContentsChanged*. These represent the three kinds of changes that can occur in a list box; here, each sends its own message to the JList display.

The class diagram in Figure 22.4 clearly shows the Observer pattern. It also illustrates the Observer relationship between the ColorList class and its JListdata observer.

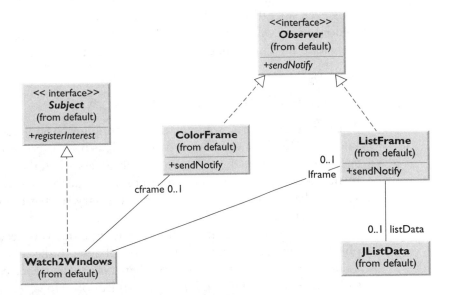

Figure 22.4   The Observer interface and Subject interface implementation of the Observer pattern.

The MVC Architecture as an Observer

As noted in Section 5, the JList, JTable, and JTree objects all operate as Observers of a data model. In fact, all of the visual components derived from JComponent can have this same division of labor between the data and the visual representation. In JFC parlance, this is called the MVC architecture (Model-View-Controller), whereby the data are represented by the Model and the View by the visual component. The Controller is the communication between the Model and View objects and may be a separate class or may be inherent in either the Model or the View. This is the case for the JFC components, which are all examples of the Observer pattern.

The Observer Interface and Observable Class

Java has an Observer interface built into the java.util package that has one method:

```
public void update(Observable o, Object arg)
```

This method is intended to be called whenever the observed object changes. The second argument can be used to describe the nature of the change.

Unfortunately, Observable is implemented as a class rather than an interface, so you can use it only when your base class is not already determined. However, since this is rarely the case in GUI applications, the Observable class is seldom used. On the other hand, you could easily use this Observer interface instead of the simpler one developed in this chapter.

Consequences of the Observer Pattern

The Observer pattern promotes abstract coupling to Subjects. A Subject doesn't know the details of any of its Observers. This has the potential disadvantage of successive or repeated updates to the Observers when there is a series of incremental changes to the data. If the cost of these updates is high, introducing some sort of change management might be necessary so that the Observers are not notified too soon or too often.

When one client changes the underlying data, you need to decide which object will initiate the notification of the change to the other Observers. If the Subject notifies all of the Observers when it is changed, each client is not responsible for remembering to initiate the notification. However, this can result in a number of small successive updates being triggered. If the clients tell the Subject when to notify the other clients, this cascading notification can be avoided;

however, the clients are left with the responsibility to tell the Subject when to send the notifications. If one client "forgets," the program simply won't work properly.

Finally, you can specify the kind of notification to send by defining a number of *update* methods for the Observers to receive, depending on the type or scope of change. In some cases, the clients will thus be able to ignore some of these notifications.

THOUGHT QUESTIONS

1. Rewrite the Watch2Windows program in this chapter to use the java.util.Observer interface.

2. Write a program using the Observable class and Observable interface.

Programs on the CD-ROM

Program	Description
\Observer\Watch2Windows.java	Illustrates the Observer pattern between a main window and two observing windows.
\Observer\Ltest\Ltest.java	A simple example of how a JList observes a JListData object.

CHAPTER 23

The State Pattern

The State pattern allows you to have an object represent the state of your application and to switch application states by switching objects. For example, you can have an enclosing class switch between a number of related contained classes and pass method calls on to the current contained class. *Design Patterns* suggests that the State pattern switches between internal classes in such a way that the enclosing object appears to change its class. In Java, at least, this is a bit of an exaggeration, but the actual purpose to which the classes are put can change significantly.

Many programmers have had the experience of creating a class that performs slightly different computations or displays different information based on the arguments passed into the class. This often leads to some sort of switch or if-else statement inside of the class that determines which behavior to carry out. It is this inelegance that the State pattern seeks to replace.

Sample Code

Let's consider the case of a drawing program similar to the one we developed for the Memento class in Chapter 21. This program has toolbar buttons for Select, Rectangle, Fill, Circle, and Clear, as shown in Figure 23.1.

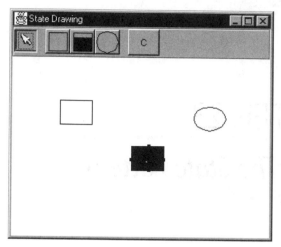

Figure 23.1   A simple drawing program for illustrating the State pattern.

Each toolbar button does something different when it is selected and the mouse is clicked or dragged across the screen. Thus the *state* of the graphical editor affects the behavior that the program should exhibit. This suggests some sort of design using the State pattern.

Initially, we might design our program like this, with a Mediator managing the actions of five command buttons, as shown in Figure 23.2.

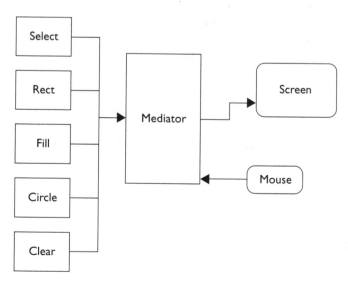

Figure 23.2   One possible interaction between the classes needed to support the simple drawing program.

However, this initial design puts the entire burden of maintaining the state of the program on the Mediator, when the main purpose of a Mediator is to coordinate activities between various controls, such as the buttons. Keeping the state of the buttons and the desired mouse activity inside the Mediator can make it unduly complicated as well as lead to a set of if or switch tests, which make the program difficult to read and maintain.

Further, this set of large, monolithic conditional statements might have to be repeated for each action that the Mediator interprets, such as mouseUp, mouseDrag, rightClick, and so on. This, too, makes the program very hard to read and maintain. Instead, let's analyze the expected behavior for each button.

1. If the Pick button is selected, then clicking inside a drawing element should cause it to be highlighted or appear with handles. If the mouse is dragged and a drawing element is already selected, the element should move on the screen.

2. If the Rect button is selected, then clicking on the screen should cause a new rectangle drawing element to be created.

3. If the Fill button is selected and a drawing element is already selected, then that element should be filled with the current color. If no drawing is selected, then clicking inside a drawing should cause it to be filled with the current color.

4. If the Circle button is selected, then clicking on the screen should cause a new circle drawing element to be created.

5. If the Clear button is selected, then all of the drawing elements are removed.

Several of these actions share some common threads. Four use the mouse click event to cause actions, and one uses the mouse drag event to cause an action. Thus we really want to create a system that can help us redirect these events based on which button is currently selected. Let's create a State object that handles mouse activities.

```
public class State {
    public void mouseDown(int x, int y) { }
    public void mouseUp(int x, int y) { }
    public void mouseDrag(int x, int y) { }
}
```

We include the mouseUp event in case we need it later. Because none of the cases described need all of these events, we give the base class empty methods rather than create an abstract base class. Then we create four derived State classes for Pick, Rect, Circle, and Fill, and put instances of all of them inside a

StateManager class that sets the current state and executes methods on that State object. In *Design Patterns*, this StateManager class is called a *Context* object, as illustrated in Figure 23.3.

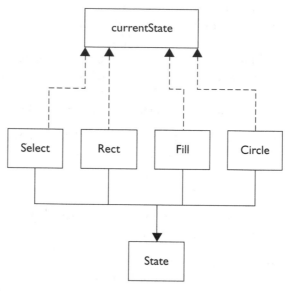

Figure 23.3   A StateManager class that keeps track of the current state.

A typical State object simply overrides those event methods that it must handle specially. For example, following is the complete Rectangle state object:

```
public class RectState extends State {
    private Mediator med;      //save the Mediator here
    public RectState(Mediator md) {
        med = md;
    }
    //create a new Rectangle where mouse clicks
    public void mouseDown(int x, int y) {
        med.addDrawing(new visRectangle(x, y));
    }
}
```

The RectState object tells the Mediator to add a rectangle to the drawing list. Similarly, the Circle state object tells the Mediator to add a circle to the drawing list.

```
public class CircleState extends State {
    private Mediator med;      //save the Mediator
    public CircleState(Mediator md) {
        med = md;
    }
```

```
        //draw a circle where the mouse clicks
        public void mouseDown(int x, int y) {
            med.addDrawing(new visCircle(x, y));
        }
    }
```

The only tricky button is the Fill button because we have defined two actions for it:

1. If an object is already selected, fill it.

2. If the mouse is clicked inside an object, fill the object.

To carry out these tasks, we need to add the *select* method to the base State class. This method is called when each toolbar button is selected.

```
public class State {
    public void mouseDown(int x, int y) { }
    public void mouseUp(int x, int y) { }
    public void mouseDrag(int x, int y) { }
    public void select (Drawing d, Color c) { }
}
```

The Drawing argument is either the currently selected Drawing or null if none is selected, and the color is the current fill color. In this program, we have arbitrarily set the fill color to red. So the Fill state class is as follows:

```
public class FillState extends State {
    private Mediator med;              //state the Mediator
    private Color color;               //save the current color
    public FillState(Mediator md) {
        med = md;
    }
    //fill the drawing if selected
    public void select(Drawing d, Color c) {
        color = c;
        if (d!= null) {
            d.setFill(c);              //fill that drawing
        }
    }
    //fill the drawing if you click inside of one
    public void mouseDown (int x, int y) {
        Vector drawings = med.getDrawings();
        for (int i = 0; i < drawings.size(); i++) {
            Drawing d = (Drawing)drawings.elementAt(i);
            if (d.contains(x, y))
                d.setFill(color);      //fill the drawing
        }
    }
}
```

Switching between States

Now that we have defined how each state behaves when mouse events are sent to it, we need to decide how the StateManager switches between states. We set the currentState variable to the state that is indicated by the selected button.

```
public class StateManager {
    private State           currentState;
    private RectState       rState;
    private ArrowState      aState;
    private CircleState     cState;
    private FillState       fState;

public StateManager(Mediator med) {
        rState = new RectState(med);
        cState = new CircleState(med);
        aState = new ArrowState(med);
        fState = new FillState(med);
        currentState = aState;
    }
    //these methods are called when the toolbar buttons
    //are selected
    public void setRect() {currentState = rState;}
    public void setCircle() {currentState = cState;}
    public void setFill() {currentState = fState;}
    public void setArrow() {currentState = aState;}
```

Note that in this version of the StateManager, we create an instance of each state during the constructor and copy the correct one into the state variable when the *set* methods are called. We also could create these states on demand. This might be advisable if a large number of states exists, each of which consumes a fair number of resources.

The remainder of the StateManager code calls the methods of whichever state object is current. This is the critical piece of code; there is no conditional testing. Instead, the correct state is already in place, and its methods are ready to be called.

```
public void mouseDown(int x, int y) {
    currentState.mouseDown(x, y);
}
public void mouseUp(int x, int y) {
    currentState.mouseUp(x, y);
}
public void mouseDrag(int x, int y) {
    currentState.mouseDrag(x, y);
}
public void select(Drawing d, Color c) {
    currentState.select(d, c);
    }
}
```

How the Mediator Interacts with the StateManager

Recall that it is clearer to separate the state management from the Mediator's button and mouse event management. The Mediator is the critical class, however, because it tells the StateManager when the current program state changes. The beginning part of the Mediator illustrates how this stage change takes place. Note that each button click calls one of these methods and changes the application's state. The remaining statements in each method simply turn off the other toggle buttons so that only one button at a time may be depressed.

```java
public class Mediator {
    private boolean          startRect;
    private boolean          dSelected;
    private Vector           drawings;
    private Vector           undoList;
    private Rectbutton       rectButton;
    private FillButton       fillButton;
    private CircleButton     circButton;
    private PickButton       arrowButton;
    private JPanel           canvas;
    private Drawing          selectedDrawing;
    private StateManager     stMgr;

    public Mediator() {
        startRect  =  false;
        dSelected  =  false;
        drawings   =  new Vector();
        undoList   =  new Vector();
        stMgr      =  new StateManager(this);
    }
//--------------
    public void startRectangle() {
        stMgr.setRect();
        arrowButton.setSelected(false);
        circButton.setSelected(false);
        fillButton.setSelected(false);
    }
//--------------
    public void startCircle() {
        stMgr.setCircle();
        rectButton.setSelected(false);
        arrowButton.setSelected(false);
        fillButton.setSelected(false);
    }
}
```

These *startXxx* methods are called from the *Execute* method of each button as a Command object.

The class diagram for this program, illustrating the State pattern, is given in two parts. The State section is shown in Figure 23.4.

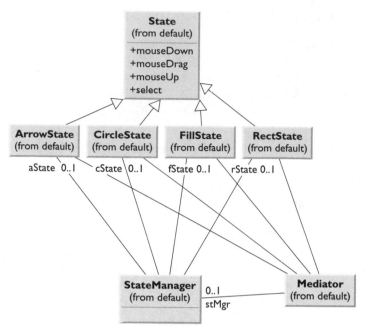

Figure 23.4   The StateManager and the Mediator.

The interaction of the Mediator with the buttons is depicted in Figure 23.5.

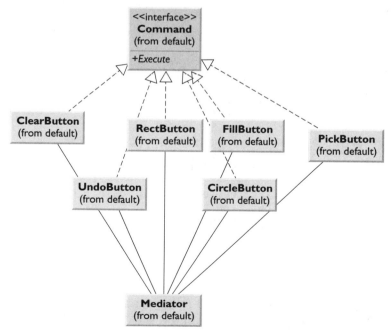

Figure 23.5   Interaction between the buttons and the Mediator.

State Transitions

The transition between states can be specified internally or externally. In the previous example, the Mediator tells the StateManager when to switch between states. However, it is also possible that each state can decide automatically what each successor state will be. For example, when a rectangle or circle drawing object is created, the program could automatically switch back to the arrow object State.

Mediators and the God Class

One real problem with programs that have this many objects interacting is that too much knowledge of the system is placed into the Mediator. This makes it a "god class." In the previous example, the Mediator communicates with the six buttons, the drawing list, and the StateManager. We can write this program another way so that the button Command objects communicate with the StateManager, while the Mediator deals only with the buttons and the drawing list. Each button creates an instance of the required state and sends it to the StateManager. For example, when we select the Circle button, the following code executes:

```
public void Execute() {
    stateMgr.setState (new CircleState(med));   //new State
    med.startCircle();              //toggle buttons
}
```

Consequences of the State Pattern

Using the State pattern has the following consequences:

1. The State pattern creates a subclass of a basic State object for each state that an application may have and switches between them as the application changes state.

2. You don't need to have a long set of conditional if or switch statements associated with the various states because each state is encapsulated in a class.

3. No variable specifies which state a program is in, so this approach reduces errors caused by programmers who forget to test this state variable.

4. You could share State objects between several parts of an application, such as separate windows, as long as none of the State objects have specific instance variables. In this example, only the FillState class has an instance

variable, and this could be easily rewritten to be an argument passed in each time.

5. This approach generates a number of small class objects, but in the process, it simplifies and clarifies the program.

6. In Java, all of the State objects must inherit from a common base class, and all must have common methods, although some of those methods may be empty. In other languages, the States can be implemented by function pointers with much less type checking and, of course, a greater chance of error.

 ## Thought Questions

1. Rewrite the StateManager to use a Factory pattern to produce the states on demand.

2. While visual graphics programs provide obvious examples of State patterns, Java server programs can benefit by this approach. Outline a simple server that uses a State pattern.

Programs on the CD-ROM

Program	Description
\State\StateDraw.java	A simple drawing program that draws and moves rectangles and circles and allows you to fill the shapes with a solid color.
\State\StateFactory\ StateDraw.java	A drawing program that creates new instances of each state whenever the state changes. These states are created in the button Command objects rather than in the Mediator.

CHAPTER 24

The Strategy Pattern

The Strategy pattern is much like the State pattern in outline but a little different in intent. The Strategy pattern consists of a number of related algorithms encapsulated in a driver class called Context. Your client program can select one of these algorithms, or in some cases Context might select the best one for you. The intent is to make these algorithms interchangeable and provide a way to choose the most appropriate one. The State and Strategy differ in that the user generally chooses which of several strategies to apply, and only one strategy at a time is likely to be instantiated and active within the Context class. By contrast, all of the different states could possibly be active at once, and switching between them might occur often. In addition, Strategy encapsulates several algorithms that do more or less the same thing, while State encapsulates related classes that each do something somewhat different. Finally, the concept of transition between different states is completely missing in the Strategy pattern.

Motivation

A program that requires a particular service or function and that has several ways of carrying out that function is a candidate for the Strategy pattern. Programs choose between these algorithms based on computational efficiency or user choice. There may be any number of strategies, more can be added, and any can be changed at any time.

Often, you want to do the same thing in several different ways, such as the following, mentioned in *Smalltalk Companion*:

- Save files in different formats.
- Compress files using different algorithms.
- Capture video data using different compression schemes.

229

- Use different line-breaking strategies to display text data.
- Plot the same data in different formats: line graph, bar chart, or pie chart.

In each case, the client program could tell a driver module (Context) which of these strategies to use and then ask it to carry out the operation.

The idea behind Strategy is to encapsulate the various strategies in a single module and provide a simple interface to allow a choice between them. Each strategy must have the same programming interface, but they do not need to be members of the same class hierarchy. However, they do have to implement the same programming interface.

Sample Code

Let's consider a simplified graphing program that can present data as a line graph or a bar chart. We start with an abstract PlotStrategy class and derive the two plotting classes from it, as illustrated in Figure 24.1.

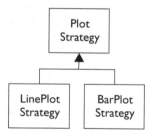

Figure 24.1   Two instances of a PlotStrategy Class.

Each plot will appear in its own frame, so the base PlotStrategy class will be derived from JFrame.

```
public abstract class PlotStrategy extends JFrame {
    protected float[]    x, y;
    protected float      minX, minY, maxX, maxY;
    protected int        width, height;
    protected Color      color;

    public PlotStrategy(String title) {
        super(title);
        width = 300;
        height = 200;
        color = Color.black;
    addWindowListener(new WindAp(this));
    }
    //---------------
    public abstract void plot(float xp[], float yp[]);
```

```
//--------------
public void setSize(Dimension sz) {
    width = sz.width;
    height = sz.height;
}
//--------------
public void setPenColor(Color c) {
    color = c;
}
```

The important part is that all of the derived classes must implement a method called *plot* with two Float arrays as arguments. Each of these classes can do any kind of plot that is appropriate.

Note that we don't derive it from the special JxFrame class because we don't want the entire program to exit if we close one of these subsidiary windows. Instead, we add a WindowAdapter class that hides the window if it is closed.

```
public class WindAp extends WindowAdapter {
    JFrame fr;
    public WindAp(JFrame f) {
        fr = f;              //copy the Jframe instance
    }
    public void windowClosing(WindowEvent e) {
        fr.setVisible(false);   //hide the window
    }
}
```

The Context Class

The Context class is the traffic cop that decides which strategy is to be called. The decision is usually based on a request from the client program, and all that Context needs to do is to set a variable to refer to one concrete strategy or another.

```
public class Context {
    //this object selects one of the strategies
    //to be used for plotting
    private PlotStrategy plotStrategy;
    private float x[], y[];
//--------------
    public Context() {
        setLinePlot();
    }
    public void setBarPlot() {
        plotStrategy = new BarPlotStrategy();
    }
    public void setLinePlot() {
        plotStrategy = new LinePlotStrategy();
    }
```

```
//---------------
    public void plot() {
        plotStrategy.plot(x, y);
    }
//---------------
    public void setPenColor(Color c) {
        plotStrategy.setPenColor(c);
    }
//---------------
    public void readData(String filename) {
    }
```

The Context class is also responsible for handling the data. Either it obtains the data from a file or database, or the data are passed in when the Context is created. Depending on the magnitude of the data, they can either be passed on to the plot strategies or the Context can pass an instance of itself into the plot strategies and provide a public method to fetch the data.

The Program Commands

The program, shown in Figure 24.2, is a panel with two buttons that call the two different plots.

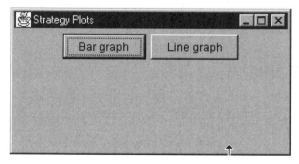

Figure 24.2   A panel to call two different plots.

Each button is a Command object that sets the correct strategy and then calls Context's plot routine. For example, following is the complete Line graph Button class:

```
public class JGraphButton extends JButton implements Command {
    Context context;
    public JGraphButton(ActionListener act, Context ctx) {
        super("Line graph");
        addActionListener(act);
        context  = ctx;
    }
```

```
    //--------------
    public void Execute() {
        context.setPenColor(Color.red);      //set the color of the
                                                 plot
        context.setLinePlot();               //set the kind of the
                                                 plot
        context.readData("data.txt");        //read the data
        context.plot();                      //plot the data
    }
}
```

The Line and Bar Graph Strategies

The two Strategy classes are pretty much the same: They set up the window size for plotting and call a plot method specific for that display panel. Here is the Line graph Strategy:

```
public class LinePlotStrategy extends PlotStrategy {
    private LinePlotPanel lp;

    public LinePlotStrategy() {
        super("Line plot");
        lp = new LinePlotPanel();
        getContentPane().add(lp);
    }
//--------------
    public void plot(float[] xp, float[] yp) {
        x = xp; y = yp;              //copy in data
        findBounds();                //sets maxes and mins
        setSize(width, height);
        setVisible(true);
        setBackground(Color.white);
        lp.setBounds(minX, minY, maxX, maxY);
        lp.plot(xp, yp, color);      //set up the plot data
        repaint();                   //call paint to plot
    }
}
```

Drawing Plots in Java

The Java GUI is event-driven, so we don't actually write a routine that draws lines on the screen in the direct response to the plot command event. Instead, we provide a panel whose paint event carries out the plotting when that event is called. The previous *repaint* method ensures that it will be called right away.

We create a PlotPanel class based on JPanel and derive two classes from it for the actual line and bar plots (Figure 24.3).

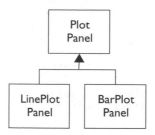

Figure 24.3   The two plot Panel classes derived from PlotPanel.

The base PlotPanel class contains the common code for scaling the data to the window.

```
public class PlotPanel extends JPanel {
    private float xfactor, yfactor;
    private int   xpmin, ypmin, xpmax, ypmax;
    private float minX, maxX, minY, maxY;
    private float x[], y[];
    private Color color;
//---------------
    public void setBounds(float minx, float miny, float maxx,
            float maxy) {
        minX = minx;
        maxX = maxx;
        minY = miny;
        maxY = maxy;
    }
//---------------
    public void plot(float[] xp, float[] yp, Color c) {
        x =    xp;         //copy in the arrays
        y =    yp;
        color = c;         //and color

        //compute bounds and scaling factors
        int w = getWidth() - getInsets().left - getInsets().right;
        int h = getHeight() - getInsets().top -
                getInsets().bottom;

        xfactor = (0.9f * w) / (maxX - minX);
        yfactor = (0.9f * h)/ (maxY - minY);

        xpmin = (int) (0.05f * w);
        ypmin = (int) (0.05f * h);
        xpmax = w - xpmin;
        ypmax = h - ypmin;
        repaint();         //this causes the actual plot
    }
```

```
//---------------
    protected int calcx(float xp) {
        return(int) ((xp-minX) * xfactor + xpmin);
    }
//---------------
    protected int calcy(float yp) {
        int ypnt = (int)((yp-minY) * yfactor);
        return ypmax - ypnt;
    }
}
```

The two derived classes implement the *paint* method for the two kinds of graphs. Here is the one for the Line plot:

```
public class LinePlotPanel extends PlotPanel {

    public void paint(Graphics g) {
        Super.paint(g);
        int xp = calcx(x[0]);              //get the first point
        int yp = calcy(y[0]);
        g.setColor(Color.white);           //flood the background
        g.fillRect(0,0,getWidth(),         getHeight());
        g.setColor(Color.black);

        //draw bounding rectangle
        g.drawRect(xpmin, ypmin, xpmax, ypmax);
        g.setColor(color);

        //draw line graph
        for (int i = 1; i < x.length; i++) {
            int xp1 = calcx(x[i]);
            int yp1 = calcy(y[i]);
            g.drawLine(xp, yp, xp1, yp1);
            xp = xp1;
            yp = yp1;
        }
    }
}
```

The final two plots are shown in Figure 24.4.

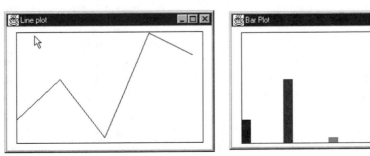

Figure 24.4 The line graph (left) and the bar graph (right).

The class diagram is given in Figure 24.5.

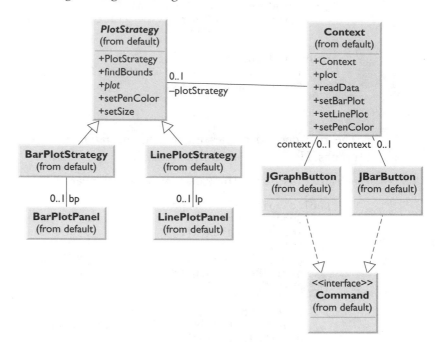

Figure 24.5   The UML class diagram for the PlotStrategy classes. Note that the Command pattern is again used.

PlotStrategy is the abstract class, and BarPlotStrategy and LinePlotStrategy are subclasses. The containers BarPlotPanel and LinePlotPanel contain instances of these two classes. The Context class contains code to select a strategy based on the request from either of the two Command buttons.

Consequences of the Strategy Pattern

The Strategy pattern allows you to select one of several algorithms dynamically. These algorithms may be related in an inheritance hierarchy, or they may be unrelated as long as they implement a common interface. Since the Context switches between strategies at your request, you have more flexibility than if you simply call the desired derived class. This approach also avoids the sort of condition statements that can make code hard to read and maintain.

However, Strategies don't hide everything. The client code is usually aware that there are a number of alternative strategies, and it has some criteria for choosing from among them. This shifts an algorithmic decision to the client programmer or the user.

You could pass any number of different parameters to different algorithms, so you must develop a Context interface and strategy methods that are broad enough to allow for passing in parameters that are not used by that particular algorithm. For example, the *setPenColor* method in PlotStrategy is actually used only by the LineGraph strategy. The BarGraph strategy ignores that method, since it sets up its own list of colors for the successive bars that it draws.

THOUGHT QUESTION

1. Use the Strategy pattern in a program to read in text and display it in a JTextField either in a monospaced font without wrapping or in a proportional font with wrapping set.

Programs on the CD-ROM

Program	Description
\Strategy\StrategyPlot.java	Selects algorithms for drawing data as line or bar plots.

CHAPTER 25

The Template Pattern

In this chapter, we take up the Template pattern—a very simple pattern that you will discover you use all the time. Whenever you write a parent class and leave one or more of the methods to be implemented by derived classes, you are in essence using the Template pattern. This pattern formalizes the idea of defining an algorithm in a class, while leaving some of the details to be implemented in subclasses. In other words, if your base class is an abstract class, as often happens in these design patterns, you are using a simple form of the Template pattern. We note that *Design Patterns* refers to this as the Template Method Pattern, but we shorten the name in this chapter for convenience.

Motivation

Templates are so fundamental, you have probably used them dozens of times without even thinking about it. The idea behind the Template pattern is that some parts of the algorithm are well defined and can be implemented in the base class, while other parts may have several implementations and are best left to derived classes. Another main idea is recognizing that there are some basic parts of a class that can be factored out and put in a base class so that they do not need to be repeated in several subclasses.

For example, in developing the PlotPanel classes used in the Strategy pattern examples, we discovered that in plotting both line graphs and bar charts we needed similar code to scale the data and compute the x- and y-pixel positions.

```
public class PlotPanel extends JPanel {
    private float xfactor, yfactor;
    private int   xpmin, ypmin, xpmax, ypmax;
    private float minX, maxX, minY, maxY;
```

```
        private float x[], y[];
        private Color color;
//---------------
    public void setBounds(float minx, float miny,
            float maxx, float maxy) {
        minX = minx;
        maxX = maxx;
        minY = miny;
        maxY = maxy;
    }
//---------------
    public void plot(float[] xp, float[] yp, Color c) {
        x = xp;           //copy in the arrays
        y = yp;
        color = c;      //and color

        //compute the bounds and scaling factors
        int w = getWidth() - getInsets().left - getInsets().right;
        int h = getHeight() - getInsets().top -
            getInsets().bottom;

        xfactor = (0.9f * w) /(maxX - minX);
        yfactor = (0.9f * h)/ (maxY - minY);

        xpmin = (int)(0.05f * w);
        ypmin = (int)(0.05f * h);
        xpmax = w - xpmin;
        ypmax = h - ypmin;
        repaint();        //this causes the actual plot
    }
//---------------
    protected int calcx(float xp) {
        return(int)((xp-minX) * xfactor + xpmin);
    }
//---------------
    protected int calcy(float yp) {
        int ypnt = (int)((yp-minY) * yfactor);
        return ypmax - ypnt;
    }
}
```

Thus these methods all belong in a base PlotPanel class without any actual plotting capabilities. Note that the *plot* method sets up all of the scaling constants and then calls *repaint*. The actual *paint* method is deferred to the derived classes. Since the JPanel class always has a *paint* method, we don't want to declare it as an abstract method in the base class, but we do need to override it in the derived classes.

Kinds of Methods in a Template Class

As set out in *Design Patterns*, the Template pattern has four kinds of methods that you can make use of in derived classes:

1. Complete methods that carry out some basic function that all of the subclasses will want to use, such as *calcx* and *calcy* in the previous example. These are called *Concrete methods*.

2. Methods that are not filled in at all and must be implemented in derived classes. In Java, you would declare these as *abstract methods,* and that is how they are referred to in the pattern description.

3. Methods that contain a default implementation of some operations but which may be overridden in derived classes. These are called *Hook methods*. Of course, this is somewhat arbitrary because in Java you can override any public or protected method in the derived class. But Hook methods are intended to be overridden, whereas Concrete methods are not.

4. Finally, a Template class may contain methods that call any combination of abstract, hook, and concrete methods. These methods are not intended to be overridden but describe an algorithm without actually implementing its details. *Design Patterns* refers to these as Template methods.

Template Method Patterns in Java

Java abounds with Template patterns. A large number of classes start out with an abstract class with only a few methods filled in and have subclasses where these methods are implemented.

AbstractTableModel

The TableModel interface defines all of the required methods for the data class for handling data for a JTable display. The AbstractTableModel provides default implementations for all but three of these methods. When you create the data class, you must provide implementations for *getRowCount(), getColumnCount(),* and *getValueAt(int row, int column)*.

AbstractBorder

The Border interface defines the methods for a border to surround any JComponent. The AbstractBorder class provides default implementations of all of these methods for a border having no width. You can then create your own border subclasses by reimplementing the AbstractBorder methods to handle an actual border.

AbstractListModel

Similar to the TableModel, the AbstractListModel provides a default implementation of the ListModel interface. You can create your own list data models by subclassing AbstractListModel. You can also use the DefaultListModel class as a simple Vector data repository.

Sample Code

Let's consider a program for drawing triangles on a screen. We start with an abstract Triangle class and then derive some special triangle types from it, as shown in Figure 25.1.

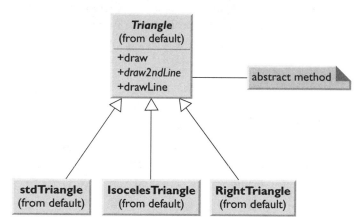

Figure 25.1   The abstract Triangle class and three of its subclasses.

Our abstract Triangle class illustrates the Template pattern.

```java
public abstract class Triangle {
    private Point p1, p2, p3;
    //---------------------
    public Triangle(Point a, Point b, Point c) {
        //save
        p1 = a; p2 = b; p3 = c;
    }
    //---------------------
    public void draw(Graphics g) {
        //This routine draws a general triangle
        drawLine(g, p1, p2);
```

```
        Point current = draw2ndLine(g, p2, p3);
        closeTriangle(g, current);
    }
    //--------------------
    public void drawLine(Graphics g, Point a, Point b) {
        g.drawLine(a.x, a.y, b.x, b.y);
    }
    //--------------------
    //this routine is the "Hook" that has to be implemented
    //for each triangle type.
    abstract public Point draw2ndLine(Graphics g,
                    Point a, Point b);
    //--------------------
    public void closeTriangle(Graphics g, Point c) {
        //draw back to first point
        g.drawLine(c.x, c.y, p1.x, p1.y);
    }

}
```

This Triangle class saves the coordinates of three lines, but the *draw* routine draws only the first and the last lines. The all-important *draw2ndLine* method that draws a line to the third point is left as an abstract method. In that way, the derived class can move the third point to create the kind of rectangle that you wish to draw.

This is a general example of a class's using the Template pattern. The *draw* method calls two Concrete base class methods and one abstract method that must be overridden in any concrete class derived from Triangle.

Another very similar way to implement the case triangle class is to include default code for the *draw2ndLine* method.

```
public Point draw2ndLine(Graphics g, Point a, Point b) {
    g.drawLine(a.x, a.y, b.x, b.y);
    return b;
}
```

In this case, the *draw2ndLine* method becomes a Hook method that can be overridden for other classes.

Drawing a Standard Triangle

To draw a general triangle with no restrictions on its shape, we implement the *draw2ndLine* method in a derived stdTriangle class.

```
public class stdTriangle extends Triangle {
    public stdTriangle(Point a, Point b, Point c) {
        super(a, b, c);
    }
```

```
public Point draw2ndLine(Graphics g, Point a, Point b) {
    g.drawLine(a.x, a.y, b.x, b.y);
    return b;
}
}
```

Drawing an Isoceles Triangle

This class computes a new third data point that will make the two sides equal in length and saves that new point inside of the class.

```
public class IsocelesTriangle extends Triangle {
    private Point newc;
    private int nexcx, newcy;
    private int incr;

    public IsocelesTriangle(Point a, Point b, Point c) {
        super(a, b, c);
        double dx1 = b.x - a.x;
        double dy1 = b.y - a.y;
        double dx2 = c.x - b.x;
        double dy2 = c.y - b.y;

        double side1 = calcSide(dx1, dy1);
        double side2 = calcSide(dx2, dy2);

        if (side2 < side1)
                incr = -1;
        else
                incr = 1;
        double slope = dy2 / dx2;
        double intercept = c.y - slope* c.x;

        //move to point c so that this is an isoceles triangle
        newcx = c.x; newcy = c.y;
        while (Math.abs(side1 - side2) > 1) {
            newcx += incr;     //iterate a pixel at a time
            newcy = (int)(slope* newcx + intercept);
            dx2 = newcx - b.x;
            dy2 = newcy - b.y;
            side2 = calcSide(dx2, dy2);
        }
        newc = new Point(newcx, newcy);
}
//----------------------
//calculate the length of the side
private double calcSide(double dx, double dy) {
    return Math.sqrt(dx*dx + dy*dy);
}
```

When the Triangle class calls the *draw* method, it calls this new version of *draw2ndLine* and draws a line to the new third point. Further, it returns that new point to the *draw* method so that it will draw the closing side of the triangle correctly.

```
//draws a second line using the saved new point
    public Point draw2ndLine(Graphics g, Point b, Point c) {
        g.drawLine(b.x, b.y, newc.x, newc.y);
        return newc;
    }
}
```

The Triangle Drawing Program

The main program creates instances of the triangles that we want to draw and adds them to a Vector in the TPanel class.

```
public class TriangleDrawing extends JxFrame {
    private stdTriangle t, t1;
    private IsocelesTriangle it;

    public TriangleDrawing() {
        super("Draw triangles");
        TPanel tp = new TPanel();
        t = new stdTriangle(new Point(10,10), new Point (150,50),
                new Point(100, 75));
        it = new IsocelesTriangle(new Point(150,100),
                new Point(240,40), new Point(175, 150));
        t1 = new stdTriangle(new Point(150, 100),
                new Point(240,40), new Point(175, 150));
        tp.addTriangle(t);
        tp.addTriangle(it);
        getContentPane().add(tp);
        setSize(300, 200);
        setBackground(Color.white);
        setVisible(true);
        }
```

It is the *paint* routine in this class that actually draws the triangles.

```
public class TPanel extends JPanel {
    private Vector triangles;
    public TPanel() {
        triangles = new Vector();
    }
    public void addTriangle(Triangle t) {
        triangles.addElement(t);
    }
    public void paint(Graphics g) {
```

```
        for (int i = 0; i < triangles.size(); i++) {
            Triangle tng1 = (Triangle) triangles.elementAt(i);
            tng1.draw(g);
        }
    }
}
```

Figure 25.2 offers an example of two standard triangles in the left window and the same code using an isoceles triangle in the right window.

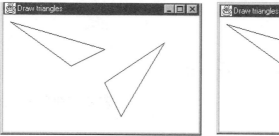 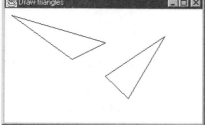

Figure 25.2   Two standard triangles (left) and a standard triangle and an isoceles triangle (right).

Templates and Callbacks

Design Patterns points out that Templates can exemplify the "Hollywood Principle," or "Don't call us, we'll call you." The idea here is that methods in the base class seem to call methods in the derived classes. The operative word here is *seem*. If we consider the *draw* code in the base Triangle class, we see that there are three method calls:

```
drawLine(g, p1, p2);
Point current = draw2ndLine(g, p2, p3);
closeTriangle(g, current);
```

Now *drawLine* and *closeTriangle* are implemented in the base class. However, as we have seen, the *draw2ndLine* method is not implemented at all in the base class, and various derived classes can implement it differently. Since the actual methods that are being called are in the derived classes, they appear to be called from the base class.

If this idea makes you uncomfortable, you will probably take solace in recognizing that *all* of the method calls originate from the derived class and that those calls move up the inheritance chain until they find the first class that implements them. If this class is the base class, fine. If it is not, then it could be any other class in between. Now, when we call the *draw* method, the derived class moves up the inheritance tree until it finds an implementation of *draw*. Likewise, for each method called from within *draw*, the derived class starts at the current class and moves up the tree to find each method. When it gets to the *draw2ndLine* method, it finds it immediately in the current class. So it isn't really called from the base class, although it does sort of seem that way.

Consequences of the Template Pattern

Template patterns occur all of the time in OO software and are neither complex nor obscure in intent. They are a normal part of OO programming, and you shouldn't try to make them into more than they actually are.

1. The first significant point is that your base class may define only some of the methods that it will be using, leaving the rest to be implemented in the derived classes.

2. The second point is that there might be methods in the base class that call a sequence of methods, some implemented in the base class and some implemented in the derived class. This Template method defines a general algorithm, although the details might not be worked out completely in the base class.

3. Template classes often have some abstract methods that you must override in the derived classes. They might also have some classes with a simple placeholder implementation that you are free to override where appropriate. If these placeholder classes are called from another method in the base class, then these overridable methods are called Hook methods.

 THOUGHT QUESTION

1. The Abstract Collection class in the java.util package is an example of a Template pattern. To use a collection derived from it, you must provide an implementation of the *iterator* and *size* methods. Write a program utilizing a collection derived from AbstractCollection.

Programs on the CD-ROM

Program	Description
\Template\TriangleDrawing.java	Draws generic and isoceles triangles using the Triangle template pattern.

CHAPTER 26

The Visitor Pattern

The Visitor pattern turns the tables on our OO model and creates an external class to act on data in other classes. This is useful when you have a polymorphic operation that cannot reside in the class hierarchy for some reason. For example, the operation wasn't considered when the hierarchy was designed or because it would clutter the interface of the classes unnecessarily.

Motivation

While at first it might seem "unclean" to put operations that should be inside of a class in another class instead, there are good reasons for doing this. Suppose that each of a number of drawing object classes has similar code for drawing itself. The drawing methods might differ, but they probably all use underlying utility functions that you might have to duplicate in each class. Further, a set of closely related functions is scattered throughout a number of different classes, as shown in Figure 26.1.

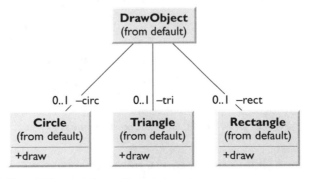

Figure 26.1　A DrawObject and three of its subclasses.

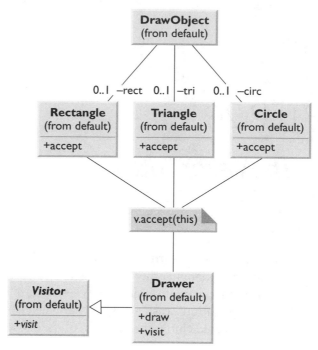

Figure 26.2   A Visitor class (Drawer) that visits each of three triangle classes.

Instead, you can write a Visitor class that contains all of the related *draw* methods and have it visit each object in succession (Figure 26.2).

Most people who first read about this pattern typically ask, "What does visiting mean?" An outside class can gain access to another class in only one way: by calling its public methods. In the Visitor's case, visiting each case means that you call a method already installed for this purpose, called *accept*. The *accept* method has one argument: the instance of the visitor. It then calls the *visit* method of the Visitor, passing itself as an argument, as shown in Figure 26.3.

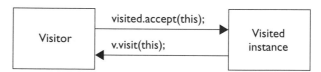

Figure 26.3   How the *visit* and *accept* methods interact.

Put in simple code terms, every object that you want to visit must have the following method:

```
public void accept(Visitor v) {
      v.visit(this);
   }
```

In this way, the Visitor object receives a reference to each instance, one by one, and can then call its public methods to obtain data, perform calculations, generate reports, or only draw the object on the screen. Of course, if the class does not have an *accept* method, you can subclass it and add one.

When to Use the Visitor Pattern

You should consider using a Visitor pattern when you want to perform an operation on the data contained in a number of objects that have different interfaces. Visitors are also valuable if you must perform a number of unrelated operations on these classes. Visitors are a useful way to add function to class libraries or frameworks for which you either do not have the source or cannot change the source for other technical (or political) reasons. In these latter cases, you simply subclass the classes of the framework and add the *accept* method to each subclass.

Visitors are a good choice, however, only when you do not expect many new classes to be added to your program. This is shown shortly.

Sample Code

Let's consider a simple subset of the Employee problem discussed in the Composite pattern. We have a simple Employee object that maintains a record of the employee's name, salary, number of vacation days taken, and number of sick days taken. A simple version of this class is the following:

```
public class Employee {
    private int      sickDays, vacDays;
    private float    Salary;
    private String   Name;

    public Employee(String name, float salary, int vacdays,
                    int sickdays) {
        vacDays = vacdays;
        sickDays = sickdays;
        Salary = salary
        Name = name;
    }
    public String getName() {
        return Name;
    }
```

```
    public int getSickdays() {
        return sickDays;
    }
    public int getVacDays() {
        return vacDays;
    }
    public float getSalary() {
        return Salary;
    }
    public void accept(Visitor v) {
        v.visit(this);
    }
}
```

Note that we have included the *accept* method in this class. Now let's suppose that we want to prepare a report of the number of vacation days that all employees have taken so far this year. We could just write some code in the client to sum the results of calls to each Employee's *getVacDays* function, or we could put this function into a Visitor.

Since Java is a strongly typed language, our base Visitor class needs to have a suitable abstract *visit* method for each kind of class in the program. In the following first example of our basic abstract visitor class, we have only Employees.

```
public abstract class Visitor {
    public abstract void visit(Employee emp);
    public abstract void visit(Boss emp);
}
```

Notice that there is no indication what the Visitor does with each class in either the client classes or the abstract Visitor class. We can in fact write a whole lot of Visitors that do different things to the classes in our program. The first Visitor that we write sums the vacation data for all employees.

```
public class VacationVisitor extends Visitor {
    protected int total_days;
    public VacationVisitor() {
        total_days = 0;
    }
    //---------------
    public void visit(Employee emp) {
        total_days += emp.getVacDays();
    }
    //---------------
    public void visit(Boss boss) {
        total_days += boss.getVacDays();
    }
    //---------------
    public int getTotalDays() {
        return total_days;
    }
}
```

Visiting the Classes

Now all that we must do to compute the total vacation days taken is to go through a list of the employees, visit each of them, and then ask the Visitor for the total.

```
        VacationVisitor vac = new VacationVisitor();
        for (int i = 0; i < employees.length; i++) {
            employees[i].accept(vac);
}
total.setText(new Integer(vac.getTotalDays()).toString());
```

Here's what happens for each visit:

1. We move through a loop of all Employees.

2. The Visitor calls each Employee's *accept* method.

3. That instance of Employee calls the Visitor's *visit* method.

4. The Visitor fetches the value for the number of vacation days and adds that number to the total.

5. The main program prints out the total number of days when the loop is complete.

Visiting Several Classes

The Visitor becomes more useful when we have several different classes with different interfaces and we want to encapsulate how we get data from these classes. Let's extend our vacation days model by introducing a new Employee type called Boss. We further suppose that at this company, Bosses are rewarded with bonus vacation days (instead of money). So the Boss class has a couple of extra methods to set and obtain the bonus vacation days information.

```
public class Boss extends Employee {
    private int bonusDays;

    public Boss(String name, float salary, int vacdays,
            int sickdays) {
        super(name, salary, vacdays, sickdays);
    }
    public void setBonusDays (int bonus) {
        bonusDays = bonus;
    }
    public int getBonusDays() {
        return bonusDays;
    }
    public void accept(Visitor v) {
```

```
        v.visit(this);
    }
}
```

When we add a class to this program, we must add it to our Visitor as well. The abstract template for the Visitor is now as follows:

```
public abstract class Visitor {
    public abstract void visit(Employee emp);
    public abstract void visit(Boss emp);
}
```

This says that any concrete Visitor classes that we write must provide polymorphic *visit* methods for both the Employee and the Boss classes. In the case of the vacation day counter, we need to ask the Boss for both regular and bonus days taken, so the visits are now different. We'll write a new bVacationVisitor class that takes this difference into account.

```
public class bVacationVisitor extends Visitor {
    int total_days;

    public bVacationVisitor() {
        total_days = 0;
    }
    //---------------
    public int getTotalDays() {
        return total_days;
    }
    //---------------
    public void visit(Boss boss) {
        total_days += boss.getVacDays();
        total_days += boss.getBonusDays();
    }
    //---------------
    public void visit(Employee emp) {
        total_days += emp.getVacDays();
    }
}
```

While in this case Boss is derived from Employee, it need not be related at all as long as it has an *accept* method for the Visitor class. It is important, however, that you implement a *visit* method in the Visitor for *every class* you will be visiting and not count on inheriting this behavior, since the *visit* method from the parent class is an Employee rather than a Boss *visit* method. Likewise, each of our derived classes (Boss, Employee, and so on) must have its own *accept* method rather than calling one in its parent class. This is illustrated in the class diagram in Figure 26.4.

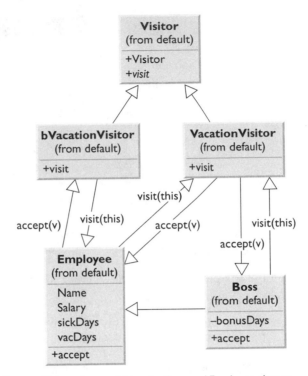

Figure 26.4   The two Visitor classes visiting the Boss and Employee classes.

Bosses Are Employees, Too

Figure 26.5 shows an application that carries out both Employee visits and Boss visits on the collection of Employees and Bosses. The original VacationVisitor will treat Bosses as Employees and get only their ordinary vacation data. The bVacationVisitor will get both ordinary and bonus vacation days.

```
VacationVisitor vac = new VacationVisitor();
bVacationVisitor bvac = new bVacationVisitor();
    for (int i = 0; i < employees.length; i++)      {
        employees[i].accept(vac);
        employees[i].accept(bvac);
    }
total.setText(new Integer(vac.getTotalDays()).toString());
btotal.setText(new Integer(bvac.getTotalDays()).toString());
```

The two lines of displayed data represent the two sums that are computed when the user clicks on the Vacation button.

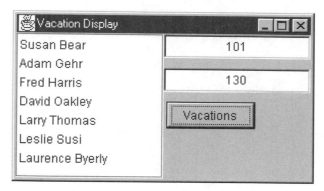

Figure 26.5 An application that performs the vacation visits.

Catch-All Operations Using Visitors

In all of the previous cases, the Visitor class had a *visit* method for each visiting class, such as the following:

```
public void visit(Employee emp) {}
public void visit(Boss emp) {}
```

However, if you start subclassing your Visitor classes and adding new classes that might visit, you should recognize that some *visit* methods might not be satisfied by the methods in the derived class. These might instead "fall through" to methods in one of the parent classes in which that object type is recognized. This provides a way of specifying default Visitor behavior.

Note that every class must override *accept(v)* with its own implementation so that the return call *v.visit(this)* returns an object *this* of the correct type and not of the superclass's type.

Let's suppose that we introduce another layer of management into the company, discussed earlier in the chapter: the Manager. Managers are subclasses of Employees, and now they have the privileges formerly reserved for Bosses, that is, extra vacation days. And Bosses now have an additional reward: stock options. If we run the same program to compute vacation days but do not revise out Visitor to look for Managers, it will recognize Managers as mere Employees and count only their regular vacation days and not their extra vacation days. However, the catch-all parent class is good to have if subclasses might be added to the application from time to time and we want the Visitor operations to continue to run without modification.

There are three ways to integrate the new Manager class into the visitor system. In one, we could define a ManagerVisitor. In the second, we could use the BossVisitor to handle both. However, there could be conditions when it is not desirable to modify the Visitor structure continually. In that third case, you could simply test for this in the EmployeeVisitor class.

```
public void visit (Employee emp) {
    total_days += emp.getVacDays();
    //special test in catch-all parent class
    if(emp instanceof Manager)
        total_days += ((Manager) emp).getBonusDays ();
}
```

While this seems "unclean" at first compared to defining classes properly, it can provide a method of catching special cases in derived classes without writing whole new Visitor program hierarchies. This catch-all approach is discussed in some detail in the book *Pattern Hatching* [Vlissides, 1998].

Double Dispatching

No discussion of the Visitor pattern is complete without mentioning that you are really dispatching a method twice in order for the Visitor to work. The Visitor calls the polymorphic *accept* method of a given object, and the *accept* method calls the polymorphic *visit* method of the Visitor. It is this bidirectional calling that allows you to add more operations on any class that has an *accept* method, since each new visitor class can carry out whatever operations you might think of using the data available in these classes.

Traversing a Series of Classes

In order to visit a series of classes, the calling program that passes the class instances to the Visitor must know about all of the existing instances of classes to be visited and must keep them in a simple structure such as an array or Vector. Another possibility would be to create an Enumeration of these classes and pass it to the Visitor. Finally, the Visitor itself could keep the list of objects that it is to visit. In the earlier example program, we used an array of objects, but any of the other methods would work equally well.

Consequences of the Visitor Pattern

The Visitor pattern is useful when you want to encapsulate fetching data from a number of instances of several classes. *Design Patterns* suggest that the Visitor can provide additional functionality to a class without changing it. However, it's preferable to say that a Visitor can add functionality to a collection of classes and encapsulate the methods that it uses.

The Visitor is not magic, however, and cannot obtain private data from classes; it is limited to the data available from public methods. This might force you to provide public methods that you would otherwise not provide. However, the Visitor can obtain data from a disparate collection of unrelated classes and utilize it to present the results of a global calculation to the user program.

It is easy to add new operations to a program using Visitors, since the Visitor contains the code instead of each of the individual classes. Further, Visitors can gather related operations into a single class rather than forcing you to change or derive classes to add these operations. This can make the program simpler to write and maintain.

Visitors are less helpful during a program's growth stage. This is because each time that you add new classes that must be visited, you must add an abstract visit operation to the abstract Visitor class and an implementation for that class to each concrete Visitor that you've written. Visitors can be powerful additions when the program reaches the point at which many new classes are unlikely.

They also can be used very effectively in Composite systems. For example, the boss-employee system just illustrated could well be a Composite like the one used in Chapter 11, The Composite Pattern.

THOUGHT QUESTION

1. An investment firm's customer records consist of an object for each stock or other financial instrument that each investor owns. The object contains a history of the purchase, sale, and dividend activities for that stock. Design a Visitor pattern to report on net end-of-year profit or loss on stocks sold during the year.

Programs on the CD-ROM

Program	Description
\Visitor\VacationDisplay.java	Displays the result of visiting a series of Employee and Boss objects and shows their vacation days.
\Visitor\CatchAll\ VacationDisplay.java	Displays vacation days for Employee, Manager, and Boss classes, using Employee as a catch-all.

SECTION 5

Design Patterns and the Java Foundation Classes

In this section we discuss how to use the principal Swing classes, and in the process, point out a number of the design patterns they use.

CHAPTER 27

The JFC, or Swing

The Java Foundation Classes (JFC, or Swing) are a complete set of lightweight user interface components that enhance, extend, and, to a large degree, replace the AWT components such as buttons, panels, list boxes and check boxes. In addition to the buttons, lists, tables, and trees in the JFC, you will also find a pluggable look and feel that allows the components to take on the appearance of several popular windowing systems. The JFC actually uses a few common design patterns that we used for most of the examples in this book. Thus in this section, we review how to use the JFC and point out a number of patterns it encompasses. If you haven't used these powerful classes yet, this is a simple introduction. If you have, read through this chapter to see how many patterns you can discover in them.

We should note at the outset that this package was called "Swing" during development, and it was intended that it be referred to as "JFC" upon release. However, the nickname has stuck, and this has led to the Java programmer's explanation, "It's spelled JFC, but it's pronounced Swing."

Installing and Using Swing

All programs that are to use Swing must import

```
import javax.swing.*;
```

and might require one or more of the following, depending on the components used:

```
import javax.swing.event.*;
import javax.swing.border.*;
import javax.swing.text.*;
```

Ideas behind Swing

The Swing components are called lightweight because they don't rely on native user-interface components. They are, in fact, 100 percent pure Java. Thus a Swing JButton does not rely on a Windows button or a Motif button or a Macintosh button to implement its functionality. The components also use fewer classes to achieve this interface than did the heavier-weight AWT classes. In addition, Swing has many more user-interface components than did the AWT, including image buttons, hover buttons, tooltips, tables, trees, splitter panels, and customizable dialog boxes.

Because Swing components create their look and feel completely within the Swing class hierarchy, you can have a pluggable look and feel to emulate Windows, Motif, Macintosh, or the native Swing look.

Swing components also use an architecture derived from the MVC design pattern discussed in Chapter 1. Recall that the MVC pattern keeps the data in a *Model* class, displays the data in a *view* class, and varies the data and view using a *Controller* class. We'll see that this is exactly how the JList and JTable handle their data.

The Swing Class Hierarchy

All Swing components inherit from the JComponent class. JComponent is much like the AWT's Component class in its position in the hierarchy; however, it provides the pluggable look and feel. It also provides

- keystroke handling that works with nested components,
- a border property that defines both the border and the component's insets,
- tooltips that pop up when the mouse hovers over components, and
- automatic scrolling of any component when placed in a scroller container.

Because of this interaction with the user interface environment, Swing's JComponent is actually more like the AWT's Canvas class than its Component class.

CHAPTER 28

Writing a Simple JFC Program

Getting started using the Swing classes is pretty simple. Application windows inherit from JFrame, and applets inherit from JApplet. The only difference between Frame and JFrame is that you cannot add components or set the layout directly for JFrame. Instead, you must use the *getContentPane* method to obtain the container in which you can add components and vary the layout.

```
getContentPane().setLayout(new BorderLayout());
JButton b = new JButton ("Hi");
getContentPane().add(b);        //add a button to the layout
```

This is sometimes a bit tedious to type each time, so we recommend retrieving the JPanel from the content pane and then adding all the components to that panel.

```
JPanel jp = getContentPane()    //get the JPanel
JButton b = new JButton("Hi");
jp.add(b);                      //add components to it
```

JPanels are containers much like the AWT Panel object, except that they are automatically double-buffered and repaint more quickly and smoothly.

Setting the Look and Feel

If you do not select a look and feel, Swing programs will start up in their own default native look and feel rather than that of Windows, Motif, or the Mac. If you don't want the default look and feel, you must specifically set the look and feel in each program, using a method like that following:

```
private void setLF() {
        // Force SwingApp to come up in the System L&F
        String laf = UIManager.getSystemLookAndFeelClassName();
        try {
            UIManager.setLookAndFeel(laf);
        } catch (UnsupportedLookAndFeelException exc) {
            System.err.println("UnsupportedLookAndFeel: " + laf);
        } catch (Exception exc) {
            System.err.println("Error " + laf + ": " + exc);
        }
    }
```

The system that generates one of several look and feels and returns self-consistent classes of visual objects for a given look and feel is an example of an Abstract Factory pattern, discussed in Chapter 5.

Setting the Window Close Box

Like the Frame component, the system exit procedure is *not* called automatically when a user clicks on the Close box. To enable that behavior, you must add a WindowListener to the frame and catch the WindowClosing event. This can be done most effectively by subclassing the WindowAdapter class.

```
private void setCloseClick() {
        //create a WindowListener to respond to the window close
          click
        addWindowListener(new WindowAdapter() {
                public void windowClosing(WindowEvent e) {
                    System.exit(0);
                }
        });
    }
```

Making a JxFrame Class

Because you will probably always set the look and feel and must always create a Window Adapter to close the JFrame, we have created a JxFrame class that contains those two functions and calls them as part of initialization.

```
public class JxFrame extends Jframe {
    public JxFrame(String title) Jframe {
        super(title);
        setCloseClick();
        setLF();
    }
}
```

The *setLF* and *setCloseClick* methods are included as well. It is this JxFrame class that we use in virtually all of our examples in this book, to avoid always having to retype the same code.

A Simple Two-Button Program

With these fundamentals taken care of, we can write a simple program with two buttons in a frame, like the one in Figure 28.1.

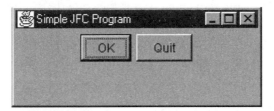

Figure 28.1 A simple two-button Swing program.

One button switches the color of the background, and the other causes the program to exit. We start by initializing our GUI and catching both button clicks in an *actionPerformed* method.

```java
public class SimpleJFC extends JxFrame
implements ActionListener {
    private JButton OK, Quit;
    private Color    color;
    private JPanel  jp;

    public SimpleJFC() {
        super("Simple JFC Program");
        color = Color.yellow;
        setGUI();
    }
    //---------------
    private void setGUI() {
        jp = new JPanel();
        getContentPane().add(jp);

        //create and add the buttons
        OK =   new JButton("OK");
        Quit = new JButton("Quit");
        OK.addActionListener(this);
        Quit.addActionListener(this);

        jp.add(OK);
        jp.add(Quit);

        setSize(new Dimension(250,100));
```

```
        setVisible(true);
    }
    //——————————————
    public void actionPerformed(ActionEvent e) {
        Object obj = e.getSource();
        if (obj == OK)
            switchColors();
        if (obj == Quit)
            System.exit(0);
    }
```

The only remaining part is the code that switches the background colors.

```
    private void switchColors() {
        if (color == Color.green)
            color = Color.yellow;
        else
            color = Color.green;
        jp.setBackground(color);
        repaint();
    }
```

That's all there is to writing a basic JFC application. Writing JFC applets are identical except that the applet's *init* routine replaces the constructor. Now let's look at some of the power of the more common JFC components.

More on JButton

The JButton has several constructors to specify text, an icon, or both:

```
JButton(String text);
JButton(Icon icon);
JButton(String text, Icon icon);
```

You can also set two other images to go with the button:

```
set SelectedIcon(Icon icon);        //shown when clicked
setRolloverIcon(Icon icon);         //shown when mouse over
```

Finally, like all other JComponents, you can use *setToolTipText* to set the text of a tooltip which will be displayed when the mouse hovers over the button. Here is the code to implement these improvements:

```
    OK = new JButton("OK", new ImageIcon("color.gif"));
    OK.setRolloverIcon(new ImageIcon("overColor.gif"));
    OK.setToolTipText("Change background color");
    Quit = new JButton("Quit", new ImageIcon("exit.gif"));
    Quit.setToolTipText("Exit from program");
```

The resulting application window is shown in Figure 28.2 with the tooltip up.

Figure 28.2   Two picture buttons with the hover tooltip showing.

Programs on the CD-ROM

Program	Description
\Swing\Simple\SimpleJFC.java	Basic two-button program using JxFrame.
\Swing\Simple\SimpleJFC2.java	Two-button program with button images and tooltips.

CHAPTER 29

Radio Buttons and Toolbars

Swing provides separate implementations of both the JRadioButton and the JCheckBox. A check box has two states, and within a group of check boxes, any number can be selected or deselected. Radio buttons should be grouped into a ButtonGroup object so that only one radio button of a group can be selected at a time.

Radio Buttons

Both radio buttons and check boxes can be instantiated with an image as well as a title, and both čan have rollover icons. The JCheckBox component is derived from the simpler JToggleButton object. JToggleButton is a button that can be switched between two states by clicking but which stays in that new state (up or down) like a two-state check box does. Further, the JToggle Button can take on the exclusive aspects of a radio button by adding it to a ButtonGroup.

```
//create radio buttons in the right panel
JRadioButton Rep, Dem, Flat;
right.add(Rep   =   new JRadioButton("Republicrat"));
right.add(Dem   =   new JRadioButton("Demmican"));
right.add(Flat  =   new JRadioButton("Flat Earth"));
ButtonGroup bgroup = new ButtonGroup();
bgroup.add(Rep);          //add to a button group
bgroup.add(Dem);
bgroup.add(Flat);
```

If you neglect to add the radio buttons to a ButtonGroup, you can have several of them turned on at once. It is the ButtonGroup that assures that only one button at a time can be turned on. The ButtonGroup object enforces this only-one-on protocol by keeping track of the state of all of the radio buttons in the group. This is an example of the Mediator pattern discussed in Chapter 20.

The JToolBar

The JToolBar is a container bar for tool buttons of the type you see in many programs. Normally, the JDK documentation recommends that you add the JTool-Bar as the only component on one side of a BorderLayout (typically the North side) and that you not add components to the other three sides. The buttons you add to the toolbar are small JButtons with picture icons and without text. The JToolBar class has two important methods: *add* and *addSeparator.*

```
JToolBar toolbar = new JToolBar();
JButton Open = new JButton("open.gif");
toolbar.add(Open);
toolbar.addSeparator();
```

By default the JButton has a rectangular shape. To make the usual square-looking buttons, you need to use square icons and set the insets of the button to zero. On most toolbars, the icons are 25×25 pixels. Following is a ToolButton class that handles both the insets and the size:

```
public class ToolButton extends JButton {
    public ToolButton(Icon img) {
        super(img);
        setMargin(new Insets(0,0,0,0));
        setSize(25,25);
    }
}
```

You also can detach the JToolBar from its anchored position along the top side of the program and attach it to another side, or you can leave it floating. This allows some user customization of the running program but otherwise is not terribly useful. It also is not particularly well implemented and can be confusing to the user. Thus we recommend that you use the *setFloatable(false)* method to turn this feature off.

JToggleButton

The JToggleButton class is actually the parent class for check boxes and radio buttons. It is a two-state button that will stay in an up or down position when clicked, and you can use it just like a check box. While toggle buttons look rather strange on most screens, they look very reasonable as part of toolbars. You can use individual toggle buttons to indicate the state of actions that the user might select. By themselves, toggle buttons behave like check boxes, so you can click on as many as you want and uncheck, or raise, toggle buttons by using the *setSelected(false)* method.

You can also add toggle buttons to a ButtonGroup so that they behave like radio buttons; that is, only one at a time may be indented. However, once a ButtonGroup object is mediating them, you can't raise the buttons using the *setSelected* method. If you want to be able to raise them but still allow only one at a time to be indented, you need to write your own Mediator class to replace the ButtonGroup object.

A Sample Button Program

Figure 29.1 illustrates a program that has check boxes, radio buttons, toolbar buttons, and toggle buttons.

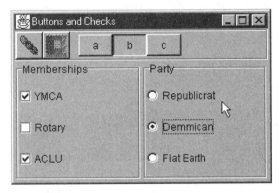

Figure 29.1 A simple display of check boxes, radio buttons, toolbar buttons, and toggle buttons.

Note that the "b" JToggleButton stays depressed until another button is selected, as toggle buttons are supposed to do. While the user can select any number of organizations in which he holds memberships using the JCheckboxes, he can select only one political party from the JRadioButtons.

Programs on the CD-ROM

Program	Description
\Swing\Buttons\Buttons.java	Shows toolbar buttons, toggle buttons, check boxes, and radio buttons.

CHAPTER 30

Menus and Actions

The JMenu Bar and JMenu classes in Swing work almost the same as those in the AWT. However, the JMenuItem class adds constructors that allow you to include an image alongside the menu text. To create a menu, you create a menu bar, add top-level menus, and then add menu items to each top-level menu.

```
JMenuBar mbar = new JMenuBar();              //menu bar
setJMenuBar(mbar);                           //add it to JFrame
JMenu mFile = new JMenu("File");             //top-level menu
mbar.add(mFile);                             //add it to the menu
                                             //  bar

JMenuItem Open = new JMenuItem("Open");      //menu items
JMenuItem Exit = new JMenuItem("Exit");
mFile.add(Open);                             //add them to the
                                             //  menu
mFile.addSeparator();                        //put in a separator
mFile.add(Exit);
```

The JMenuItem object also generates an ActionEvent, and thus menu clicks cause these events to be generated. As with buttons, you simply add Action-Listeners to each of them.

```
Open.addActionListener(this);                //for example
Exit.addActionListener(this);
```

Action Objects

Menus and toolbars are really two ways of representing the same thing: a single click interface to initiate some program function. Swing also provides an Action interface that encompasses both.

```
public void putValue(String key, Object value);
public Object getValue(String key);
public void actionPerformed(ActionEvent e);
```

You can add this interface to an existing class or create a JComponent with these methods and use it as an object that you can add to either a JMenu or a JToolBar. The most effective way is simply to extend the AbstractAction class. The JMenu and JToolBar will then display it as either a menu item or a button, respectively. Further, since an Action object has a single ActionListener built in, you can be sure that selecting either one will have exactly the same effect. In addition, disabling the Action object has the advantage of disabling both representations on the screen.

Let's see how this works. We start with a basic abstract ActionButton class and use a Hashtable to store and retrieve the properties.

```
public abstract class ActionButton extends AbstractAction {
    Hashtable properties;

    public ActionButton(String caption, Icon img) {
        properties = new Hashtable();
        properties.put(DEFAULT, caption);
        properties.put(NAME, caption);
        properties,put(SHORT_DESCRIPTION, caption);

        properties.put(SMALL_ICON, img);
    }
    public void putValue(String key, Object value) {
        properties.put(key, value);
    }
    public Object getValue(String key) {
        return properties.get(key);
    }
    public abstract avoid actionPerformed(ActionEvent e);
}
```

Following are the properties that Action objects recognize by key name:

```
DEFAULT
LONG_DESCRIPTION
NAME
SHORT_DESCRIPTION
SMALL_ICON
```

The NAME property determines the label for the menu item and the button. The LONG_DESCRIPTION is not used at present. The SMALL_ICON property does work correctly.

Now we can derive an ExitButton from the ActionButton like this.

```
public class ExitButton extends ActionButton {

    JFrame fr;
    public ExitButton(String caption. Icon img) {
```

```
        super(caption, img);
    }
    public void actionPerformed(ActionEvent e) {
        System.exit(0);
    }
}
```

We do the same for the FileButton, adding these to the toolbar and menu as follows:

```
//add the File menu
        JMenu mFile = new JMenu("File");
        mbar.add(mFile);

        //create two Action Objects
        Action Open = new FileButton("Open",
                new ImageIcon("open.gif"), this);
        mFile.add(Open);

        Action Exit = new ExitButton("Exit",
                new ImageIcon("exit.gif"));
        mFile.addSeparator();
        mFile.add(Exit);
//now create a toolbar that fixes up the buttons as you add them
        toolbar = new JToolBar();
        getContentPane().add(jp = new JPanel());
        jp.setLayout(new BorderLayout());
        jp.add("North", toolbar);

        //add the two action objects
        toolbar.add(Open);
        toolbar.addSeparator();
        toolbar.add(Exit);
```

This code produces the program window shown in Figure 30.1.

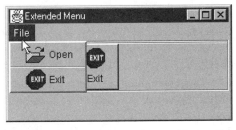

Figure 30.1   A menu with pictures using the same Action object as the toolbar buttons.

The problem with this approach is that we don't usually want the images in the menu or the text on the toolbar. However, the *add* methods of the toolbar and menu have a unique feature when used to add an action object: They return an object of type JButton or JMenuItem, respectively. We can use these to set the features the way that we want them. For the menu, we want to remove the icon.

```
Action Open = new FileButton("Open",
            new ImageIcon("open.gif"), this);
menuitem = mFile.add(Open);
menuitem.setIcon(null);
```

For the button, we want to remove the text and add a tooltip.

```
JButton button = toolbar.add(act);
button.setText("");
button.setToolTipText(tip);
button.setMargin(new Insets(0,0,0,0));
```

This gives us the screen look that we want, shown in Figure 30.2.

Figure 30.2   The menu items with the Action object's images turned off.

Design Patterns in the Action Object

Objects that implement the Action interface deserve discussion because they exemplify at least two design patterns. First, each Action object must have its own *actionListener* method and thus can directly launch the code to respond to that action. In addition, even though these Action objects might have two (or more) visual instantiations, they provide a single point that launches this code. This is an excellent example of the Command pattern.

In addition, the Action object takes on different visual aspects depending on whether it is added to a menu or to a toolbar. In fact, you could decide that the Action object is a Factory pattern, which produces a button or menu object depending on where it is added. It does seem to be a Factory because the toolbar and menu *add* methods return instances on those objects. On the other hand, the Action object seems to be a single object and gives different appearances depending on its environment. This is a description of the State pattern, according to which an object seems to change class (or methods) depending on the object's internal state.

One interesting and challenging aspect of the design patterns discussed in this book is that once you start looking at a pattern, you discover that it is represented far more widely that you first assumed. In some cases, the application and implementation are obvious; in other cases, the implementation is more subtle. In these cases, you step back, tilt your head, squint, and realize that from that angle it *looks* like a pattern where you hadn't noticed one before. Again, being able to label the code as exemplifying a pattern makes it easier for you to remember how it works and easier for you to communicate to others how that code is constructed.

Programs on the CD-ROM

Program	Description
\Swing\Menu\simpleMenu.java	Basic implementation of the JMenu.
\Swing\Menu\xMenu.java	Action objects used as a menu and tool buttons.
\Swing\Menu\xtendMenu.java	Action objects used as a menu and tool buttons, with icons suppressed in the menu.

CHAPTER 31

The JList Class

The JList class is a more powerful replacement for the AWT's List class. A JList can be instantiated using a Vector or an array to represent its contents. It does not support scrolling and thus must be added to a JScrollPane to allow scrolling to take place.

In the simplest program that you can write using a JList, you

1. add a JScrollPane to the Frame,

2. create a Vector of data,

3. create a JList using the Vector, and

4. add the JList to the JScrollPane's viewport.

This program is shown next.

```
JPanel jp = new JPanel();          //a panel in Frame
getContentPane().add(jp);

//create a scroll pane
JScrollPane sp = new JScrollPane();
jp.add(sp);                        //add the pane to the layout
Vector dlist = new Vector();       //create a Vector
dlist.addElement("Anchovies");     //and add data
dlist.addElement("Bananas");
dlist.addElement("Cilantro");
dlist.addElement("Doughnuts");
dlist.addElement("Escarole");
JList list = new JList(dlist);     //create a list with data
sp.getViewport().add(list);        //add the list to the
                                     JScrollpane
```

This produces the display shown in Figure 31.1.

Figure 31.1   A simple JList.

You could just as easily use an array instead of a Vector and get the same result.

List Selections and Events

You can set the JList to allow users to select a single line, multiple contiguous lines, or separated multiple lines by using the *setSelectionMode* method, where the arguments can be

```
SINGLE_SELECTION
SINGLE_INTERVAL_SELECTION
MULTIPLE_INTERVAL_SELECTION
```

You can then receive these events by using the *addListSelectionListener* method. Your program must implement the following method from the ListSelectionListener interface:

```
public void valueChanged(ListSelectionEvent e)
```

In the following example, we display the selected list item in a text field:

```
public void valueChanged(ListSelectionEvent e)    {
    text.setText((String)list.getSelectedValue());
}
```

This is shown in Figure 31.2.

Figure 31.2   A JList with the selected item displayed in the JTextField.

Changing a List Display Dynamically

For a list to change dynamically while your program is running, the problem is somewhat more involved because the JList displays the data that it is initially loaded with and does not update the display unless you tell it to. One simple way to accomplish this is to use the *setListData* method of JList to keep passing it a new version of the updated Vector after you change it. In the JListDemo.java program, the contents of the top text field are added to the list each time that the Add button is clicked. All of this place in the *action* routine for that button.

```
public void actionPerformed(ActionEvent e)        {
    dlist.addElement(text.getText());    //add text from the field
    list.setListData(dlist);        //send a new Vector to the list
    list.repaint();                 //and tell it to redraw
}
```

One drawback to this solution is that you are passing the entire Vector to the list each time and it must update its entire contents each time rather than updating only the portion that changed. This brings us to the underlying List-Model that contains the data that the JList displays.

When you create a JList using an array or a Vector, the JList automatically creates a ListModel object that contains those data. Each ListModel object is a concrete subclass of the AbstractListModel class that defines the following methods:

```
void fireContentsChanged(Object source, int index0, int index1);
void fireIntervalAdded(Object source, int index0, int index1);
void fireIntervalRemoved(Object source, int index0, int index1);
```

The AbstractListModel class is declared as *abstract,* so you must subclass it and create your own class, but there are no abstract methods that you must implement. All of them have default implementations. You need only call those *fire* methods that your program will be using, for example, the *fireInterval-Added* method in the following. The ListModel is an objcet that contains the data (in a Vector or other suitable structure) and notifies the JList whenever it changes. Here, the ListModel is the following:

```
class JListData extends AbstractListModel {
    private Vector dlist;                         //the color name list

    public JListData()      {
        dlist = new Vector();
        makeData();
    }
    public int getSize()      {
        return dlist.size();
    }
    private Vector makeData()
    {
        dlist = new Vector();                 //create the Vector
        dlist = addElement("Anchovies")   //and add data
         //then add the rest of the names as before
        return dlist;
    }
    public Object getElementAt(int index)      {
        return dlist.elementAt(index);
    }
    //add a string to the list and tell the list about it
    public void addElement(String s)      {
        dlist.addElement(s);
        fireIntervalAdded(this, dlist.size()-1, dlist.size());
    }
}
```

The ListModel approach is really an implementation of the Observer pattern discussed in Chapter 15. The data are in one class, the rendering or display methods in another, and the communication between them triggers new display activity.

A Sorted JList with a ListModel

To display a list that is always sorted, you can use the DefaultListModel class to contain the data. This class implements the same methods as the Vector class and notifies the JList whenever the data change. So a complete program for a nonsorted list display can be as follows:

```java
//creates a JList based on an unsorted DefaultListModel
public class ShowList extends JxFrame implements ActionListener {
    String names[]= ("Dave", "Charlie", "Adam", "Edward", "Barry");
    JButton          Next;
    DefaultListModel ldata;
    int              index;

    public ShowList() {
        super("List of names");
        JPanel jp = new JPanel();
        getContentPane().add(jp);
        jp.setLayout(new BorderLayout());

        //create the ListModel
        ldata = new DefaultListModel();
        //Create the list
        JList nList = new JList(ldata);
        //add it to the scrollpane
        JScrollPane sc = new JScrollPane();
        sc.getViewport().setView(nList);
        jp.add ("Center", sc);
        JButton Next = new JButton ("Next");

        //add an element when the button is clicked
        JPanel bot = new JPanel();
        jp.add("South", bot);
        bot.add(Next);
        Next.addActionListener (this);

        setSize(new Dimension(150, 150));
        setVisible(true);
        index = 0;

    }
    public void actionPerformed(ActionEvent evt) {
        if(index < names.length)
            ldata.addElement (names[index++];

    }
```

In this program, we add along the bottom a Next button that adds a new name each time that it is clicked. The data are not sorted here, but obviously if we subclass the DefaultListModel, we can have our sorted list and have the elements always sorted, even when new names are added.

So, if we create a class based on DefaultListModel that extends the *addElement* method and re-sorts the data each time, we'll have our sorted list.

```java
//this list model re-sorts the data every time
public class SortedModel extends DefaultListModel {
    private String[] dataList;
```

```
public void addElement(Object obj) {
    //add to the internal Vector
    super.addElement(obj);
    //copy into the array
    dataList = new String[size()];
    for(int i = 0; i < size(); i++) {
            dataList[i] = (String)elementAt(i);
    }
    //sort the data and copy it back
    Arrays.sort (dataList); //sort the data
    clear();        //clear out the Vector

    //reload the sorted data
    for(int i = 0; i < dataList.length; i++)
        super.addElement(dataList[i]);


    //tell JList to repaint
    fireContentsChanged(this, 0, size());
    }
}
```

Figure 31.3 shows this list. The names are added one at a time in nonalphabetical order each time the Next button is clicked, but it is sorted before being displayed.

Figure 31.3   Sorted data using SortedListModel.

Sorting More-Complicated Objects

Suppose now that we want to display both first and last names and want to sort by the last names. In order to do this, we must create an object that holds first and last names but which can be sorted by last name. And how do we do this sort? We could do it by brute force, but in Java any class that implements the Comparable interface can be sorted by the *Arrays.sort* method. And the Comparable interface consists of only one method:

```
public int compareTo(Object obj)
```

Here, the class returns a negative value, zero, or a positive value, depending on whether the existing object is less than, equal to, or greater than the argument object. Thus we can create a Person class with this interface as follows:

```
public class Person implements Comparable {

    private String frname, lname;

    public Person(String name) {
        //split the name apart
            int i = name.indexOf (" ");
            frname = name.substring (0, i).trim();
            lname = name.substring (i).trim();
        }
        public int compareTo(Object obj) {
            Person to = (Person)obj;
            return lname.compareTo (to.getLname ());
        }
        public String getLname() {
            return lname;
        }
        public String getFrname() {
            return frname;
        }
        public String getName() {
            return getFrname()+" "+getLname();
    }
}
```

Note that the compareTo method simply invokes the *compareTo* method of the last name String objects.

The other change to make is to have the data model return both names. So we extend the *getElementAt* method.

```
//data model that uses and sorts Person objects
public class SortedModel extends DefaultListModel {
    private Person[] dataList;

    public void addElement(Object obj) {
        Person per = new Person((String) obj);
        super.addElement(per);
        dataList = new Person[size()];
    //copy the Person into an array
    for(int i = 0; i < size(); i++) {
        dataList[i] = (Person)elementAt(i);
    }

    //sort them
    Arrays.sort (dataList);
```

```
      //and put them back
        clear();
        for(int i = 0; i < dataList.length; i++)
            super.addElement(dataList[i]);
        fireContentsChanged(this, 0, size());
      }
      public Object getElementAt(int index) {
          //returns both names as a string
          Person p = dataList[index];
          return p.getName();
      }
      public Object get(int index) {
          return getElementAt(index);
      }
  }
```

Figure 31.4 shows the resulting sorted names.

Figure 31.4   Sorted list using the Comparable interface to sort on last names.

Getting Database Keys

One disadvantage of a sorted list is that clicking on the *n*th element does not correspond to selecting the *n*th element, since the sorted elements can be in an order that differs from the order in which they were added to the list. Thus if you want to get a database key corresponding to a particular list element (here, a person) in order to display detailed information about that person, you must keep the database key inside the Person object. This is analogous to, but considerably more flexible than, the Visual Basic approach whereby you can keep only one key value for each list element. Here, you could keep several items in the Person object if that is desirable. In Figure 31.5, we double-click on one person's name and pop up a window containing his or her phone number.

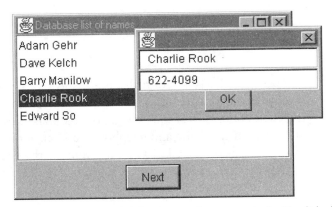

Figure 31.5   A pop-up list showing details appears when a name is double-clicked.

When you double-click on a JList, you must add a mouse listener to the JList object in order to pop up a window. In our code, we create a class called ListMouseListener, which carries out the listening and produces the pop-up. First we add the ListMouseListener by

```
nList.addMouseListener(new ListMouseListener(nList, ldata, db, this));
```

where db represents our database and ldata the list data model. Following is the complete mouseListener class:

```
public class ListMouseListener extends MouseAdapter {
    private JList          nList;
    private DataBase       db;
    private SortedModel    lData;
    private JFrame         jxf;

    public ListMouseListener(JList list, SortedModel ldata,
                    DataBase dbase, JFrame jf) {

        nList = list;
        db    = dbase;
        jxf   = jf;
        lData = ldata;
    }
    //
    public void mouseClicked(MouseEvent e) {
        if (e.getClickCount () == 2) {
        //a mouse double-click
        //gets the database key for this person
            int index = nList.locationToIndex (e.getPoint());
            int key   = lData.getKey (index);
        //display pop up dialog box
            Details details = new Details(jxf,
                db.getName (key), db.getPhone (key));
```

```
                    details.setVisible(true);
            }
        }
    }
```

Because the JList control has no specific methods for detecting a mouse double-click, we check the *mouseClicked* event method to determine whether the click count is 2. If it is, we get the database key for that line and query the database for the name and telephone number of the person with that key. In the example code on the CD-ROM, we simulate the database with a simple text file so that the code example does not become unwieldy.

Adding Pictures in List Boxes

The JList is flexible in yet another way. You can write your own cell rendering code to display anything you want in a line of a list box. So you can include images, graphs, or dancing babies if you want. All you have to do is create a cell rendering class that implements the ListCellRenderer interface. This interface has only one method—getListCellRendererComponent—and is easy to write. By extending the JLabel class, which itself allows for images as well as text, we can display names and images alongside each name. We assume that each Person object now contains the image to display.

```
public class cellRenderer extends JLabel implements
ListCellRenderer {

    public Component getListCellRendererComponent(JList list,
            Object value, int index, boolean isSelected,
            boolean hasFocus) {
        Person p = (Person)value;       //get the person
        setText(p.getName ());          //display name
        setIcon(p.getIcon ());          //and image
        if(isSelected)
            setBackground(Color.lightGray );
        else
            setBackground(Color.white);
        return this;
    }
}
```

We also connect this cell renderer class to the JList with the following method call:

```
nList.setCellRenderer (new cellRenderer());
```

The resulting display is shown in Figure 31.6.

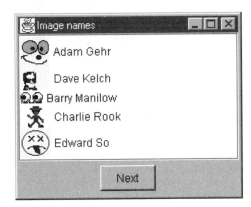

Figure 31.6 A sorted list with pictures added via a custom cell renderer.

Programs on the CD-ROM

Program	Description
\Swing\JList\JlistDemo.java	Simple demonstration of JList.
\Swing\JList\JlistDemo.java	JList, where clicking on an entry copies it to the text field.
\Swing\JList\JListADemo.java	JList, where entering text in a text field and clicking on the Add button adds data to a Vector and then causes a repaint.
\Swing\JList\JListMDemo.java	JList, where entering text in a text field and clicking on the Add button adds data to a JListModel.
\Swing\JList\BaseSorted\ShowList.java	A simple sorted list.
\Swing\JList\TwoNames\Showlist.java	A list sorted by two names based on last names.
\Swing\JList\Database\ShowList.java	A list sorted with the database key.
\Swing\JList\ImageList\ShowList.java	A sorted list with images.

CHAPTER 32

The JTable Class

The JTable class is much like the JList class in that you can very easily program it to do simple things. Similarly, to do more sophisticated things, you can create a class derived from the AbstractTableModel class to hold your data.

A Simple JTable Program

In the simplest program, you can create a rectangular array of objects and use it in the constructor for the JTable. You can also include an array of strings to be used as column labels for the table.

```java
public class SimpleTable extends JxFrame {
    public SimpleTable() {
        super("Simple table");
        JPanel jp = new JPanel();
        getContentPane().add(jp);
        Object[] [] musicData = {
            {"Tschaikovsky", "1812 Overture", new Boolean(true)},
            {"Stravinsky", "Le Sacre", new Boolean(true)}
            {"Lennon", "Eleanor Rigby", new Boolean(false)}
            {"Wagner", "Gotterdammerung", new Boolean (true)}
        };
        String[] columnNames = {"Composer", "Title",
                "Orchestral"};
        JTable table   = new JTable(musicData, columnNames);
        JScrollPane sp = new JScrollPane(table);
        table.setPreferredScrollableViewportSize(
                new Dimension(250,170));
        jp.add(sp);

        setSize(300,200);
        setVisible(true);
    }
```

Figure 32.1   A simple table display.

This produces the table displayed in Figure 32.1.

This table has all cells editable and displays all of the cells using the *toString* method of each object. Like the JList interface, this interface to JTable creates a data model object under the covers. To produce a more flexible display, you need to create that data model yourself.

You can create a table model by extending the AbstractTableModel class. All of the methods have default values and operations, except the following three, which you must provide:

```
public int       getRowCount();
public int       getColumnCount();
public Object    getValueAt(int row, int column);
```

However, you can gain a good deal more control by overriding a couple of other methods. For example, you can use the method

```
public boolean isCellEditable(int row, int col)
```

to protect some cells from being edited. To allow editing of some cells, you must override the implementation for the method

```
public void setValueAt(Object obj, int row, int col)
```

Further, by adding a method that returns the data class of each object to be displayed, you can use some default cell-formatting behavior. The JTable's default cell renderer displays the following:

- Numbers as right-aligned labels
- ImageIcons as centered labels

- Booleans as check boxes
- Objects using their *toString* methods

To change this, you simply need to return the class of the objects in each column.

```
publicClass getColumnClass( int col) {
    return getValueAt(0, col).getClass();
}
```

Our complete table model class creates exactly the same array and table column captions as previously and implements the methods we just mentioned.

```
public class MusicModel extends AbstractTableModel {

    String[] columnNames = {"Composer", "Title", "Orchestral"};

    Object[] [] musicData = {
        {"Tschaikovsky", "1812 Overture", new Boolean (true)},
        {"Stravinsky", "Le Sacre", new Boolean(true)},
        {"Lennon", "Eleanor Rigby", new Boolean (false)},
        {"Wagner", "Gotterdammerung", new Boolean(true)}
    };

    private int rowCount, columnCount;
    //---------------
    public MusicModel(int rowCnt, int colCnt) {
        rowCount = rowCnt;
        columnCount = colCnt;
    }
    //---------------
    public String getColumnName(int col) {
        return columnNames[col];
    }
    //---------------
    public int getRowCount() {
        return rowCount;
    }
    public int getColumnCount() {
        return columnCount;
    }
    //---------------
    public class getColumnClass(int col) {
        return getValueAt(0, col).getClass();
    }
    //---------------
    public boolean isCellEditable(int row, int col) {
        return(col > 1);
    }
    //---------------
    public void setValueAt(Object obj, int row, int col) {
        musicData[row][col] = obj;
        fireTableCellUpdated(row, col);
```

```
    }
//———————————
    public Object getValueAt(int row, int col) {
        return musicData[row][col];
    }

}
```

The main program becomes the code called in the constructor when the class is instantiated from main.

```
public class ModelTable extends JxFrame {
    public ModelTable() {
        super("Simple table");
        JPanel jp = new JPanel();
        getContentPane().add(jp);
        JTable table = new JTable(new MusicModel(4, 3));
        JScrollPane sp = new JScrollPane(table);
        table.setPreferredScrollableViewportSize(new
                        Dimension(250,170));
        jp.add(sp);

        setSize(300,200);
        setVisible(true);
    }
//———————————
    static public void main(String argv[]) {
        new ModelTable();
    }
}
```

As Figure 32.2 shows, the boolean column is now automatically rendered as check boxes. You also allowed editing only of the right-most column, by overriding the *isCellEditable* method to disallow it for columns 0 and 1.

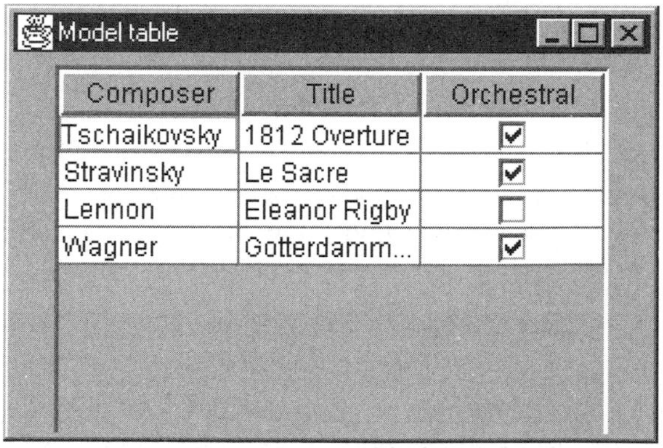

Figure 32.2   A JTable display using a data model that returns the data type of each column and controls the data display accordingly.

Just as the ListModel class does for JList objects, the TableModel class holds and manipulates the data and notifies the JTable whenever it changes. Thus the JTable is an Observer pattern, operating on the TableModel data.

Cell Renderers

Each cell in a table is rendered by a cell renderer. The default renderer is a JLabel, which may be used for all of the data in several columns. Thus these cell renderers can be thought of as Flyweight pattern implementations. The JTable class chooses the renderer according to the object's type, as discussed previously. However, you easily can change to a different renderer, such as one that uses another color, or to another visual interface.

Cell renderers are registered by type of data,

```
table.setDefaultRenderer(String.class, new ourRenderer());
```

and each renderer is passed the object, selected mode, row, and column using the only required public method.

```
public Component getTableCellRendererComponent(JTable jt,
    Object value, boolean isSelected,
    boolean hasFocus, int row, int column)
```

One common way to implement a cell renderer is to extend the JLabel type, catch each rendering request within the renderer, and return a properly configured JLabel object, usually the renderer itself. The following renderer displays cell (1, 1) in boldface and the remaining cells in plain black type:

```
public class ourRenderer extends JLabel
    implements TableCellRenderer {
        Font bold, plain;
        public ourRenderer() {
            super();
            setOpaque(true);
            setBackground(Color.white);
            bold  = new Font("SansSerif", Font.BOLD, 12);
            plain = new Font("SansSerif", Font.PLAIN, 12);
            setFont(plain);
        }
        public Component getTableCellRendererComponent(JTable jt,
                Object value, boolean isSelected,
                boolean hasFocus, int row, int column) {
        setText((String)value);
        if (row == 1 && column == 1) {
            setFont(bold);
            setForeground(Color.red);
        } else {
            setFont(plain);
```

```
            setForeground(Color.black);
        }
        return this;
    }
}
```

The results of this rendering are shown in Figure 32.3.

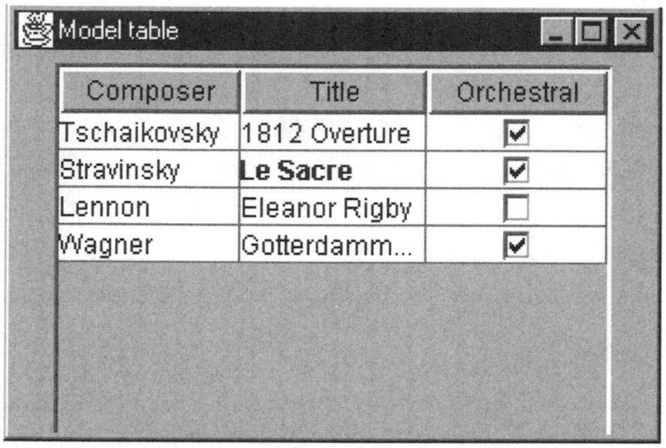

Figure 32.3   The music data using a CellRenderer that changes the font density and color in row 1, column 1 (Rows and columns are numbered starting at 0).

In this simple cell renderer, the renderer is itself a JLabel that returns a different font but the same object, depending on the row and column. More complex renderers are also possible, renderers in which one of several already instantiated objects is returned, thereby making the renderer a Component Factory pattern.

Rendering Other Kinds of Classes

Now let's suppose that we have more complicated classes that we want to render. Suppose that we have written a document mail system and want to display each document according to its type. However, the documents don't have easily located titles, and we can display them only by author and type. Since we intend that each document could be mailed, we start by creating an interface Mail to describe the properties that the various document types have in common.

```
public interface Mail {
    public ImageIcon getIcon();
    public String    getLabel();
    public String    getText();
}
```

Thus each type of document will have a simple label (the author) and a method for getting the full text (which we will not use here). Most important, each document type will have its own icon, which we can obtain with the *getIcon* method.

For example, the NewMail class would look as follows:

```java
public class NewMail implements Mail {
    private String label;

    public NewMail (String mlabel) {
        label = mlabel;
    }
    public ImageIcon getIcon () {
        return new ImageIcon("images/mail.gif");
    }
    public String getText() {
        return "";
    }
    public String getLabel() {
        return label;
    }
}
```

The renderer for these types of mail documents gets the icon and label text and uses the DefaultCellRenderer(derived from JLabel) to render them.

```java
public class myRenderer extends DefaultTableCellRenderer {
    private Mediator md;

    public myRenderer(Mediator med) {
        setHorizontalAlignment(JLabel.LEADING);
        med = med;
    }
//---------------
    public Component getTableCellRendererComponent(
            JTable table, Object value, boolean isSelected,
            boolean hasFocus, int row, int col) {
        if (hasFocus) {
            setBackground(Color.lightGray );
            md.tableClicked ();
        } else
            setBackground(new Color(0xffffce));
        if (value != null) {
            Mail ml = (Mail) value;
            String title = ml.getLabel ();
            setText(title);              //set the text
            setIcon(ml.getIcon ());      //and the icon
        }
        return this;

    }
}
```

Since one of the arguments to the *getTableCellRendererComponent* method is whether the cell is selected, we have an easy way to return a somewhat different display when the cell is selected. In this case, we return a gray background instead of a white one. We also could set a different border if we wanted. Figure 32.4 shows a display of the program. Note that the selected cell is shown with a gray background.

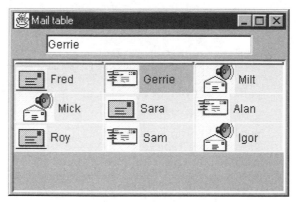

Figure 32.4   Rendering objects that implement the Mail interface, using their icon and text properties.

Selecting Cells in a Table

We can select a row, separated rows, a contiguous set of rows, or single cells of a table, depending on the list selection mode.

In the following example, we want to be able to select single cells, so we choose the single selection mode:

```
setSelectionMode(ListSelectionModel.SINGLE_SELECTION);
```

If we want to take a certain action when a table cell is selected, we get the ListSelectionModel from the table and add a list selection listener to it.

```
ListSelectModel lsm = getSelectionModel();
lsm.addListSelectionListener (new TableSelectionListener(med));
```

We also create a TableSelectionListener class that implements the *valueChanged* method and passes this information to a Mediator class.

```
public class TableSelectionListener implements
ListSelectionListener {

    private Mediator md;
```

```
    public TableSelectionListener(Mediator med) {
        md = med;
    }
    public void valueChanged(ListSelectionEvent e) {
        ListSelectionModel lsm =
            (ListSelectionModel)e.getSource();
        if( ! lsm.isSelectionEmpty ())
            md.tableClicked();
    }
}
```

The Mediator class, as discussed previously, is the only class that deals with interactions between separate visual objects. In this case, it fetches the correct label for this class and displays it in the text field at the top of the window, as shown in Figure 32.4. Here is the entire Mediator class:

```
public class Mediator {
    Ftable         ftable;
    JTextField     txt;
    int            tableRow, tableColumn;
    FolderModel    fmodel;

    public Mediator ( JTextField tx) {
        txt = tx;
    }
    public void setTable(Ftable tbl) {
        ftable = tbl;
    }
    //---------------
    public void tableClicked() {
        int row = ftable.getSelectedRow ();
        int col = ftable.getSelectedColumn ();
//don't refresh if cell not changed
        if ((row != tableRow) || (col != tableColumn)) {
            tableRow = row;
            tableColumn = col;
            fmodel = ftable.getTableModel ();
            Mail ml = fmodel.getDoc(row, col);
            txt.setText (ml.getLabel ());

        }
    }
}
```

Patterns Used in This Image Table

The UML diagram in Figure 32.5 shows the use of several common design patterns in the program in Figure 32.4. As we noted earlier, the separation of the data from the viewer in the Swing JTable is an Observer pattern. By catching the table selection in a listener and then sending the result to a Mediator class, we are implementing the Mediator pattern. Finally, the three mail classes, each producing a different icon, comprise a Factory Method pattern. These patterns occur throughout Java programming, especially when you use Swing. You'll find it extremely helpful to recognize how often you can refer to patterns in your everyday programming to simplify communication between you and your colleagues.

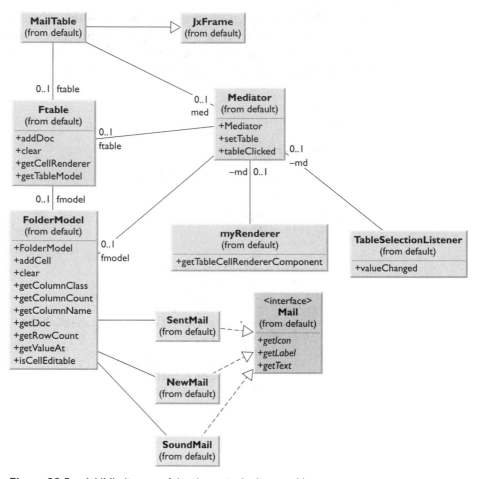

Figure 32.5   A UML diagram of the classes in the Image table.

Programs on the CD-ROM

Program	Description
\Swing\Table\SimpleTable\ SimpleTable.java	Creates a simple table from a two-dimensional String array.
\Swing\Table\RenderTable\ ModelTable.java	Creates a table using a TableModel, allowing the boolean column to be displayed as check boxes.
\Swing\Table\RenderTable\ RenderTable.java	Creates a simple table using TableModel and a cell renderer that renders one cell in bold red.
\Swing\Table\ImageTable\ MailTable.java	Creates a set of mail images in a 3×2 table.

CHAPTER 33

The JTree Class

Much like the JTable and JList, the JTree class consists of a data model and an Observer. One of the easiest ways to build the tree to display is to create a root node, then add child nodes to it, and then add child nodes to each of them as needed. The DefaultMutableTreeNode class is provided as an implementation of the TreeNode interface.

We create the JTree with a root node as its argument.

```
root = new DefaultMutableTreeNode("Foods");
JTree tree = new JTree(root);
```

Then we add each node to the root and additional nodes to those to any depth. The following program produces a food tree list by category. Note that we use the JxFrame class, derived from JFrame at the beginning of this section.

```
public class TreeDemo extends JxFrame {
    private DefaultMutableTreeNode root;
    public TreeDemo() {
        super("Tree Demo");
    JPanel jp = new JPanel();      //create the interior panel
    jp.setLayout(new BorderLayout());
    getContentPane().add(jp);

    //create a scrollpane
    JScrollPane sp = new JScrollPane();
    jp.add("Center", sp);

    //create a root node
    root = new DefaultMutableTreeNode("Foods");
    JTree tree = new JTree(root);      //create the tree
    sp.getViewport().add(tree);        //add to the scroller
```

```
        //create three nodes, each with three subnodes
        addNodes("Meats", "Beef", "Chicken", "Pork");
        addNodes("Veggies", "Broccoli", "Carrots", "Peas");
        addNodes("Desserts", "Charlotte Russe",
                "Bananas Flambe", "Peach Melba");


        setSize(200, 300);
        setVisible(true);
    }
//----------------
    private void addNodes(String b, String n1, String n2,
                String n3) {
        DefaultMutableTreeNode base =
            (new DefaultMutableTreeNode(b));
        root.add(base);
        base.add(new DefaultMutableTreeNode(n1);
        base.add(new DefaultMutableTreeNode(n2));
        base.add(new DefaultMutableTreeNode(n3));
    }
```

The tree it generated is shown in Figure 33.1.

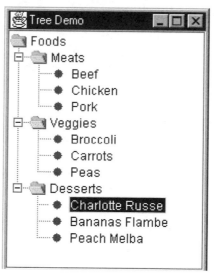

Figure 33.1   A simple JTree display.

If you want to know if a user has clicked on a particular line of this tree, you can add a TreeSelectionListener and catch the valueChanged event. The TreePath that we can obtain from the *getPath* method of the TreeSelectionEvent is the complete path back to the top of the tree. However, the *getLastPathComponent* method will return the string of the line that the user actually selected.

You will see that we use this method and display in the Composite pattern example.

```
public void valueChanged(TreeSelectionEvent evt)        {
    TreePath path = evt.getPath();
    String selectedTerm =
        path.getLastPathComponent().toString();
```

The TreeModel Interface

The previous tree was based on adding a set of nodes to make up a tree. This is an implementation of the DefaultTreeModel class that handles this structure. However, you might want to display other sorts of data structures using this tree display. To do so, you create a class of your own to hold these data that implement the TreeModel interface. This interface is very relatively simple, consisting only of the following:

```
void addTreeModelListener(TreeModelistener 1);
Object getChild(Object parent, int index);
int getChildCount(Object parent);
int getIndexOf Child(Object parent, Object child);
Object getRoot();
boolean isLeaf(Object);
void removeTreeModelListener(TreeModelListener 1);
void value ForPathChanges(TreePath path, Object newValue);
```

Note that this general interface model does not specify anything about how you add new nodes or add nodes to nodes. You can implement that in any way that is appropriate for your data.

Programs on the CD-ROM

Program	Description
\Swing\Tree\TreeDemo.java	Creates a simple tree from DefaultMutableTreeNodes.

Summary

This brief chapter touched on some of the more common Swing controls and noted how often the design patterns we've discussed in this book are represented. You might be able to use them more effectively after appreciating the patterns on which they are based.

SECTION 6

Case Studies

Sometimes design patterns leap into your consciousness after you see how others are using them. In the following case studies, we show how some programmers began using them.

CHAPTER 34

Sandy and the Mediator

Sandy and Arthur work at different branches of a large company several thousand miles apart. Sandy began writing a program to learn how to use the Swing classes and eventually integrated the program into her work assignment. She started by using a JTabbedPane component and a JTree component. Then she added the Swing JToolBar component, as well as several toolbar buttons to control the program commands.

As she began to experiment with displaying various kinds of data, she realized that she could use a JTextField to enter a search query and the JTree to display a list of suggested query refinement terms, as shown in Figure 34.1.

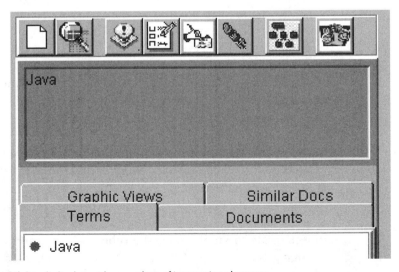

Figure 34.1   A display with a number of interacting elements.

Then she realized that she could insert a JList into another of the tabbed panes and use it to display titles of documents. Figure 34.2 shows the summary of the selected document.

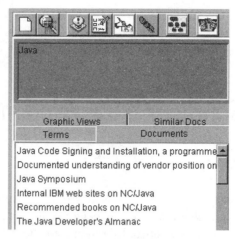

Figure 34.2   Clicking on a document title displays the summary in the lower box.

Then, just as she got these functions working and was about to leave on a trip to the West coast to work with Arthur, she obtained some code from Dick that allowed her to annotate displayed documents using the GlassPane methods of the JFrame component. This is shown in Figure 34.3.

Working under cramped conditions on the flight, she integrated that code into the working program and showed it to Arthur on her arrival. He was impressed with the program so far. After working with Sandy for a day or so and integrating her server technology, he was even more pleased with their joint work. But Sandy was less pleased because she knew that they had just hastily written a tangle of interacting classes that was nearly impossible to maintain or understand. When she expressed her concerns to Arthur, he took a familiar textbook off the shelf.

"Here's a copy of *Design Patterns*," he said. "I think you'll find some good ideas on how to modify our program to be less confusing."

Sandy took the book back to her motel room and began thumbing through the catalog of patterns. By the next day, she had the beginnings of some ideas.

"Look," she said, "we can look at this program as a set of data objects or as a set of visual objects. Either way, we have to minimize the amount that each object needs to know about the others, so we can modify an object without changing any others. If we consider the applet as a set of data interaction objects, then the toolbar buttons call on data and change display elements.

1. Clicking on the Search button produces a list of terms and documents.

2. Clicking on a document in the list causes a display of the abstract.

3. Clicking on a term and then on "Add term" causes that term to be added to the query field.

4. Clicking the document and then on the View button causes that document to display in the viewer.

5. Clicking on a term and then on the Plot button causes a plot of related terms to be generated.

6. Clicking on the annotate buttons allows you to write annotations onto the displayed document.

And every object interacts with two or three others! What a mess!"

"Well," said Arthur, "maybe we should think about the display elements as the important objects to isolate. Then we have the following:

1. The toolbar buttons

2. The toolbars

3. The query field

4. The tabbed panel

5. The document display panel

And they all communicate with the data server! It's still a tangle!"

"Let's think about those design patterns I've been reading about. It's easy to see that the toolbar buttons should communicate using the Command pattern so that we can undo that long if statement in the *actionPerformed* method. In fact, we could make the two JToolBars the ActionListeners for the buttons that they contain."

"But," said Arthur, "I don't see how that helps us keep these objects untangled. Every button needs to call methods in different objects. The Search button alone has to communicate with the text field, the search engine server, and the lists in the JTabbedPane. And the Clear button has to clear everything! Then every Command object would be calling methods in three or five other objects. That's no good. Maybe we could insert some other object that could manage this more sensibly."

"Let's see," Sandy said. "That sounds kind of familiar. You know, that Mediator pattern does just that. It says here that it

- defines how a set of objects interact,
- keeps the coupling between objects loose, and
- allows us to change object interfaces without having to change everything else.

That's just what we need. Let's look at the interactions now."

They drew them on the board together.

"See," said Sandy, "the Mediator gets the commands from all of the buttons. It decides which objects need to know about them. Then, if we change the classes, we have to change only the Mediator."

"But what about the server?" asked Arthur. "The search engine takes some time to return all of the information. How can we refresh the display later without hanging the system?"

"That sounds like an Observer pattern to me," said Sandy. "We spin off the search request in a different thread and notify the Observer when the result comes back. Then the Observer can tell the Mediator that it is time to change the display objects. That's pretty good. We've gotten most of the tangles out of this rat's nest."

"And, you know," said Arthur, "we can simplify the code that loads that display list box using an Adapter pattern. And not only that, the ListModel already is implementing the AbstractListModel. Isn't that an example of the Template pattern? Patterns aren't so hard. This is going to make this project so much easier."

To read more about Sandy's project, review the papers by Cooper and Byrd [1997, 1998] and Neff and Cooper [1999] in the bibliography.

CHAPTER 35

Herb's Text Processing Tangle

Herb was trying to rationalize a series of programs that processed text. Each of several programs operated on a stream of text and marked it in various ways: names, phrases, places, organizations, and so on. The trouble was that each of the programs made assumptions that other programs had already operated on the text stream. This made it difficult to add to or change any of the programs in any significant way.

He went to Sandy, who had just finished using Patterns in her project with Arthur. "I hear you're now an expert on design patterns," Herb said. "Is there a pattern or two in that list that can help me?"

"There might be," Sandy said. "But you should recognize that they aren't magic bullets, and you don't find them everywhere. They're just reusable software methodologies, but let's look; one might apply here."

After Herb described his problem, Sandy thumbed through *Design Patterns* for a moment. "It looks to me like this series of programs could be described as a Chain of Responsibility pattern," she said, "but you need to revise or subclass them so that they all have the same interface. Then you can send your text data down the chain and link the chain members more easily."

"That's easy enough," Herb said, "but what about the problem that some of these modules do some processing and others don't? This object recognizes some HTML tags so it can find new paragraphs, but these others don't. Wouldn't it be better if this wasn't scrambled into several classes?"

"It would be," Sandy agreed. "So early in the chain why don't you create a new object that parses out the HTML and just sends the rearranged text on to the remaining modules? You won't have to change the later modules because they will no longer see any HTML. This is still a Chain of Responsibility but with one more class in the chain."

"Well, this is a great theory," Herb agreed, "but now I have to write my own HTML parser. Thanks a lot."

"Actually," Sandy pointed out, "you only have to check for a few items and skip over and eliminate the rest. For example, you need to add a blank line wherever you find a <p> tag. The same applies to list tags and header tags. There isn't too much more to this. You might want to pull out the document titles as you go along, but that's about all."

"And how do I go about this? It still seems like a lot of work," Herb protested.

"I'd use the Interpreter pattern," Sandy answered. "Its advantage is that every item that you need to interpret is handled in a separate class, and none of them is very complicated."

"And I'll bet I can guess how you connect these little Interpreter objects," Herb replied. "Another Chain of Responsibility. This really simplifies my work." Then his face fell. "I just remembered. Some of the documents are going to be in XML. That's just enough to throw the whole design for a loop."

"Not really," Sandy pointed out. "You could use the Strategy pattern to select an HTML or XML parser as the first step in the chain. That's not hard at all, and there are lots of Java-based XML parsers available."

"Terrific!" said Herb. "I hope the rest of the project is as easy as this is turning out to be."

"Here," said Sandy, "why don't you borrow my copy of *Design Patterns* until the copy you're going to order comes in."

CHAPTER 36

Mary's Dilemma

Herb finished his Chain of Responsibility development and made the framework available for the rest of his project group. One of his first users was Mary, who suddenly discovered that she had a number of additional requirements that Herb's chain did not fulfill. She wanted to be able to produce summaries of each document.

"For example," she told Sandy, "I need to keep sentence numbers and word numbers of every term that we find in a document. Herb has that information, but he doesn't store it anywhere."

"Why don't you subclass Herb's classes and store the data in whichever class you need it?" asked Sandy.

"I don't know what else I'll need until I finish developing the algorithms, and I don't want to take a chance that I'll mess up Herb's part so that he can't fix it if we need to make basic changes," Mary explained.

"Let me see," said Sandy, reaching for the *Design Patterns*. "I think there is a pattern that just suits your situation. Yes, here it is: the Visitor."

"Sounds like Dürrenmatt," said Mary, ever the German scholar. "What does it do?"

"The idea is very simple," Sandy explained. "You write a class that visits the target class and retrieve information from it."

"And how do I visit a class that I didn't write?" Mary asked.

"That's just the situation that the Visitor is for," said Sandy. "You subclass the classes that you're going to visit and put an *accept* method in them. Then the Visitor calls each one and returns a reference to the Visitor so that you can operate on all the public methods and package-protected data in the class. You get what you want, and the original classes are unchanged."

"That's great!" said Mary. "It's like auditing the classes without paying tuition. That's the pattern for me."

BIBLIOGRAPHY

Alexander, Christopher, S. Ishikawa, et al. *A Pattern Language*. New York: Oxford University Press, 1977.

Alpert, Sherman, K. Brown, and B. Woolf. *The Design Patterns Smalltalk Companion*. Reading, Mass.: Addison-Wesley, 1998.

Arnold, Ken, and J. Gosling. *The Java Programming Language*. Reading, Mass.: Addison-Wesley, 1998.

Booch, Grady, J. Rumbaugh, and I. Jacobson. *The Unified Modeling Language User Guide*. Reading, Mass.: Addison-Wesley, 1999.

Buschman, Frank, R. Meunier, et al. *Pattern Oriented Software Architecture: A System of Patterns*. New York: John Wiley and Sons, 1996.

Cooper, James W. *Principles of Object-Oriented Programming in Java 1.1*. Research Triangle Park, N.C.: Ventana Press, 1997.

Cooper, James W. and Byrd, Roy J. "Lexical Navigation: Visually Prompted Query Refinement," presented at Digital Libraries 1997, Philadelphia, Pa.

Cooper, James W. and Neff, Mary R. "ASHRAM—Active Markup and Summarization," presented at the Hawaii International Conference of Systems Sciences, Maui, Hawaii, January, 1999.

Coplien, James O. *Advanced C++ Programming Styles and Idioms*. Reading, Mass.: Addison-Wesley, 1992.

Coplien, James O., and D. Schmidt. *Pattern Languages of Program Design*. Reading, Mass.: Addison-Wesley, 1995.

Fowler, Martin, and K. Scott. *UML Distilled: Applying the Standard Object Modeling Language*. Reading, Mass.: Addison-Wesley, 1997.

Gamma, Erich, R. Helm, R. Johnson, and J. Vlissides. *Design Patterns: Abstraction and Reuse of Object Oriented-Design.* Proceedings of ECOOP, Kaiserslautern, Germany, 1993: pp. 405–431.

Gamma, Erich, R. Helm, R. Johnson, and J. Vlissides. *Design Patterns: Elements of Reusable Object-Oriented Software.* Reading, Mass.: Addison-Wesley, 1995.

Grand, Mark. *Patterns in Java.* Vol. 1. New York: John Wiley and Sons, 1998.

Krasner, G. E., and S. T. Pope. "A Cookbook for Using the Model-View-Controller User Interface Paradigm in Smalltalk-80."*Journal of Object-Oriented Programmng* I(3), (1988).

Kurata, Deborah. "Programming with Objects." *Visual Basic Programmer's Journal* (June 1998) pp. 91–94.

Pree, Wolfgang. *Design Patterns for Object-Oriented Software Development.* Reading, Mass.: Addison-Wesley, 1994.

Riel, Arthur J. *Object-Oriented Design Heuristics.* Reading, Mass.: Addison-Wesley, 1996.

Vlissides, John. *Pattern Hatching: Design Patterns Applied.* Reading, Mass.: Addison-Wesley, 1998.

INDEX

Warranty

Addison Wesley Longman warrants the enclosed disc to be free of defects in materials and faulty workmanship under normal use for a period of ninety days after purchase. If a defect is discovered in the disc during this warranty period, a replacement disc can be obtained at no charge by sending the defective disc, postage prepaid, with proof of purchase to:

Addison Wesley Longman, Inc.
Addison-Wesley Professional
One Jacob Way
Reading, MA 01867

After the 90-day period, a replacement will be sent upon receipt of the defective disc and a check or money order for $10.00, payable to Addison Wesley Longman, Inc.

Addison Wesley Longman makes no warranty or representation, either express or implied, with respect to this software, its quality, performance, merchantability, or fitness for a particular purpose. In no event will Addison Wesley Longman, its distributors, or dealers be liable for direct, indirect, special, incidental, or consequential damages arising out of the use or inability to use the software. The exclusion of implied warranties is not permitted in some states. Therefore, the above exclusion may not apply to you. This warranty provides you with specific legal rights. There may be other rights that you may have that vary from state to state.

System Requirements

The Java programs included on the CD-ROM require JDK 1.2 and will run on any system that provides Java 1.2. The database examples will run on Windows 95/98/NT. Viewing the UML diagrams require a copy of JVISION, which is also a Java program.